Postcard History Series

Washington

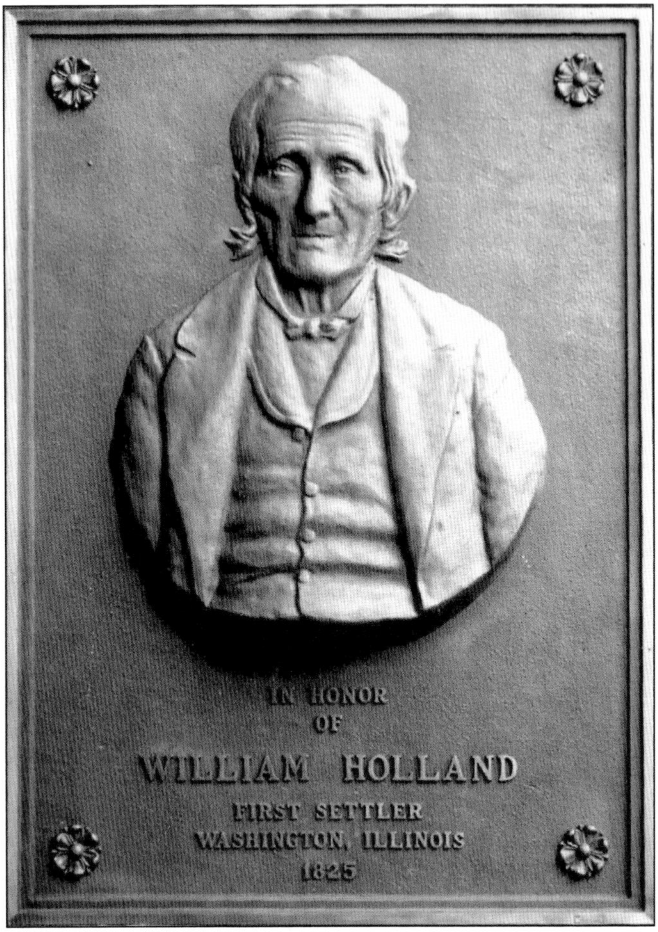

William Holland, Town Founder. This bronze placard was dedicated on October 15, 1926, and serves as a memorial to the founder and first settler of Washington. The memorial was originally placed on the west side of the bandstand that once stood in the center of the square, and faced west, towards Peoria. Today this bronze plaque is set within the bell memorial in front of the current city hall on Jefferson Street.

On the front cover: **Brick Streets of the Square.** On May 2, 1901, the 300,000 bricks that would be used to pave the streets of the square arrived. This scene, looking north from South Main Street, shows two workers beginning to lay the brick. While some believe repair of brick streets and the creation of new brick streets is cost prohibitive, it can in fact save money over the long run. Properly laid brick streets can require fewer repairs, withstand the harsh changes in weather better than asphalt, tend to encourage slower, thus safer, automobile speeds, and enhance the overall appearance of the street. (Author's collection.)

On the back cover: **Independence Day Celebration.** The Danforth Hotel, which was located on the northwest side of the square, is abundantly decorated with red, white, and blue bunting for the celebration of American independence during the 1920s. Three members of a band stand in the street with a group of youngsters while a man sells peanuts out of a street cart. An early model automobile stands parked in front of the hotel while a group of women look out onto the square from the balcony above. This street scene personifies the vibrant nature of an incredible public space. (Author's collection.)

POSTCARD HISTORY SERIES

Washington

Zachary R. Borders

ARCADIA
PUBLISHING

ISBN 978-0-7385-5105-0

Published by Arcadia Publishing
Charleston SC, Chicago IL, Portsmouth NH, San Francisco CA

Printed in the United States of America

Library of Congress Catalog Card Number: 2006937459

For all general information contact Arcadia Publishing at:
Telephone 843-853-2070
Fax 843-853-0044
E-mail sales@arcadiapublishing.com
For customer service and orders:
Toll-Free 1-888-313-2665

Visit us on the Internet at www.arcadiapublishing.com

This book is dedicated to those who built the original town of Washington, its wonderful square, and the fantastic neighborhoods that surround it, as well as those working so hard to preserve and build upon its fantastic foundation today. This book is also dedicated to my mother and father and the rest of my family and friends—especially those who went into the snowy streets one late night for a square architectural tour.

CONTENTS

Acknowledgments

I would like to thank a number of individuals who have helped me throughout the production of this book. Ann Marie Lonsdale, an acquisitions editor at Arcadia Publishing in Chicago, has been extremely helpful and has made the process of putting this book together painless and very enjoyable. The series of local history books that Arcadia Publishing and its authors produce are really wonderful and are extremely important tools for the preservation and appreciation of local histories throughout so many different communities across the country. I am very happy that *Washington* can be a part of this great collection.

Carol Dorward at the Washington Historical Society was an extraordinary source of knowledge and an incredible help in facilitating my needs as I searched for just the right images and just the right amazing stories about a community we both love. The Washington Historical Society is lucky to have such a passionate person in their midst.

The Washington Historical Society itself should be thanked as well especially for the use of their research space and the images that appear in this book. Their efforts throughout the year allow for the people of Washington and their guests to witness and learn about the history of a great place. Washington should never take this great cultural asset for granted; instead they should embrace and support its continued growth and development.

Lastly, I would like to thank my parents and anyone else that has contributed to my own personal collection of Washington postcards.

INTRODUCTION

My hometown of Washington is a very special place. At an early age I was inspired artistically by the traditional town center, the square. I took art classes in the second story of one of the many mixed-use commercial buildings that line the streets and make up this great civic space. As one looks out onto this space, with its roundabout, its park space in the center, its handsome buildings that stand alongside the one I was in, and then looks beyond into the great nearby neighborhoods, one could tell that there was an underlying plan that had made this place special from the very beginning.

There was indeed a plan, and it was relatively simple yet very intriguing. William Holland laid out the original town with the help of local teacher and surveyor John Barry. The focal point would be the square space, which would center on the community's well. The dimensions of the square space, from building face to building face interestingly enough would be 275 feet in each direction. This was a logical decision made by a blacksmith who gave the new town the name of the country's first president. This name was also shared by the nation's capitol, the District of Columbia, whose initial plan was designed by Pierre L'Enfant on top of a 10-mile-by-10-mile block of federal property.

Once a logical plan was laid out, a great civic open space for all to congregate and celebrate in was created. It was then lined with strong and very essential commercial buildings to support and enclose it. Then there grew successful residential neighborhoods with walkable tree-lined streets full of potential customers and employees for those commercial spaces. There were places to worship, go to school, publicly debate, play sports, go to the theater, and even meet up with friends for a bite to eat and drink. All of these elements were essential to life in Washington, and they are still essential today. This model of traditional urbanism and development patterns makes places beautiful and livable throughout the world. A little bit of the best of everything exists in places like this.

The following pages are not entirely about historical facts and figures. This book of postcards is a reference guide, illustrating some of Washington's finest architecture and urbanism and some of the details that have made it work so well over the years. I hope that as the reader works through the themed chapters an understanding and appreciation can be gained concerning the interconnectivity of all of a community's various elements and how the square and the neighborhoods around it serve as a great precedent for future development throughout the growing city of Washington, my hometown.

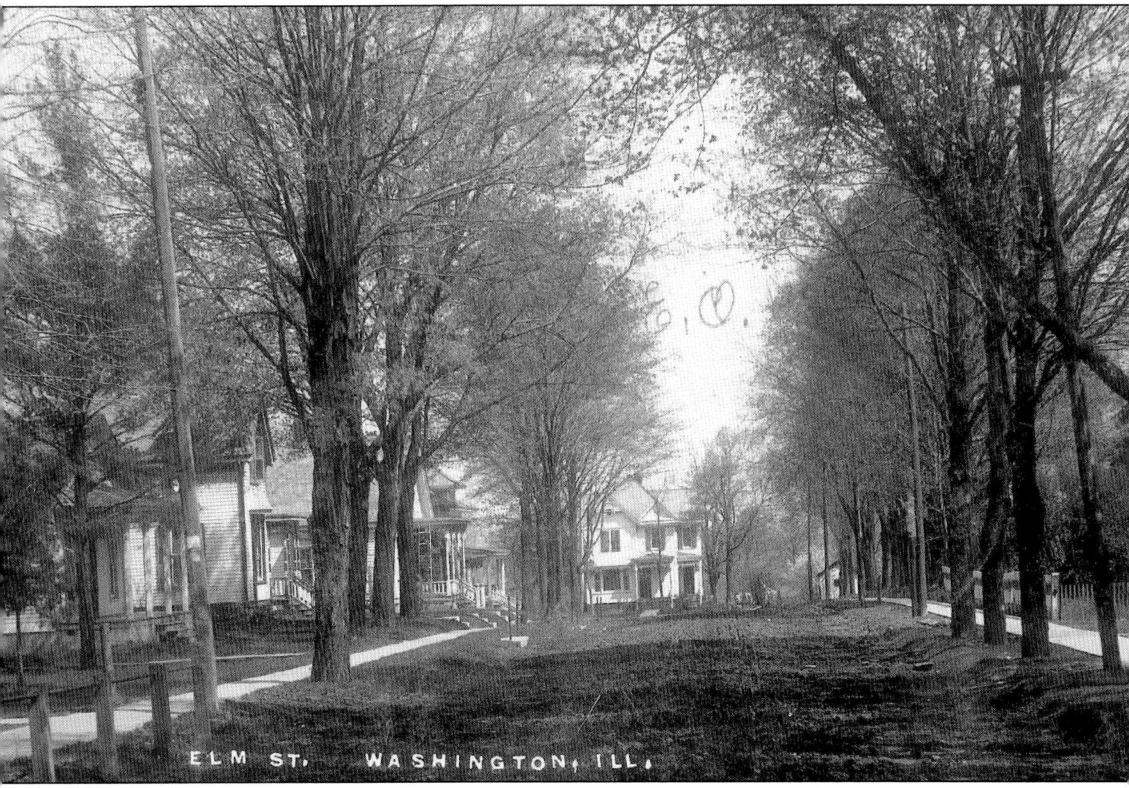

VIEW DOWN ELM STREET. This residential street was not yet paved, but the pedestrians could still enjoy the benefits of mature trees lining it on either side, providing shade and defining an enclosed space. A two-story home does a wonderful job in terminating the end of the thoroughfare off in the distance. Sidewalks on either side of the street connect to residential front porches and provide a safe place for pedestrians to travel.

One

The Town

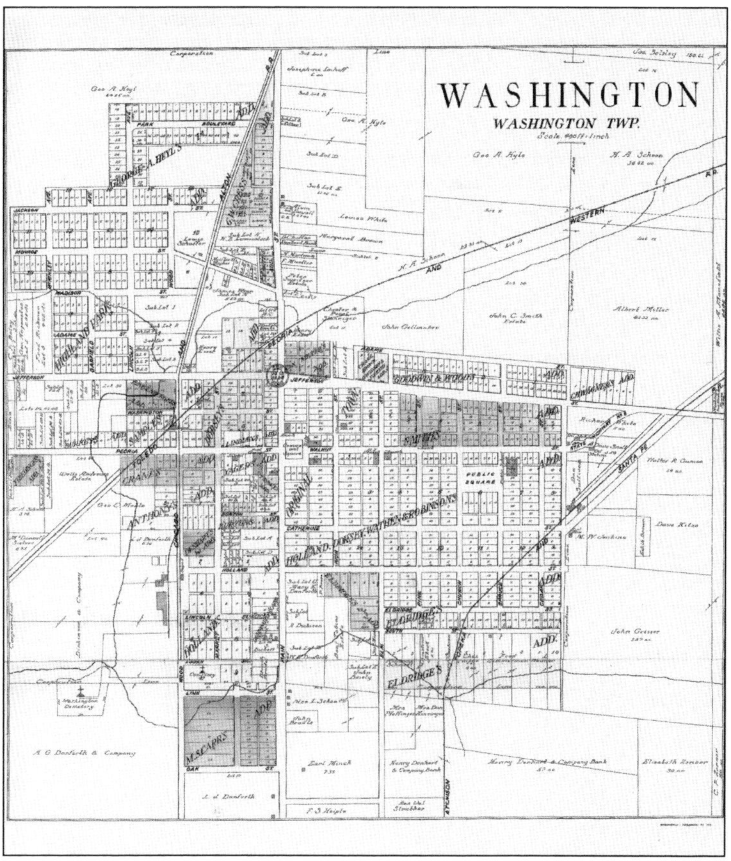

Washington, 1929. This early map illustrates the growth of Washington out from the square. North and South Main Streets intersect Peoria and Walnut Streets at the square's park space and then lead out into the walkable residential streets. The three railroad lines can be seen crisscrossing the community. Churches can be seen throughout the community, and the school nestles in amid its residential neighbors, which watch over it and the formal park space that is enjoyed by all. On the outskirts is the agricultural land, which has always been important for the community and its prosperity.

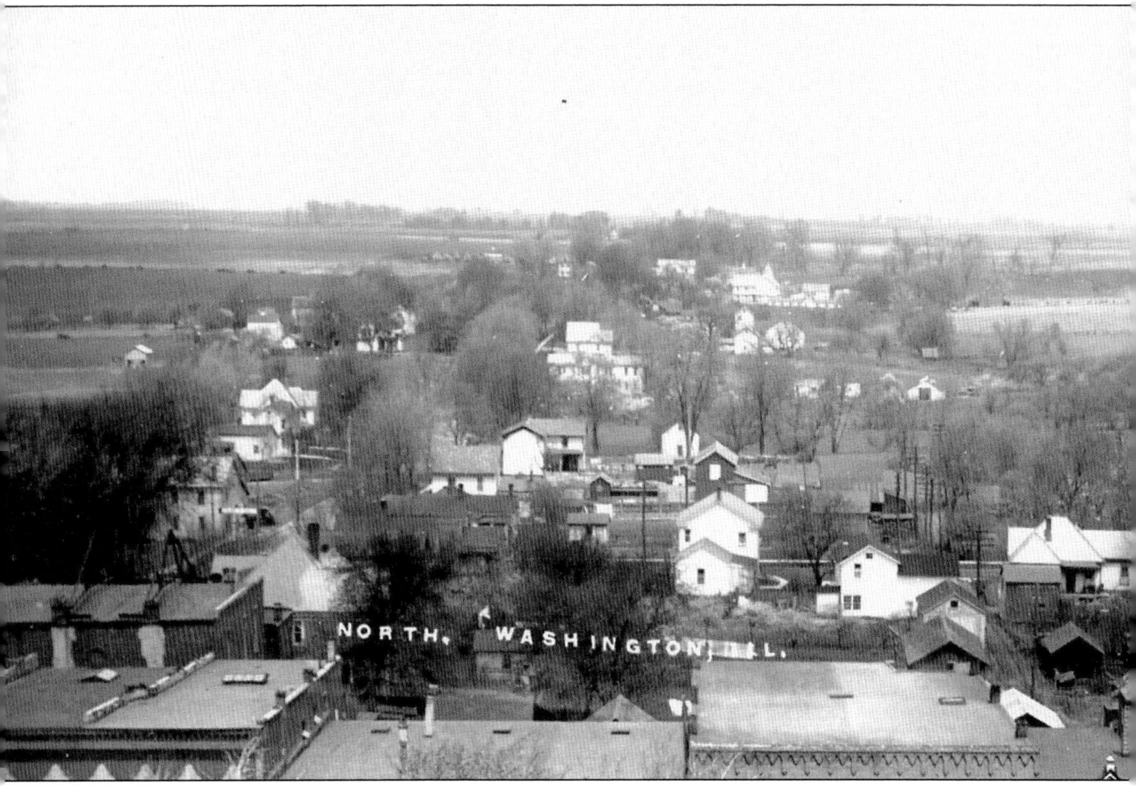

AERIAL VIEW, LOOKING NORTH. This view toward the northern portions of Washington shows the rooftops of the commercial buildings surrounding the square, extending out into the residential development and then into the agricultural areas even further north. Main Street heading north, as well as the south, was the main thoroughfare originating from the center of the town. Residential development began to grow past Main Street onto connecting streets amid the grid. One of those street was Jefferson Street as seen just north of the square near the middle of the photograph.

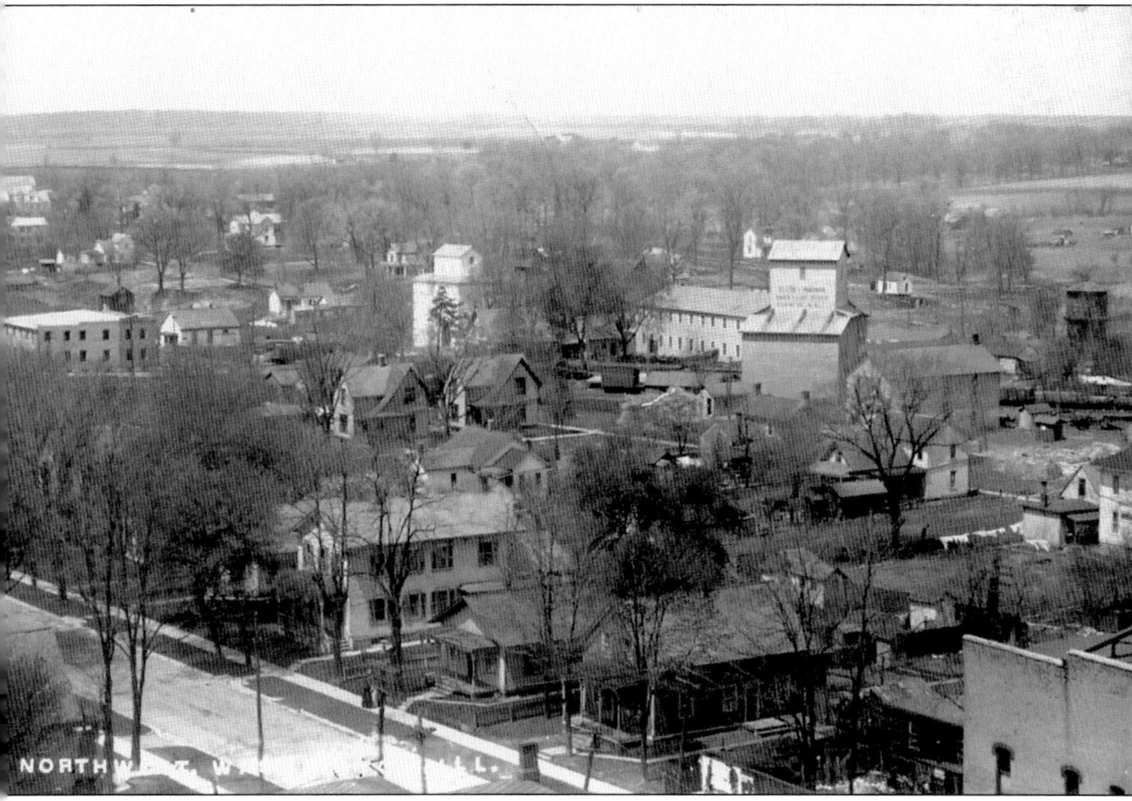

Aerial View, Looking Northwest. This view captures residential development along Peoria Street headed west from the commercial buildings of the square, the edge of which can be seen in the lower right-hand corner. Grain elevators can be seen towering over the homes that lie close to the railroad tracks that transport the goods they store. Beyond the grain elevators the frequency of homes begins to lessen as farmland begins to dominate the landscape.

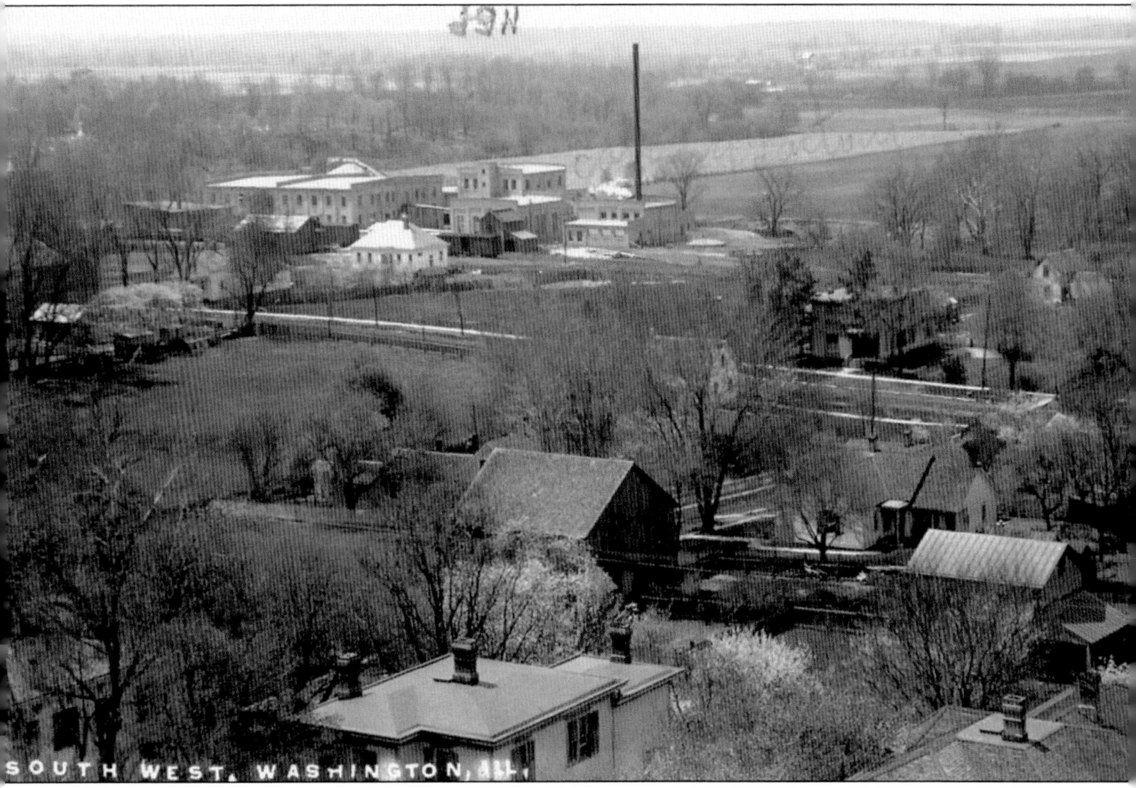

AERIAL VIEW, LOOKING SOUTHWEST. The Dickinson Cannery complex can be seen toward the top of the image past homes lying along Wood, Market, and Main Streets. Train cars on the Chicago and Alton Railroad tracks stand outside the east side of the factory buildings. Beyond the cannery, Glendale Cemetery can be seen, marking the southwest corner of the town at the time. The cemetery is the final resting place for many Washingtonians throughout the years, including many of its founders.

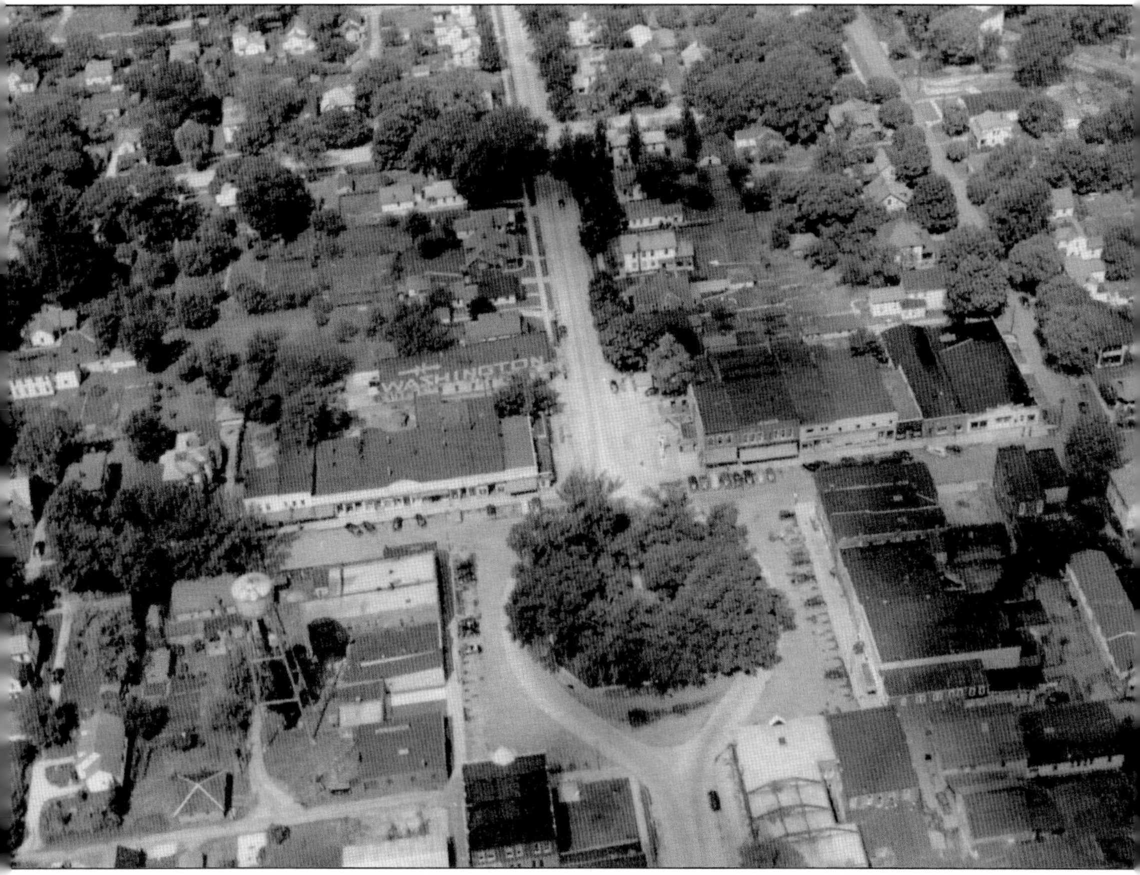

Aerial View of the Square. Taken in the 1950s, this view down toward the square from the east shows much of the commercial and residential areas built out. The image illustrates so many wonderful urban design elements at work. The commercial buildings lining the square create a strong urban street wall. The businesses provide many of the basic daily needs for residents that populate the homes within the important 10-minute walking distance surrounding the town center. The park space within the square provides relief within the space. Automobiles circle the roundabout and get a full look at all of the retail opportunities. A strong street grid surrounds the space and allows for traffic to disperse instead of compiling on the major streets: Peoria Street to the west, Walnut Street to the east, and North and South Main Streets. (Courtesy of the Washington Historical Society.)

Should auld acquaintance be forgot,
And never bro't to mind?
Should auld acquaintance be forgot,
And days o' auld lang syne.

For auld lang syne, my dear,
For auld lang syne;
Should auld acquaintance be forgot,
And days o' auld lang sang.

Tell Your Friends to Meet You

Home-Coming Week

WASHINGTON, ILL

Sept. 5 to 10, 1910

Celebration under auspices of

Commercial Club
Farmers' Club
and the Grange

How dear to my heart are the scenes of my childhood,
When fond recollections present them to view!
The orchard, the meadow, the deep tangled Wildwood
And every loved spot which my infancy knew,
The wide, spreading pond and mill that stood by it,
The bridge and the rock where the cataract fell,
The cot of my father, the dairy house nigh it,
And e'en the rude bucket that hung in the well.

Meet me at the Home Coming Celebration, Washington, Ill., Sept. 1-6, 1913

"The Isle of Long Ago."

Oh, a wonderful stream is the river Time,
As it runs through the realm of tears,
With a faultless rythm and a musical rhyme,
And a boundless sweep and surge sublime,
As it bends with the ocean of years.

How the winters, like flakes of snow,
And the summers, like buds between;
And the year in the sheaf—so they come and they go,
On the river's breast, with its ebb and flow,
As it glides in the shadow and sheen.

There's a magical isle up the river of Time,
Where the softest of airs are playing;
There's a cloudless sky and a tropical clime,
And a song as sweet as the vesper chime,
And the Junes with the roses are staying.

And the name of that Isle is the "Long Ago."
—B. F. Taylor.

Come back to Washington and meet the old friends of "Long Ago."

HOMECOMING. These two cards were used as advertisement for the community's homecoming celebrations that both occurred during the month of September in the years of 1910 and 1913. The verses on each card evoke nostalgia and a longing to return home to what was familiar. In its early days, Washington grew with the arrival of people from all over the world. As time moved on so did people. Regardless of where one travels to throughout life it is important to be proud of and to understand where one comes from—that place that shapes one's life.

Two

The Railroad

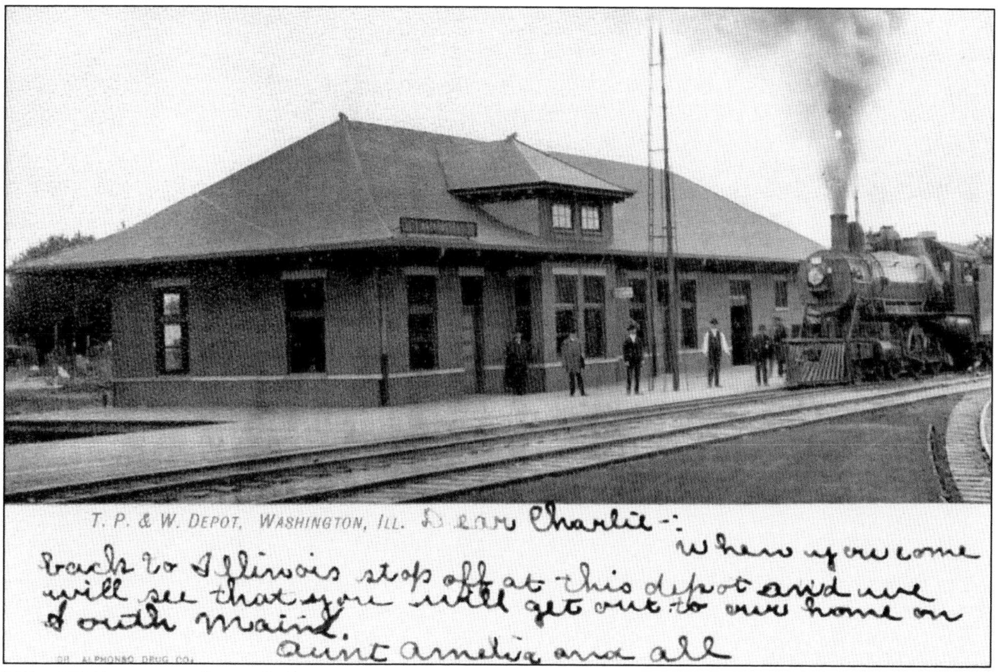

TP&W DEPOT. The Toledo, Peoria and Western Railroad (TP&W) comes into Washington from the northeast. The station was located north of Peoria Street along Wood Street and sat at the intersection of the TP&W and the Chicago and Alton Railroad, which also came from the northeast and continued south through the town toward the Dickinson Cannery.

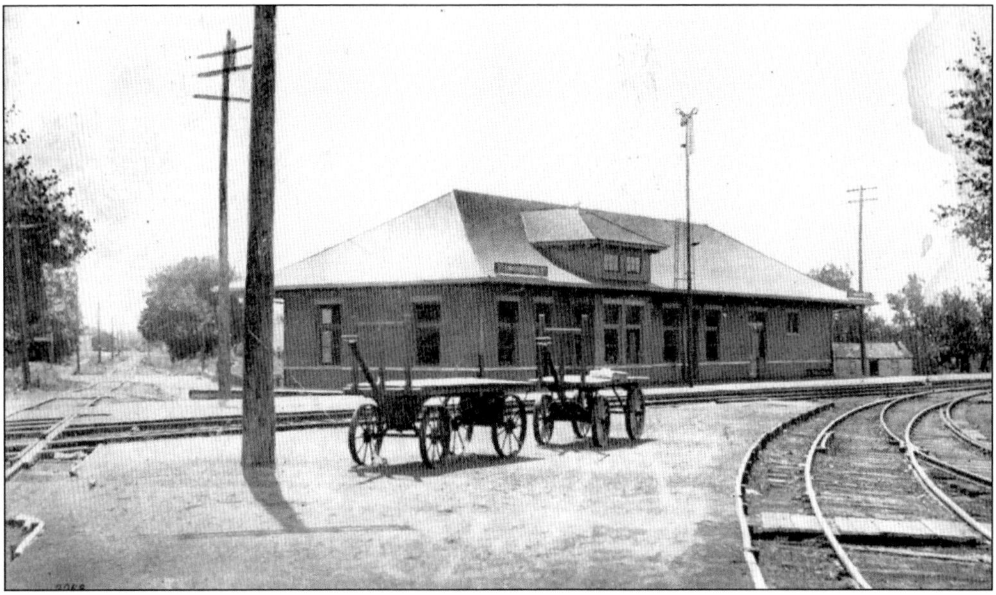

PASSENGER RAIL SERVICE. The depot for the TP&W was the main passenger railroad station in the community and served it for several decades, connecting it to the rest of the region as well as the country. Its location was convenient for visitors, because it was within walking or short transport distance from the square and its hotels and retail opportunities. The same convenience was afforded local residents, who could catch the train to any number of destinations.

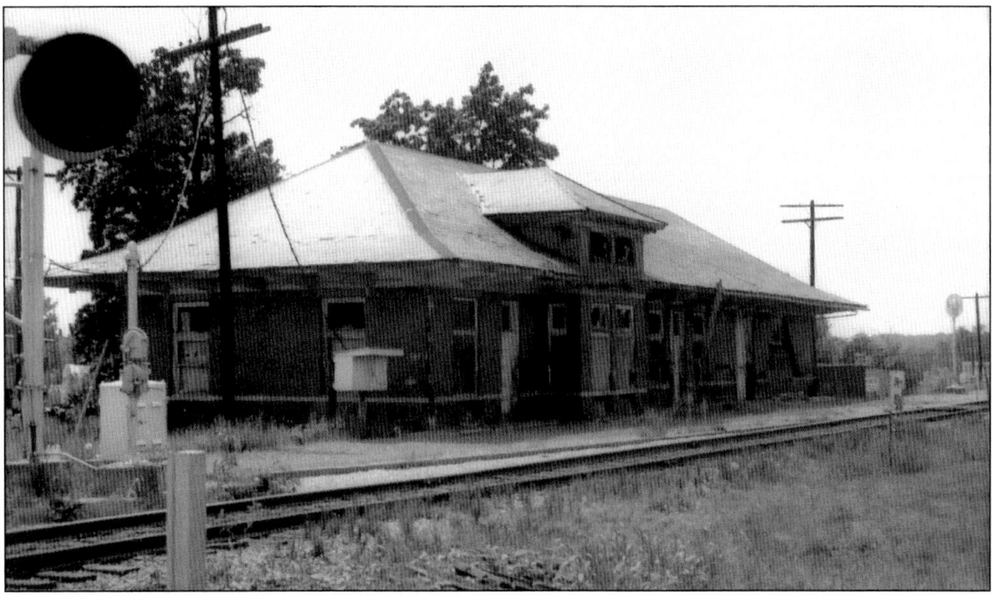

A CONVENIENCE LOST. By the 1960s, when this image was produced, passenger rail service had ended in Washington as it had in so many other communities. The increased presence of the automobile and the subsequent development of the federal highway system changed the way Americans traveled across the country. Development of the community itself would also change because of this. While trains would sail into the center of the community, the highways would bypass the community all together. Mass transit would take a serious blow. This depot no longer exists.

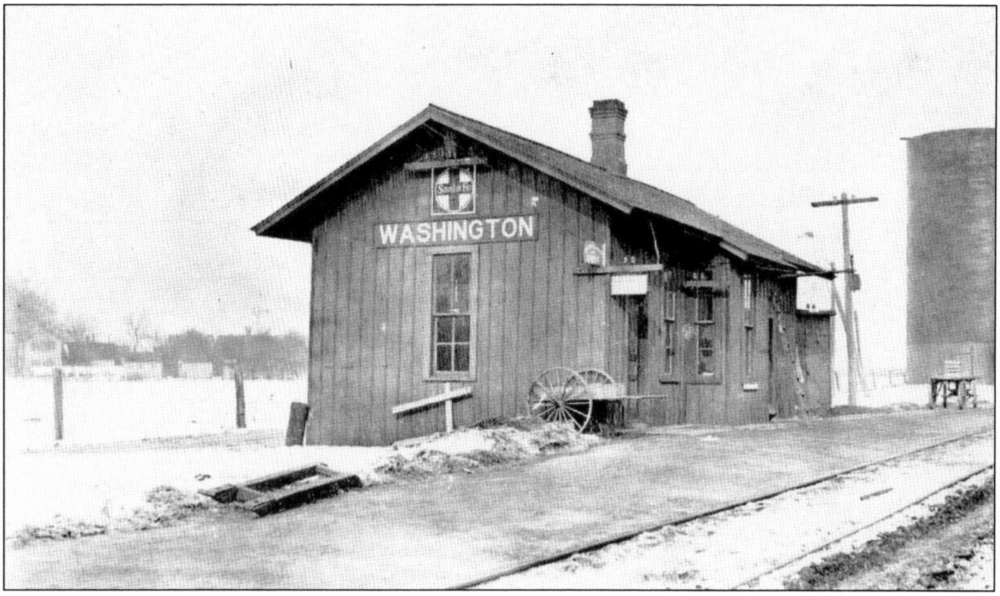

SANTA FE FREIGHT DEPOT, 1915. One of Washington's freight depots was located just off Catherine Street on the southeast side of town. The Atchison, Topeka and Santa Fe Railroad came from the northeast of Washington and provided for many of the town's agricultural shipping needs as illustrated by the presence of a grain elevator near the depot.

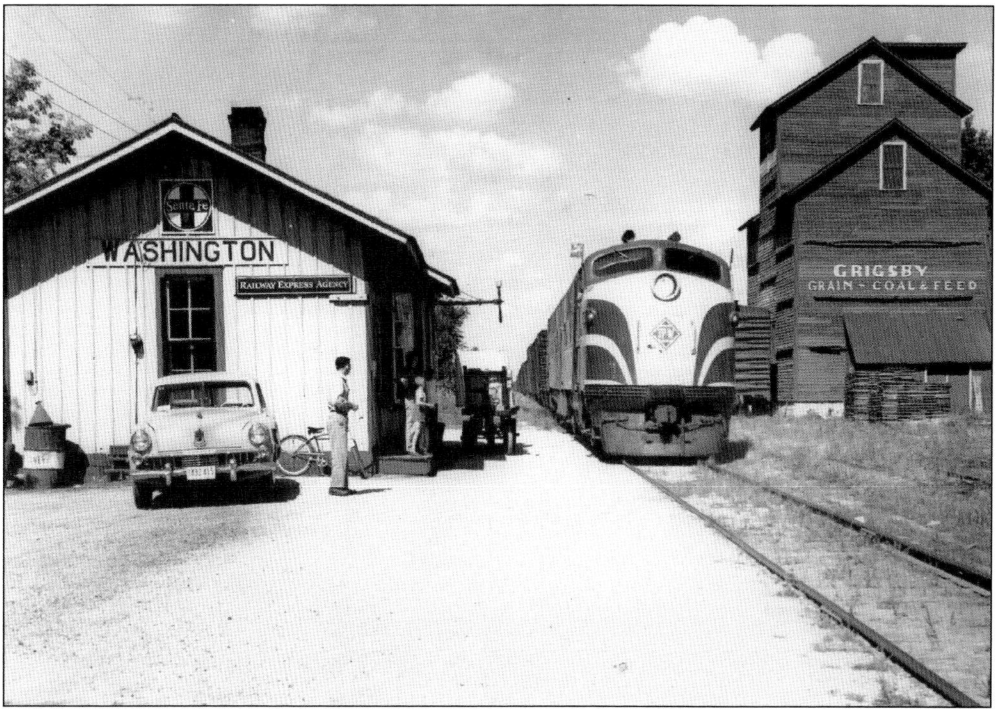

TP&W TRAIN—SANTA FE TRACKS. On July 26, 1950, the TP&W train No. 21 took a detour through Washington. Onlookers watch the engine No. 100 travel past the Santa Fe station and the Grigsby Grain Coal and Feed Elevator. (Courtesy of the Washington Historical Society, photograph by Leo Clark.)

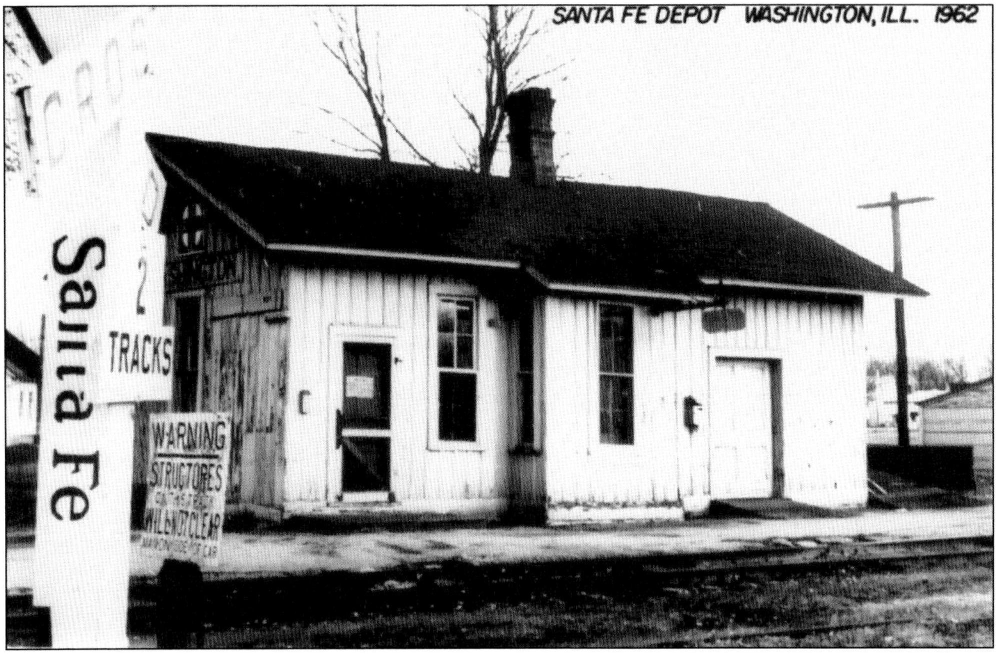

Santa Fe Freight Depot, 1962. Freight rail usage and stops were on the decline by the 1960s. The station itself, a simple wood-frame construction, began to fall into disrepair. As with passenger rail transport, freight rail service was affected by highway freight transportation, specifically the trucking industry.

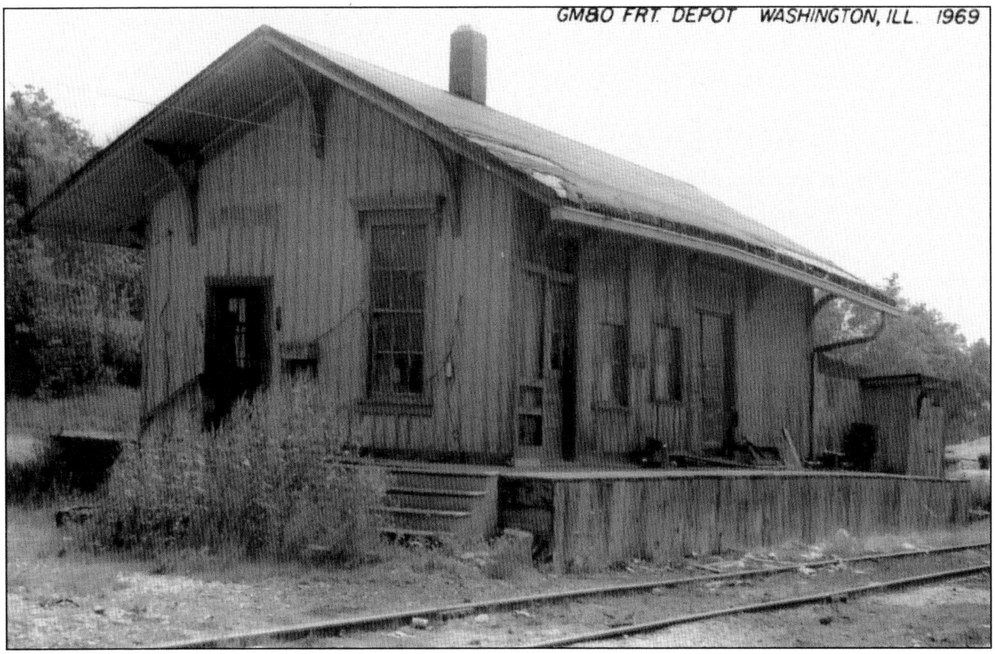

GM&O Freight Depot, 1969. This freight depot was located along what was the Chicago and Alton Railroad and east of the Dickinson Cannery. The Chicago and Alton would later become the Gulf, Mobile and Ohio while the Dickinson Cannery would become the Libby, McNeill and Libby Cannery.

Three

The Square

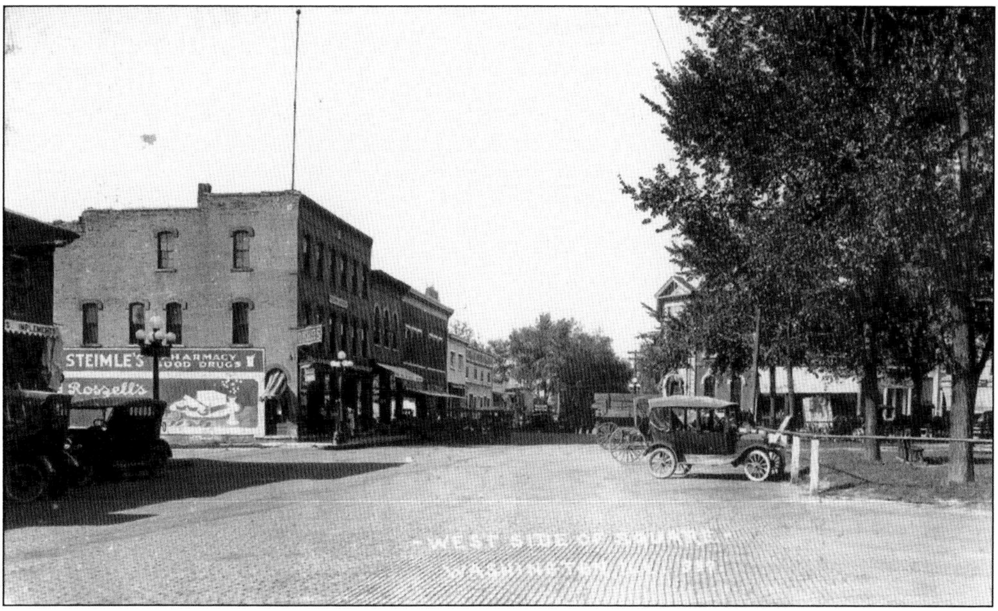

North Main Street, West Side. Brick paving around the square, the period streetlights, and the enclosure of this civic space created by the buildings and park space are shown wonderfully in this image. The multi-story Steimle Drug Store building on the north side of Peoria Street and the two-story building across the street to the south frame the entry into the square from the west. At the same time the chamfered corner of the Denhart Bank building on the north side faces this entry and greets those traveling into the space from the west. The mature trees within the square's park space act as yet another framing component and add another level of street definition. (Courtesy of the Washington Historical Society.)

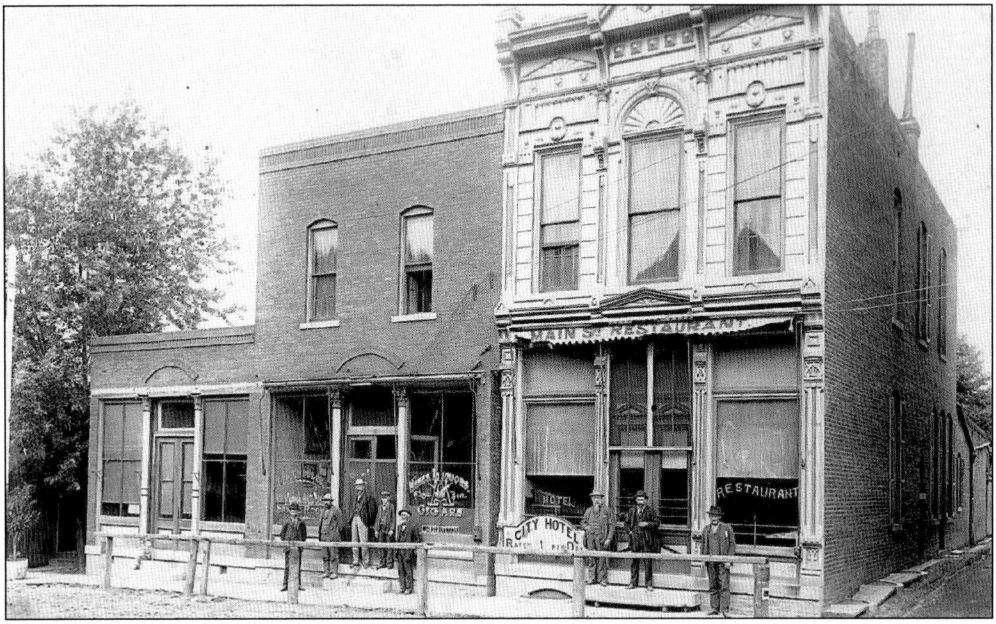

CITY HOTEL AND MAIN STREET RESTAURANT. Located on the east side of North Main Street, this series of buildings supported each other well through their uses, specifically catering to those traveling through town. While the more elaborately detailed building housed both a hotel and restaurant with a kitchen in the back, the buildings next door each contained a saloon, billiards room, and barbershop. Both buildings are primarily constructed of brick. The elaborate and finely detailed Victorian-style facade cladding the hotel and restaurant is composed of wood. As will be the case throughout square, private residences and rooms sit above a more public commercial establishment below. (Courtesy of the Washington Historical Society.)

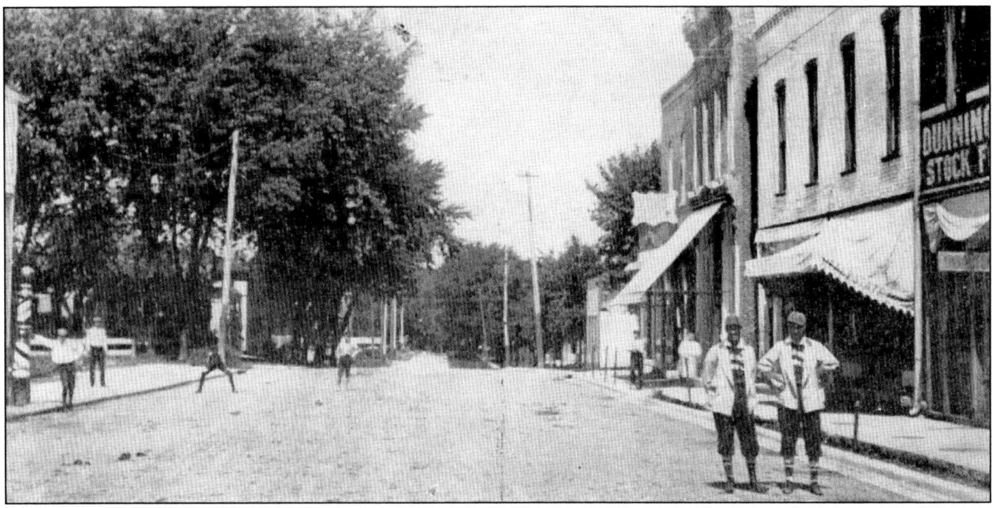

STREET BALL ON NORTH MAIN STREET. A view looking up North Main Street portrays a game between young kids. To the left sits a barber's pole that indicates not only another establishment for a shave and a trim, but also another chance to play billiards. The presence of the kids illustrates that streets, much like those in the residential areas found near the square, were not only a place for vehicles to travel, but also a place for pedestrians to travel uninhibited and enjoy the enclosed outdoor space created by the buildings.

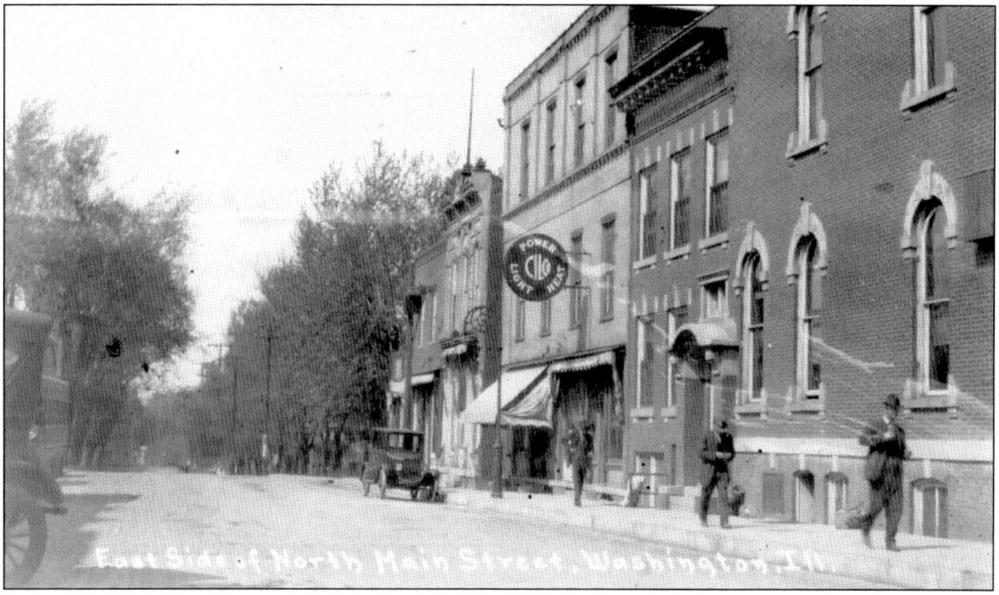

East Side of North Main Street, 1900s. This street scene portrays nearly the same view looking up North Main Street several years later. At this point in time, Main Street itself is now paved with brick, and the sidewalks and curbs are composed of a more finished concrete. The second-story blade sign for the Central Illinois Light Company illustrates an increased presence of utilities throughout the community by the beginning of the 20th century. The buildings are well detailed, and elements like varied window treatments increased the depth and interest across the facade.

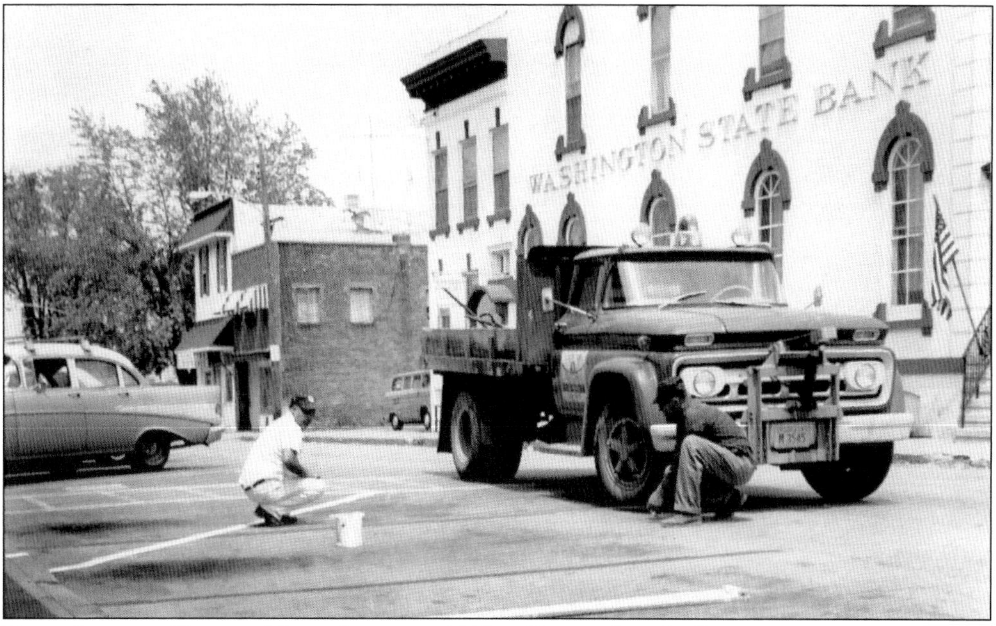

East Side of North Main Street, 1960s. Yet another similar vantage point on North Main Street shows painters striping a pedestrian crosswalk and parking spaces on the west side of the street. By this time, buildings along the east side of the street had drastically changed or disappeared. One can sense that the use of the street had changed as the presence of the automobile grew. (Courtesy of the Washington Historical Society, photograph by Leo Clark.)

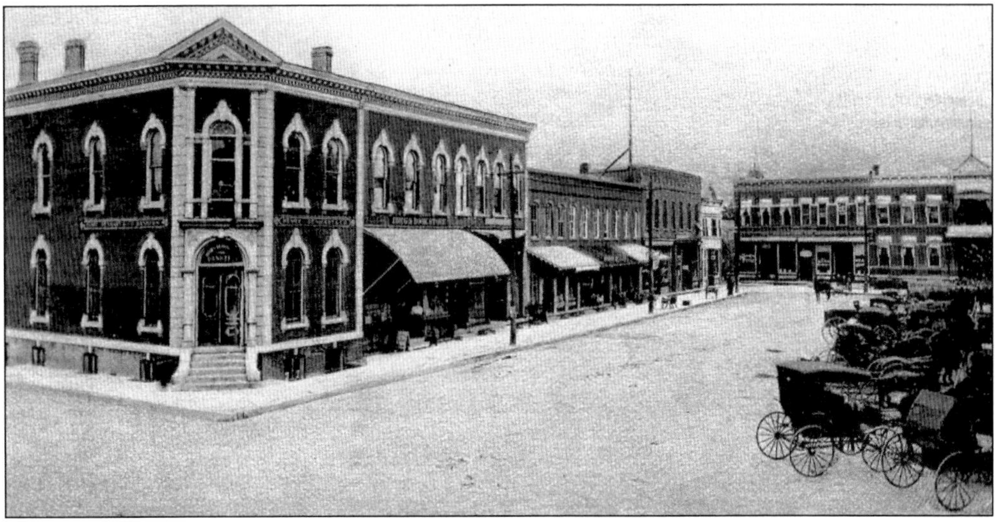

North Side of the Square. The north side of the square has undoubtedly stood as the strongest portion of this great civic space for good reason. Well-articulated, primarily brick, with stone detail facades, they are covered with large vertically oriented windows looking out onto the space. Residences can be found on the second story. Commercial spaces on the first floor face the street, and large open storefront windows display goods and provide an inviting atmosphere for those walking along the sidewalks. Awnings protruding from the building face add yet another layer of interest, advertising, and a simple way of controlling the natural light that enters the windows. The entire stretch of buildings works as a cohesive group and creates a strong street wall.

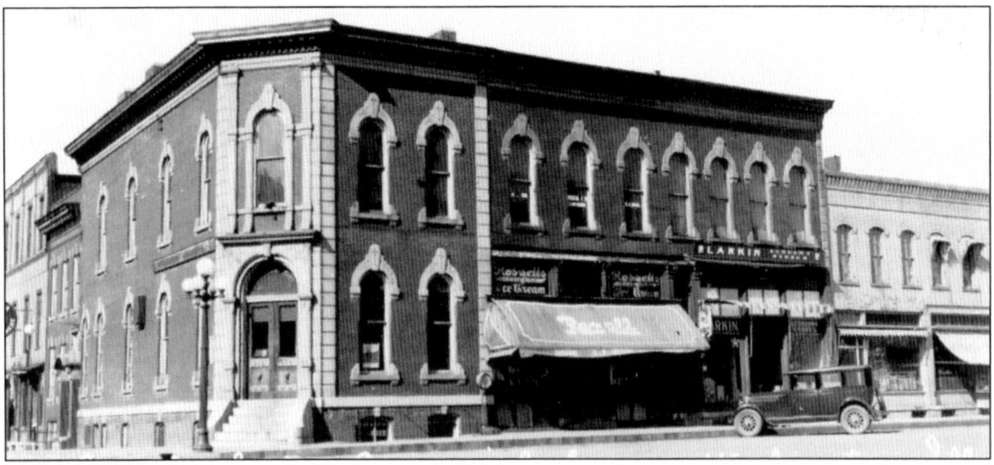

The Anchor. The Denhart Bank building stands prominently at the corner of North Main Street. Large commercial buildings, like this, that attract consistent customers serve a purpose similar to that of a large local anchor store in the conventional shopping mall. The popular building wraps the corner and leads pedestrians across its face to either the businesses of the northeast side of North Main Street or the businesses of the north side of the square. The building's front entry is prominent and handsomely designed. The chamfered corner treatment addresses the entry into the square from Peoria Street. One can see that the pediment that once sat atop the building has been removed. (Courtesy of the Washington Historical Society.)

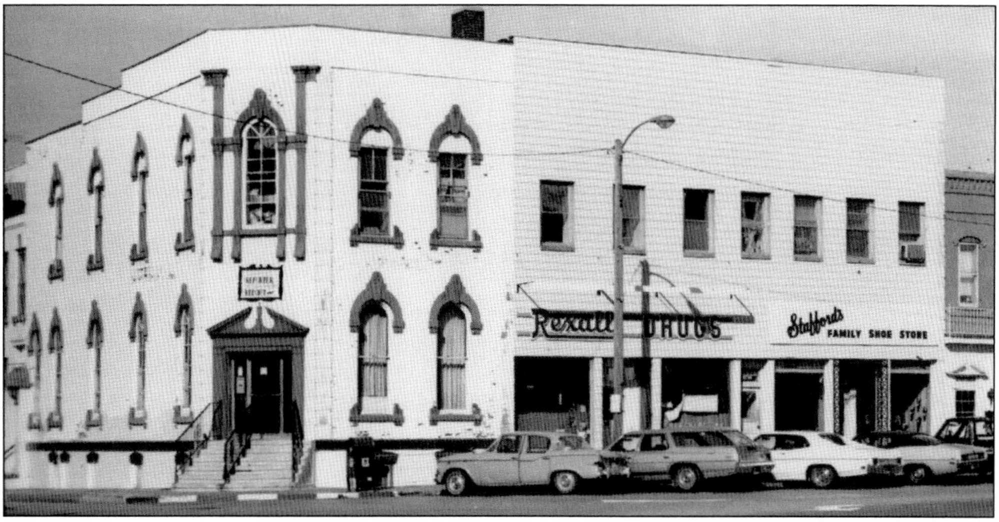

A Drastic Change. A later view of the former Denhart Bank building, at this time occupied by the *Reporter* newspaper, shows severe changes made to the facade. The cornice was completely removed, and the main entry was changed to a Colonial style. The building next door that was such a nice continuation of the corner building's exterior scheme was covered with synthetic siding, and the windows were shortened. These changes came during a period of time when suburban shopping schemes and aesthetics were in stark contrast to traditional town centers. Unfortunately the square, like so many other similar spaces during this time, changed like this in order to stay competitive. (Courtesy of the Washington Historical Society, photograph by Leo Clark.)

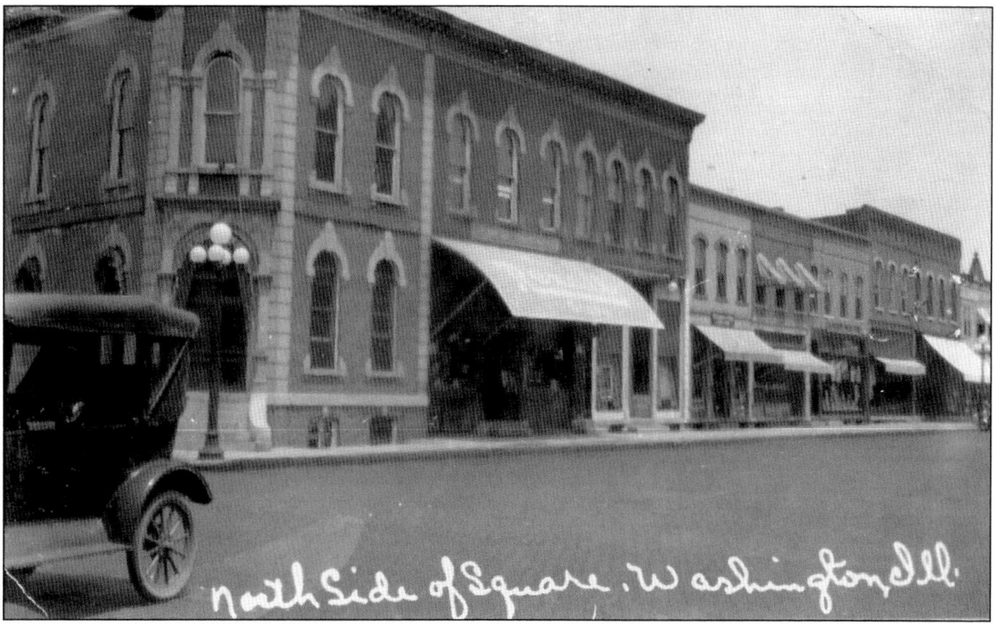

Mixed-Use Buildings. Another view looking northeast shows mixed-use buildings lining and enclosing the north side of the square. A mixed-use scheme works well in urban town centers like the square in that it provides commercial, office, and residential uses, that enhance the life of the space. A variety of different people visit the square, keeping it vibrant throughout the day and on into the night. (Courtesy of the Washington Historical Society.)

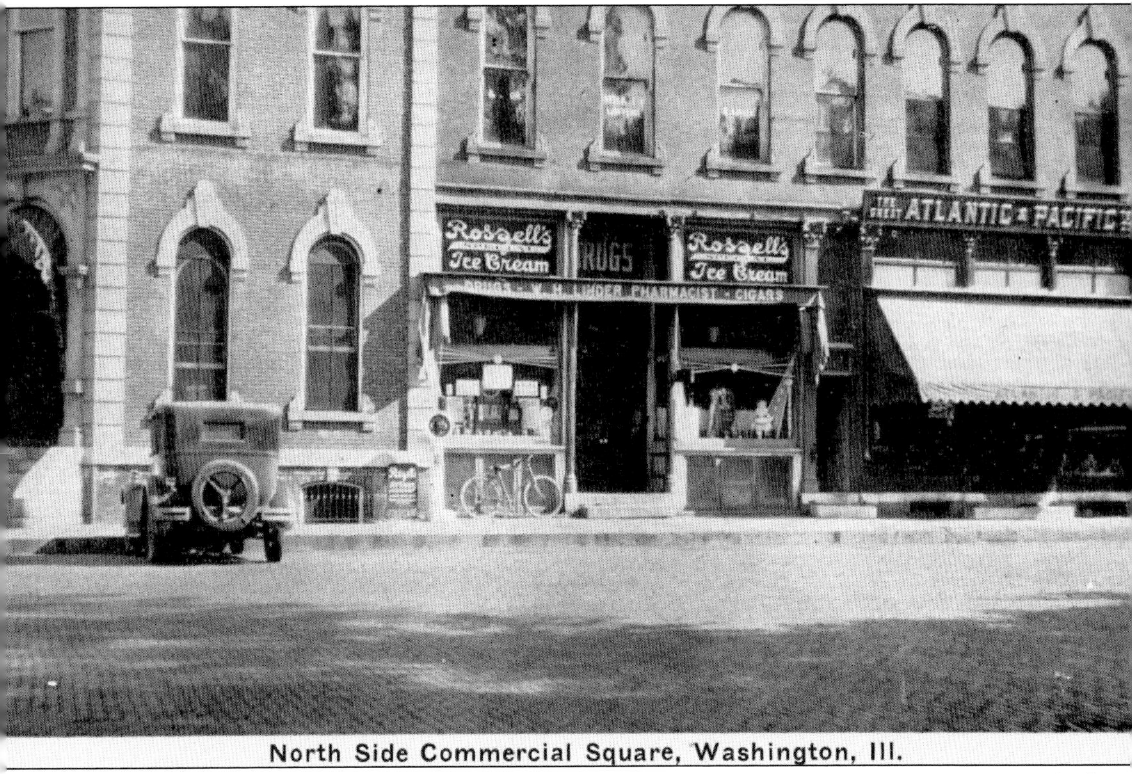

Ice Cream and Tea. To the east of the Denhart Bank the W. H. Linder Pharmacy, which prominently advertised the sale of Rossell's Ice Cream out of Peoria, and the Great Atlantic and Pacific Tea Company, were open for business each day. Although this particular store is no longer there, the Great Atlantic and Pacific Tea Company is still doing business throughout the world. The presence of popular brand names and stores of the time like these illustrates the financial success of the square at the time.

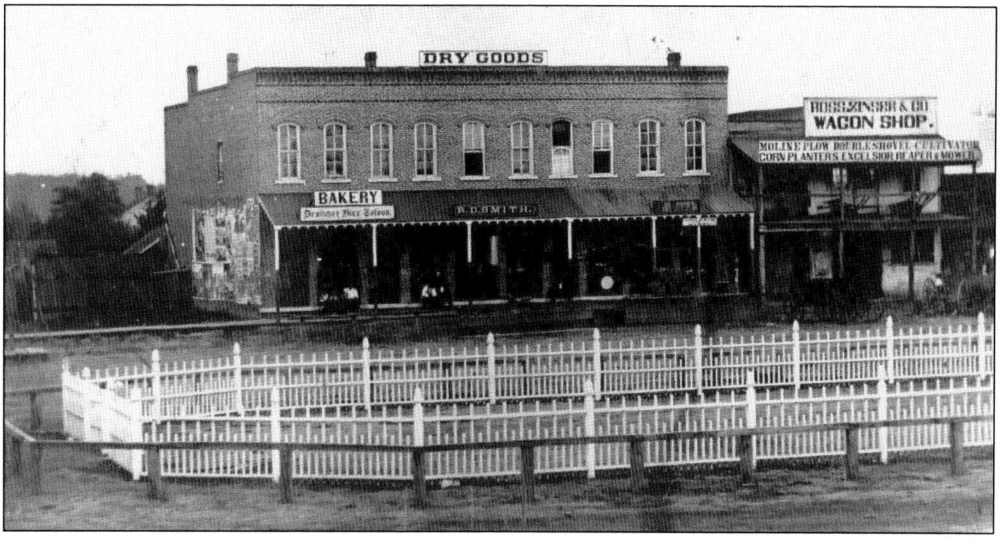

North Side, 1880s. This is one of the earliest images featuring any of the buildings on the square. The larger building shown, which still stands today, is composed of brick throughout with stone sills. Arched window treatments and varied brick patterns across the cornice area of the facade add a level of detail to an otherwise simple elevation. A German bakery and R. D. Smith's dry goods store comprise the first-floor commercial spaces. In the foreground one can see the humble beginnings of the square's inner park space, which then was a fenced-in space surrounded by hitching posts and rails. (Courtesy of the Washington Historical Society.)

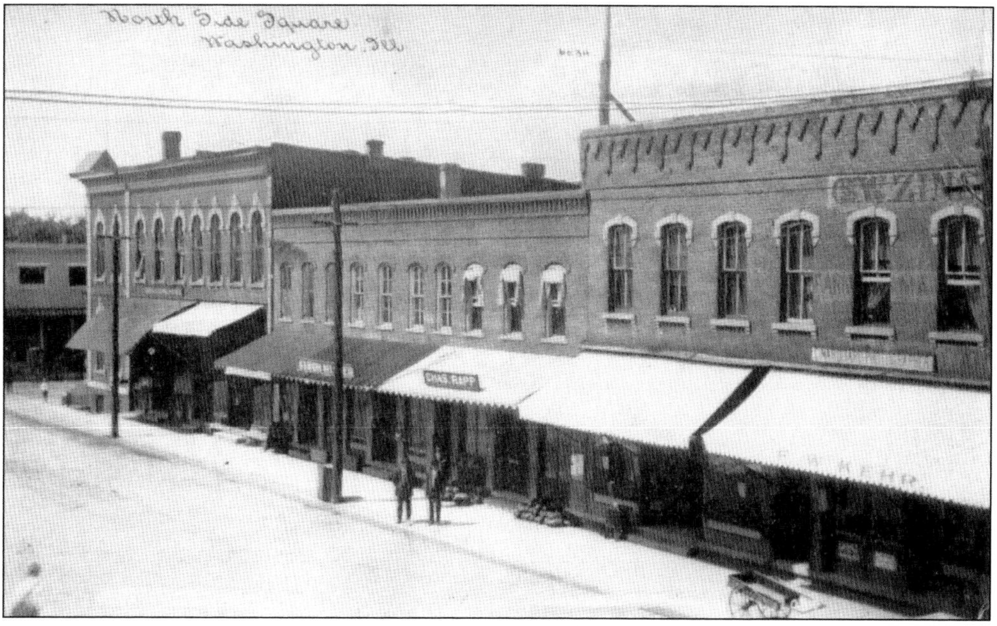

Northwest-Facing View. The series of north side buildings are similar enough in their schemes yet unique enough to be interesting across the entire street face. They act as the backdrop for many aspects of everyday life. Second-floor offices and residences possess windows that open out to the sidewalk and street below where ground-floor merchants sell their goods. All of this activity added to the vibrancy and success of the space.

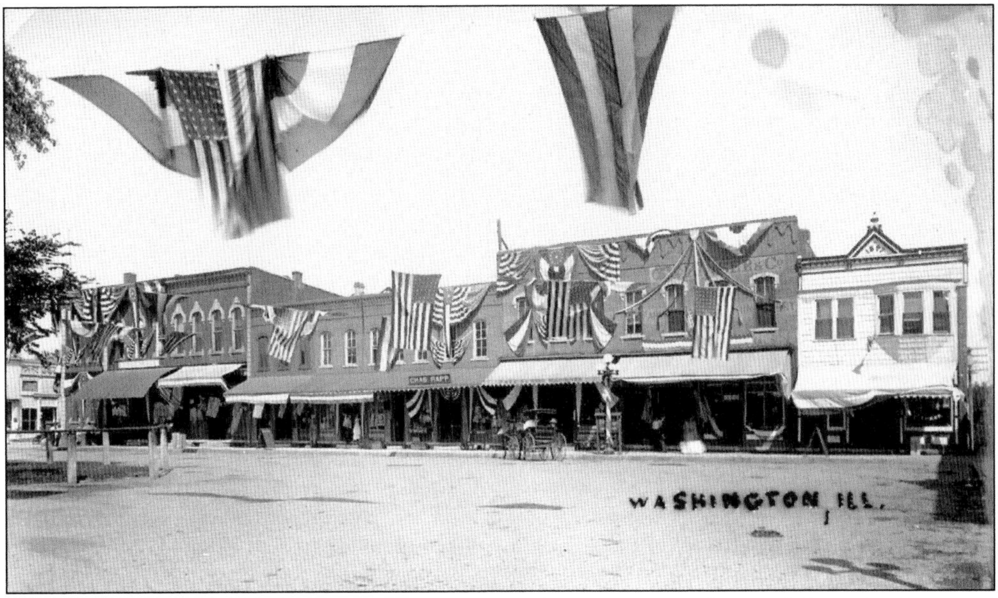

FOURTH OF JULY SCENE. The elaborate draping of the American flags and the red, white, and blue bunting over the buildings of the north side of the square create a dynamic scene during Independence Day celebrations. In 1826, there was a letter sent to Thomas Jefferson inviting him to be a part of the year-old community's Fourth of July celebration and a letter sent to John Adams asking him to provide a toast for the event. On June 24, from Monticello, Jefferson wrote back thanking Washington for the invitation but declining, while Adams would send along a toast. Both Jefferson and Adams would pass away on July 4, 1826.

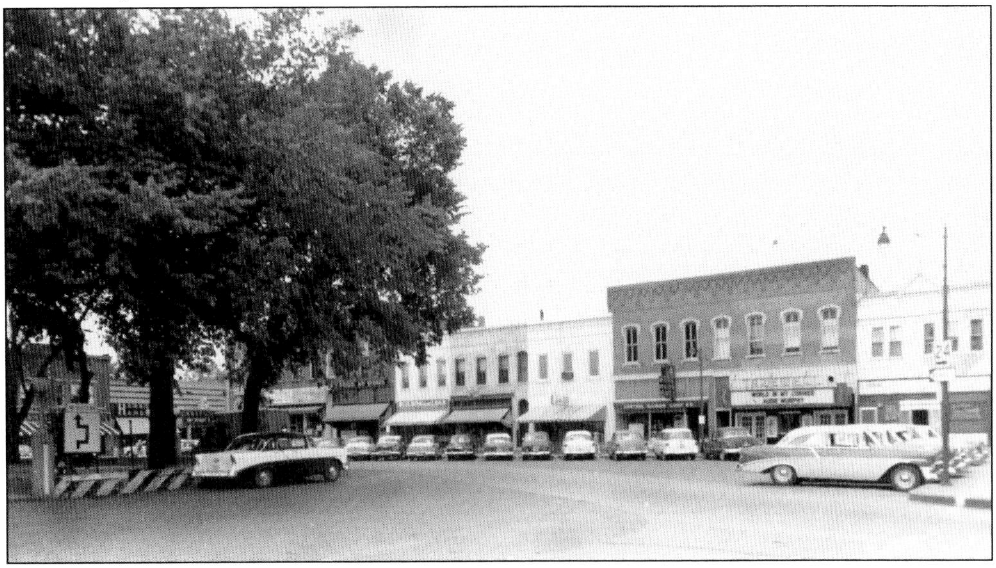

A SIMILAR VIEW NORTH, 1950S. A similar view looking north provides a familiar scene with a few noticeable changes. The addition of the automobile is the most obvious and would eventually become the most influential. The trees in the park space have matured, and a detailed retaining wall has replaced old hitching posts and rails. The buildings on the north side have new tenants, but no drastic physical changes can be seen other than individualized paint coats to each business across the face of the middle, and oldest, building.

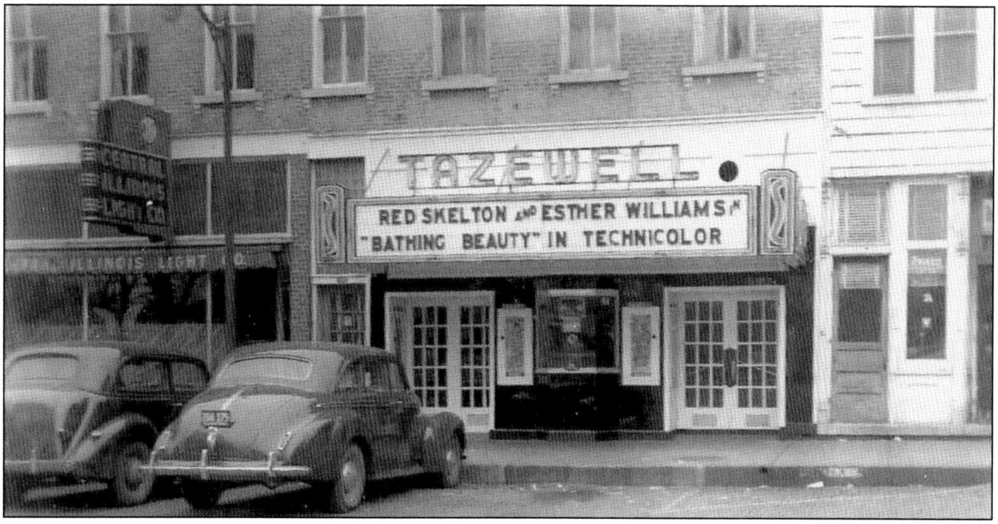

THE TAZEWELL. The sale of goods throughout the square is well known, but the many different entertainment venues found throughout the space sometimes goes forgotten. The Tazewell movie theater was located on the north side of the square for many years, providing local citizens with the opportunity to head out and enjoy the latest movies of the day. Through the years one could find opera houses, theaters, bowling alleys, and billiard rooms scattered throughout the square providing entertainment and cultural attractions while increasing the diverse uses of the space. (Courtesy of the Washington Historical Society.)

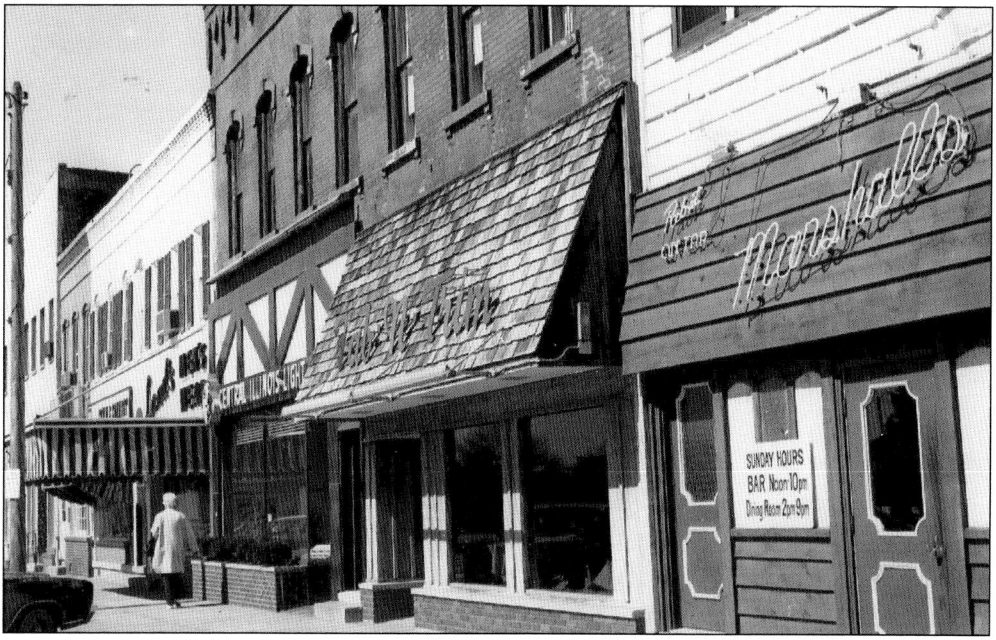

NORTH SIDE SIDEWALK VIEW, 1950S. Looking down the sidewalk one can begin to see changes to the buildings. These changes were made in response to the growing influences of the moderne movement and the developments it brought, including strip shopping centers and malls. Large windows once used for display were replaced or covered up. Simple canvas awnings were being replaced, and other less compatible elements were added. (Courtesy of the Washington Historical Society, photograph by Leo Clark.)

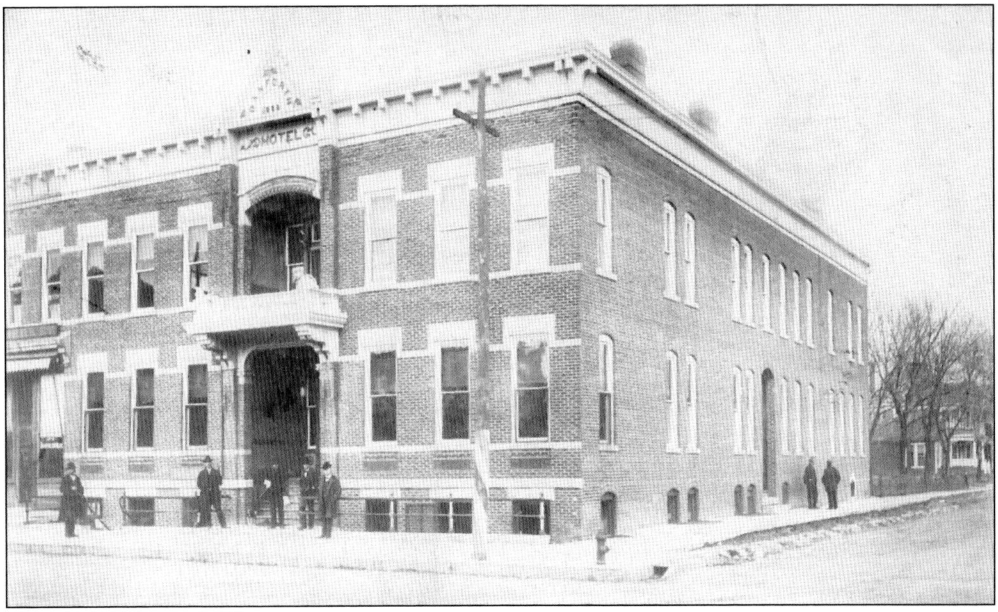

THE DANFORTH HOTEL. The large hotel proudly sat on the north side of the Walnut Street entry into the square. Composed primarily of brick with stone details, the building's facade was designed in such a way to match what was then a market next door. Windows look out on to the street on either side, and a large balcony on the second story looks out onto the square.

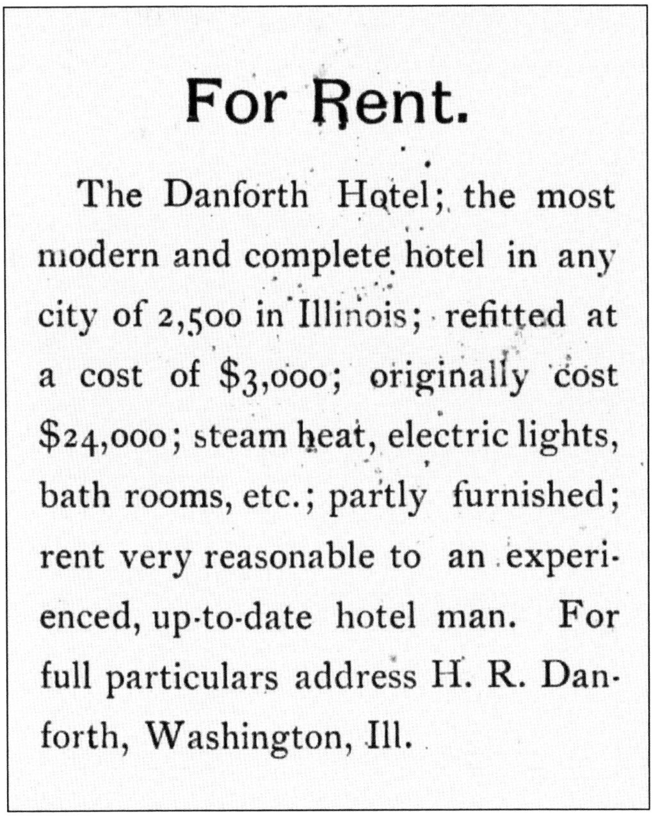

For Rent.

The Danforth Hotel; the most modern and complete hotel in any city of 2,500 in Illinois; refitted at a cost of $3,000; originally cost $24,000; steam heat, electric lights, bath rooms, etc.; partly furnished; rent very reasonable to an experienced, up-to-date hotel man. For full particulars address H. R. Danforth, Washington, Ill.

DANFORTH FOR RENT. An advertisement for the rental of the Danforth Hotel was put out by Henry R. Danforth himself. Danforth was born in Washington and became a very successful banker and farmer who was shrewd with his money and keen on investment opportunities. Along with his uncle George W. Danforth, he built the town of Danforth. When Henry constructed the hotel, the people of Washington, out of appreciation, elected him mayor.

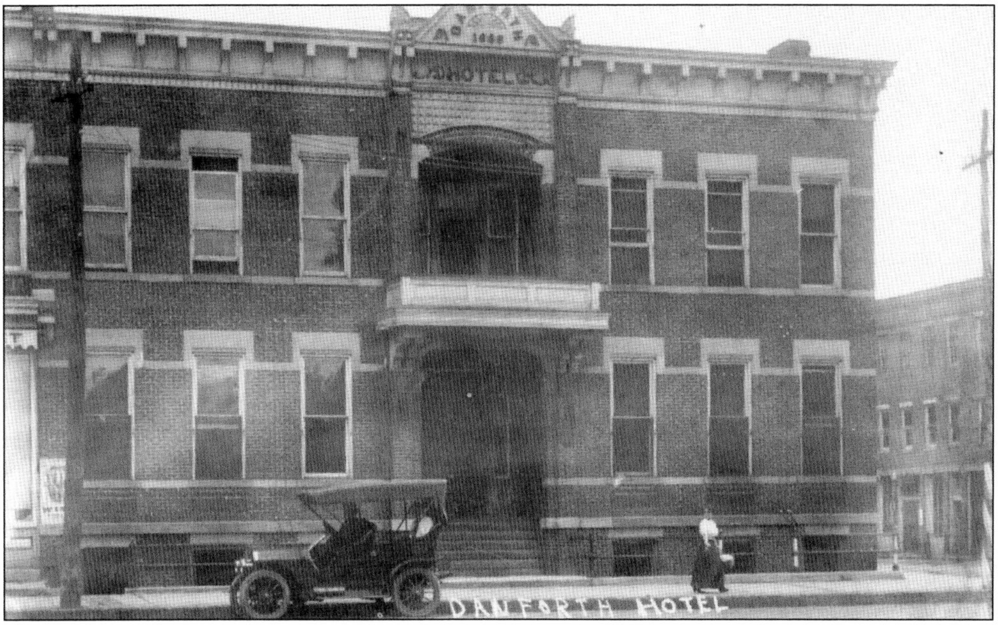

STREET SCENE AT THE DANFORTH. A symmetrical elevation composed of tall squared windows with Gothic-style stone window surrounds and banding makes up a very simple rhythmic facade. A wood cornice and elaborated pediment with the hotel name and date adds personality. The woman and the automobile below on the street illustrate the scale of the building itself.

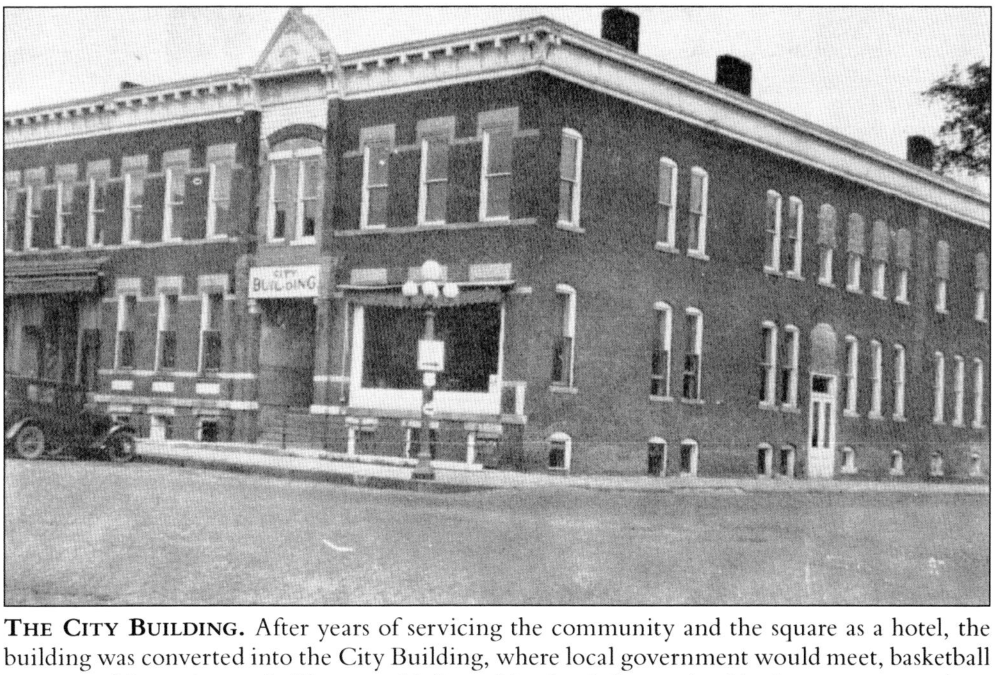

THE CITY BUILDING. After years of servicing the community and the square as a hotel, the building was converted into the City Building, where local government would meet, basketball teams would practice, and a library and jail would exist. A few noticeable changes were made to the exterior of the building when the change occurred. The second-story balcony was removed, and two windows were put in its place. One large picture window replaced three first-floor windows, and the side entry on Walnut Street was shortened.

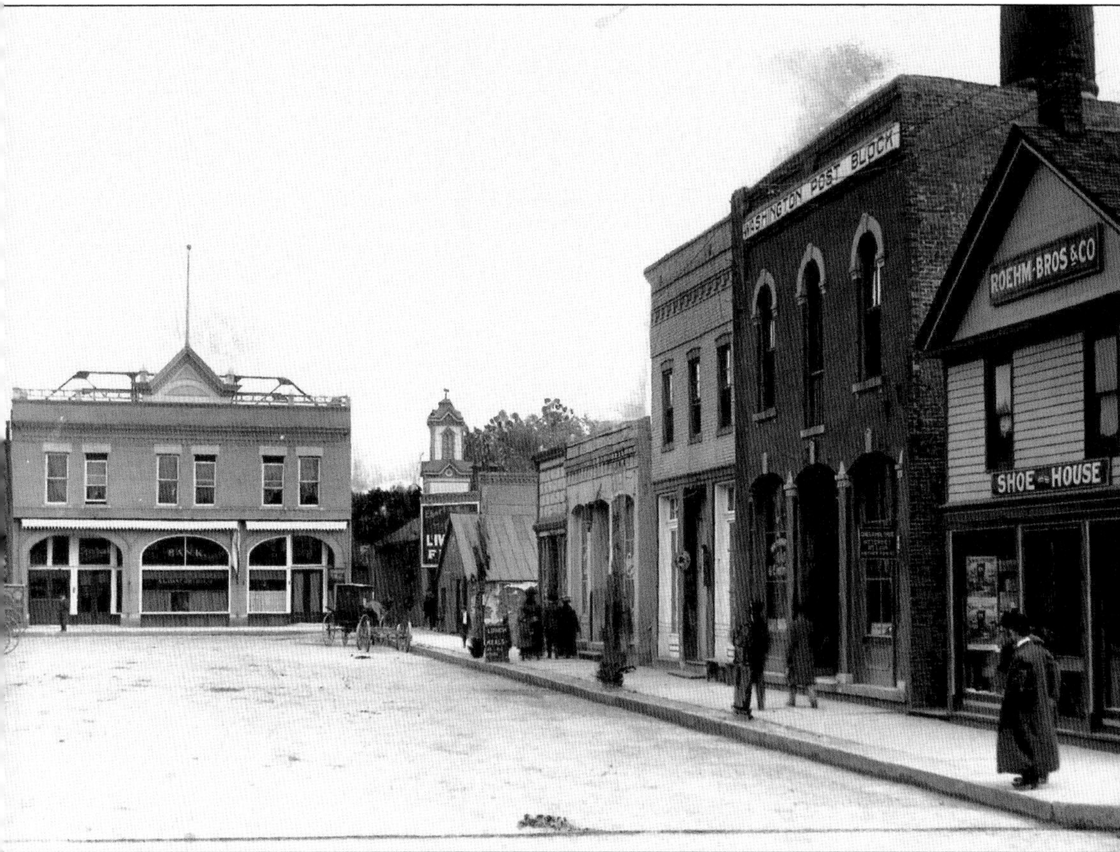

DANFORTH BANK AND THE SOUTH SIDE. The Danforth name traveled across Walnut Street to the south and the face of another building. This building, the Danforth Bank, was also a two-story structure composed primarily of brick. Paired windows sat below brick detailing on the second floor and large arched storefront windows sat below, delineating the entrance. A wood pediment-like structure was added to the top of the building and held a flagpole. This gesture was similar to that across the way at the Danforth Hotel. The rest of the buildings on the south side of the square were more modest than their counterparts to the north but still held their place and created a fine street wall.

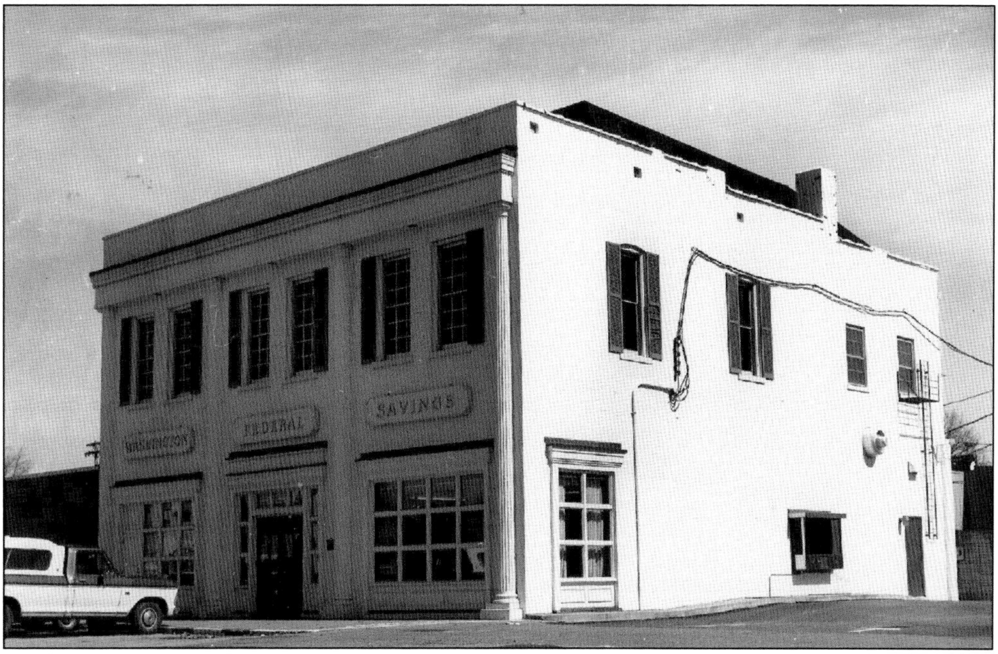

BANK FACADE REWORK. When the Washington Federal Savings moved across the square from its previous location on the north side, there was a great deal of changes made to the facade of the former Danforth Bank building. Engaged columns were added along with a entablature in order to create a classical look. (Courtesy of the Washington Historical Society, photograph by Leo Clark.)

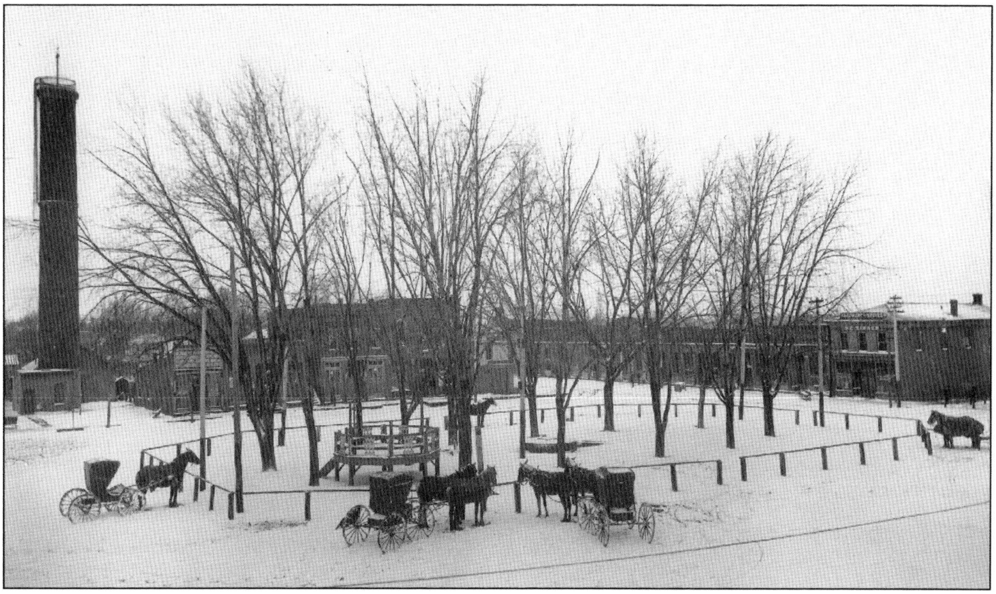

SOUTH SIDE. During the early 1900s, the park space within the square was very simply defined by a series of hitching posts and rails. To the left of the image, the City Water Works tower looms over the two-story commercial buildings. Although at a smaller scale, the corner of the south side along South Main Street and the west side of South Main Street each make up a fine street wall and provide a solid corner. (Courtesy of the Washington Historical Society.)

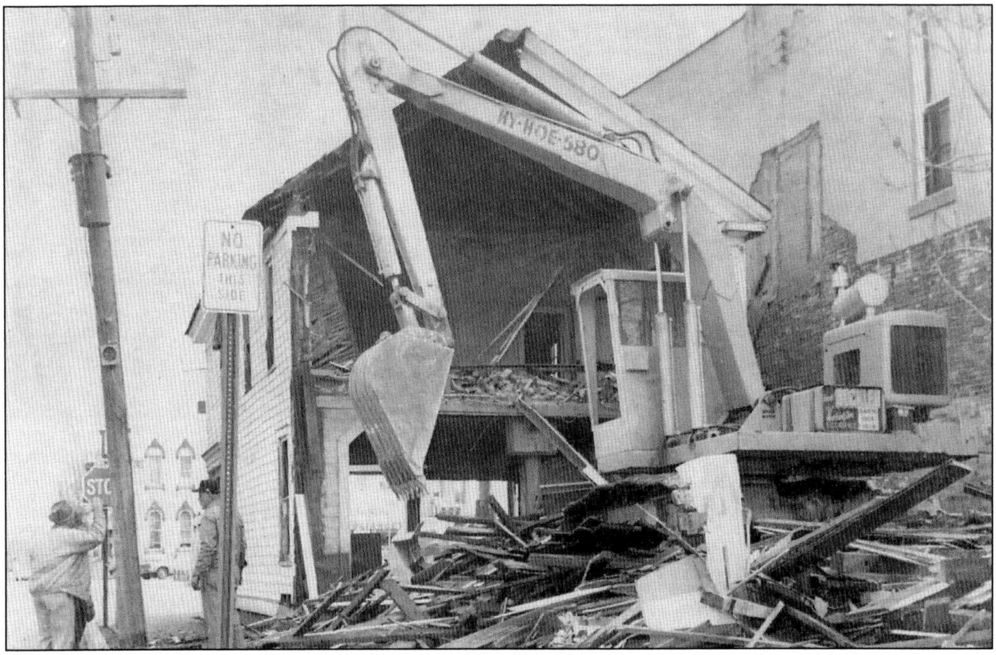

Roehm Shoe Store Demolition. The demolition of this corner building was a great loss for the entire square space. Not only was a longtime business removed, but a building that held the corner, much like the Denhart Bank building did on the north side, was lost and the south side was significantly weakened. (Courtesy of the Washington Historical Society.)

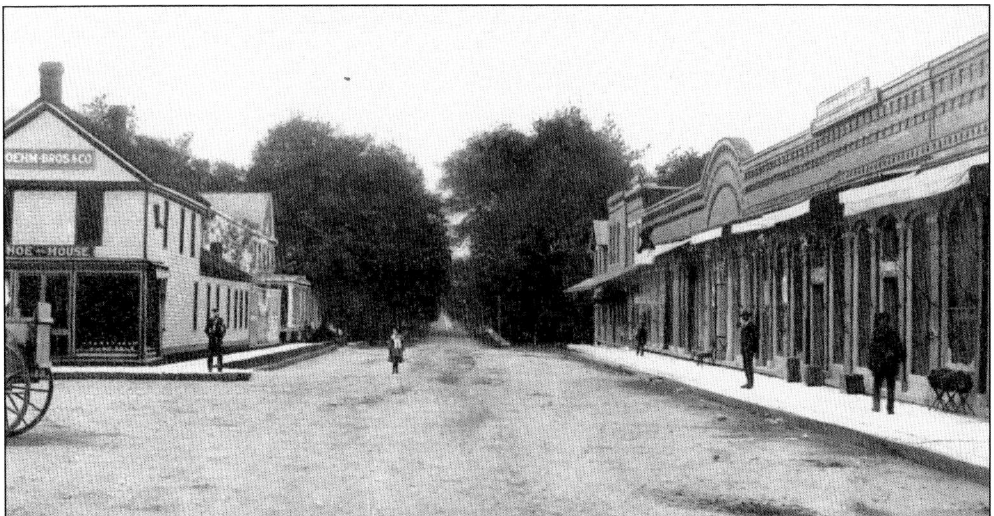

View Down South Main Street. A look down South Main Street shows a tree-lined residential street leading into the square just as it does to the north. The two-story Roehm Brothers and Company Shoe House sits on the east side while a series of one- and two-story commercial buildings line the west side. The community's early post office sits amid the storefronts on the west. The child in the street, as well as the pedestrians on the sidewalk, illustrates the scale of the one-story buildings and the intimacy that is created within the street.

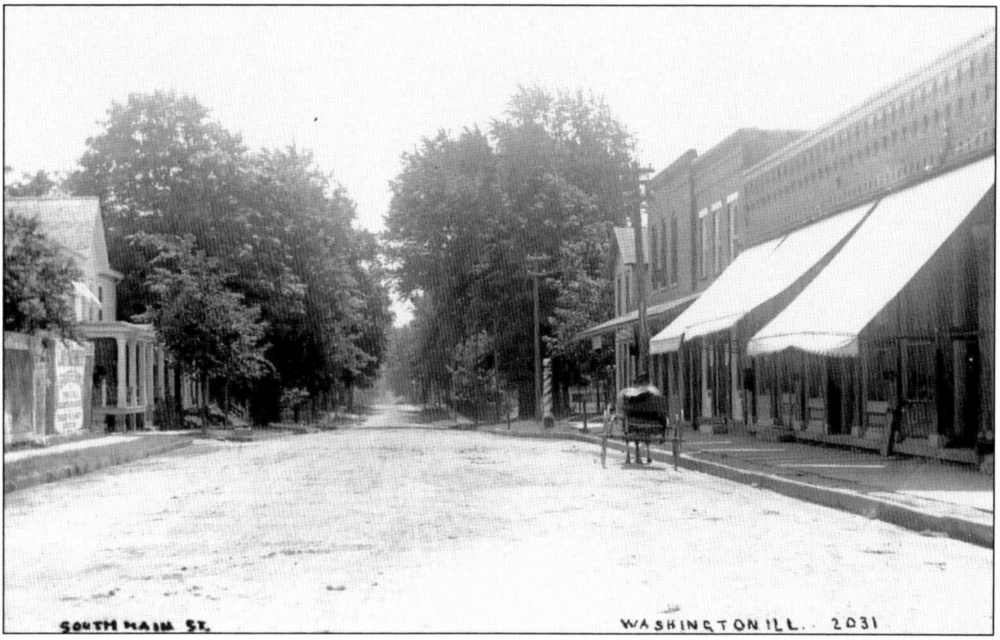

SOUTH MAIN STREET VIEW. The transition between residential homes and the commercial buildings of the square is wonderfully smooth. Grassed parkways in front of residences give way to full sidewalks in front of business, and there is very little change in scale between the built structures. The front porches of the homes that line the streets and sidewalks bleed directly into and even mirror the awnings of the open and inviting commercial storefronts.

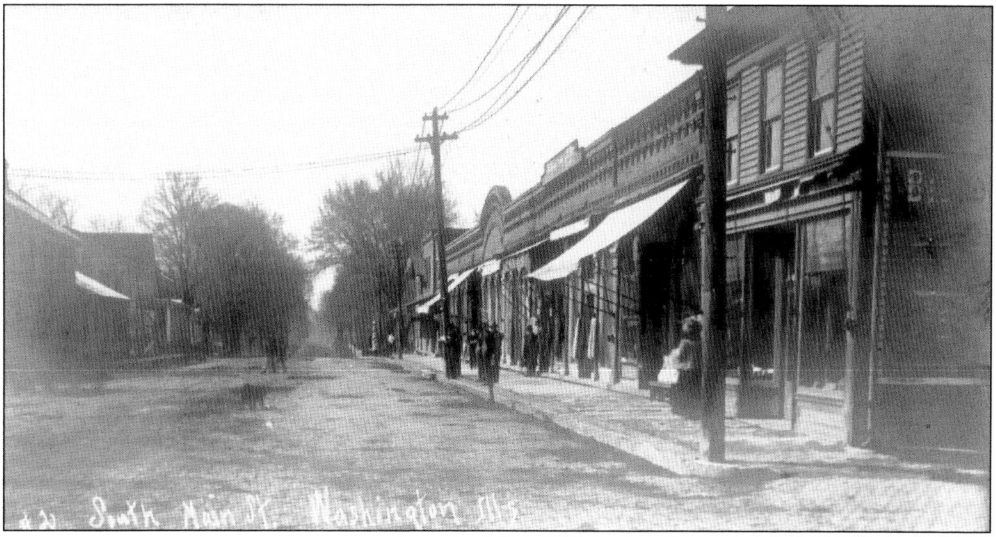

SOUTH MAIN BUSINESSES. One of the buildings that lined the west side of South Main Street was one of the most interesting on the entire square. The brick arch at the middle portion of the building indicated the entry to what was Pfeiffer's Department Store. The series of bays presumably featured those different kinds of goods, and the store would be divided as such. The brickwork itself is finely detailed, and the interesting shape and orientation of the building and its program enhances the character of the square.

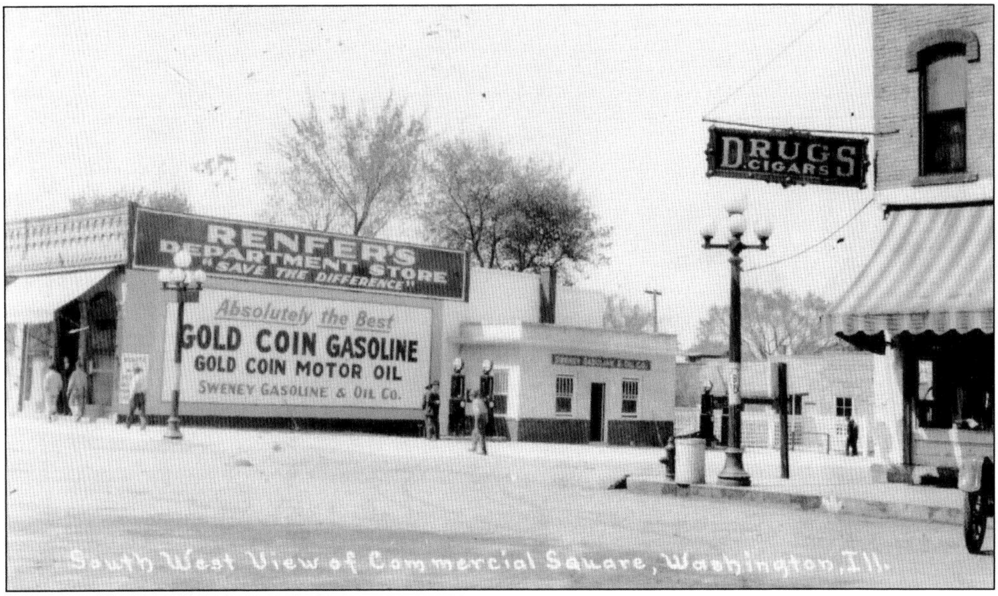

SOUTH MAIN STREET CORNER, 1920S. The loss of one of the buildings framing the Peoria Street entry into the square illustrates how important a significantly scaled building holding the corner is. A corner gas station stands in its place here in the photograph. Also present are the handsome five bulb streetlights that could be found along the sidewalks throughout the square.

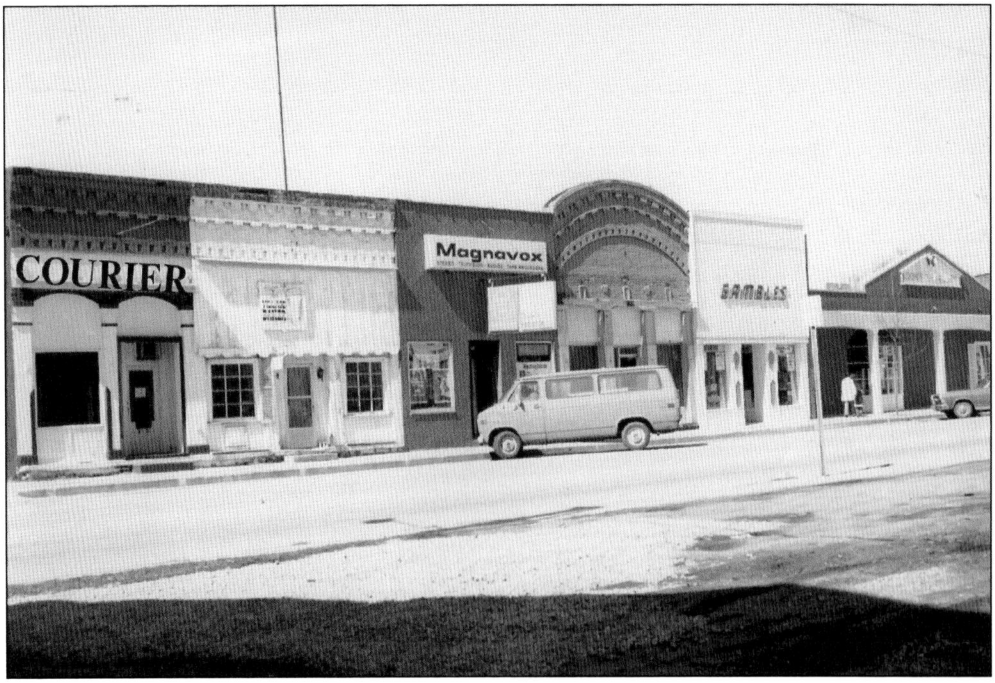

SOUTH MAIN STREET, WEST SIDE. The changes made to a once cohesive building elevation are shown here in the 1970s. As seen elsewhere on the square, the trend had been to change traditional spaces and buildings into something quite different, more streamlined and in step with stylistic trends. Ornate brickwork and detailing were either removed or covered, and windows were filled in or altered.

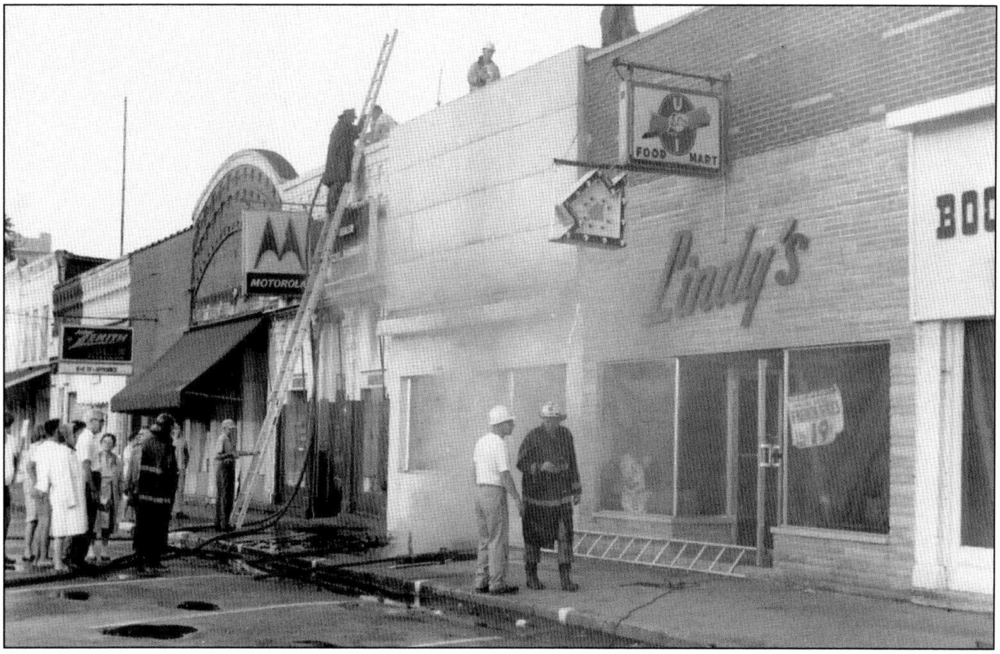

FIRE ON THE SOUTHWEST SIDE. Onlookers watch as firemen work their way onto the roof of one of the buildings along the west side of South Main Street. Smoke can be seen coming out of one of the front entries. The northernmost portion of this stretch of buildings would later be removed as well as the two separate buildings to the south near St. Mark's Lutheran Church. Today the remaining portions are largely covered by the cladding and other exterior treatments that had already begun to overwhelm the original facade. (Courtesy of the Washington Historical Society, photographs by Leo Clark.)

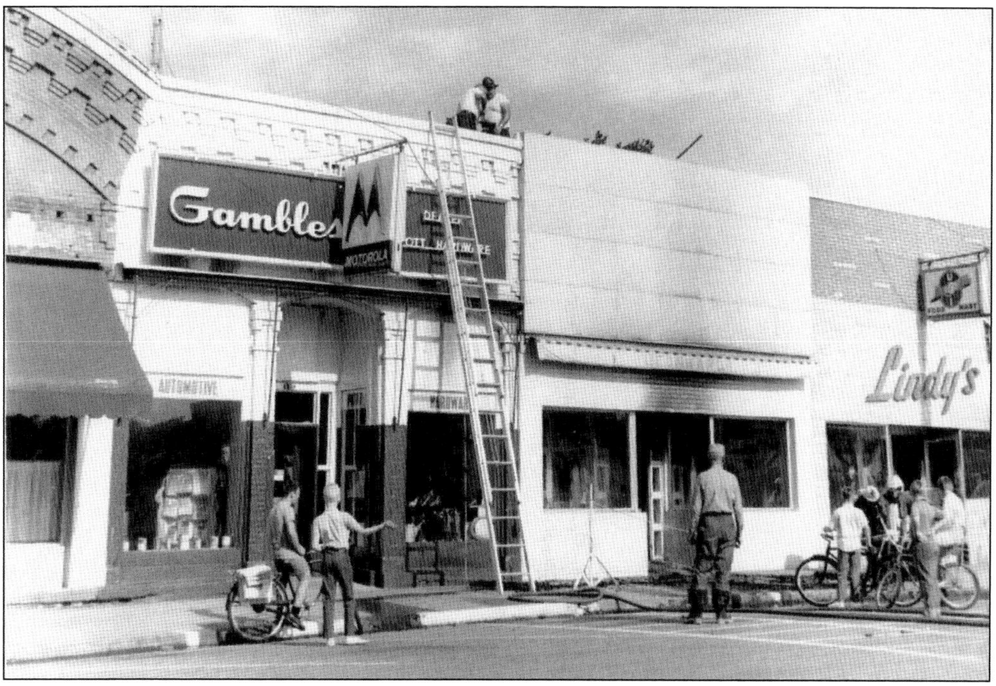

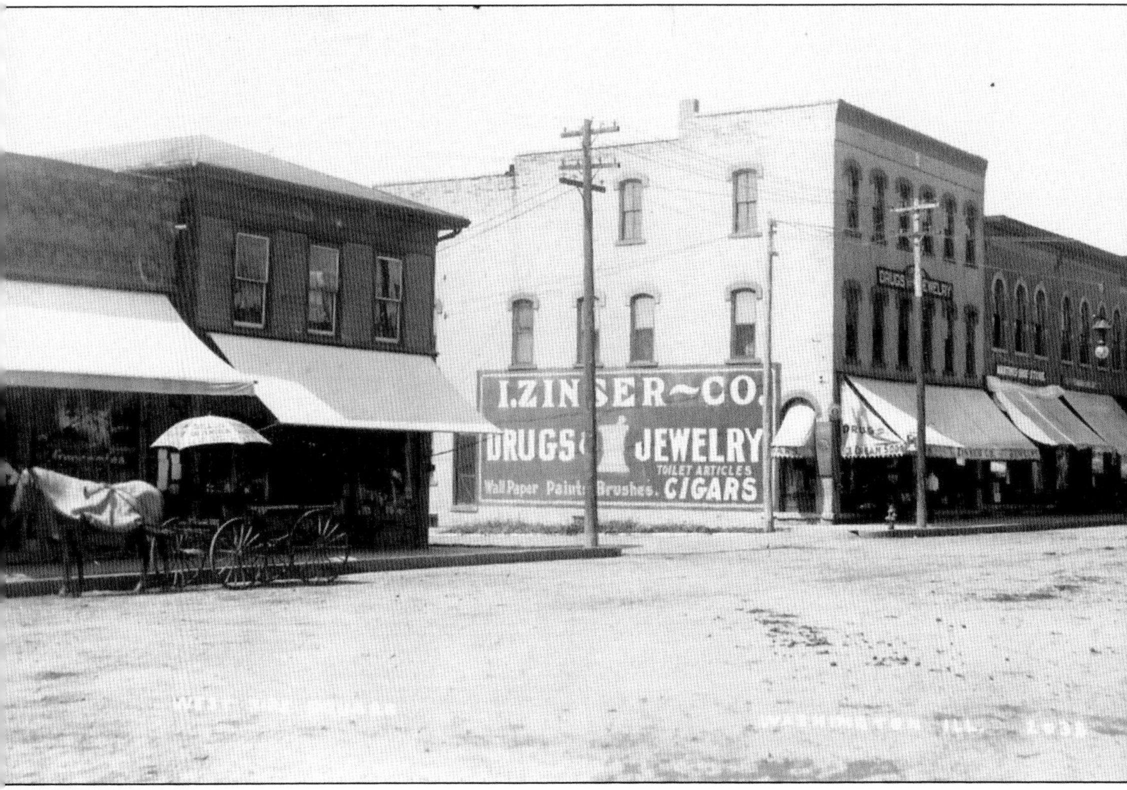

PEORIA STREET ENTRY INTO THE SQUARE. An unappreciated element of the square today has to do with how well the space is enclosed, or is not enclosed. This view of corner buildings on either side of Peoria Street along Main Street provides a glimpse into how important taller buildings are at corners and how much stronger the entire space looks with these two acting as the gateway. The three-story I. Zinser Company building was one of the tallest buildings on the square. At one time the building was an opera house, a wonderful cultural asset that was not uncommon then.

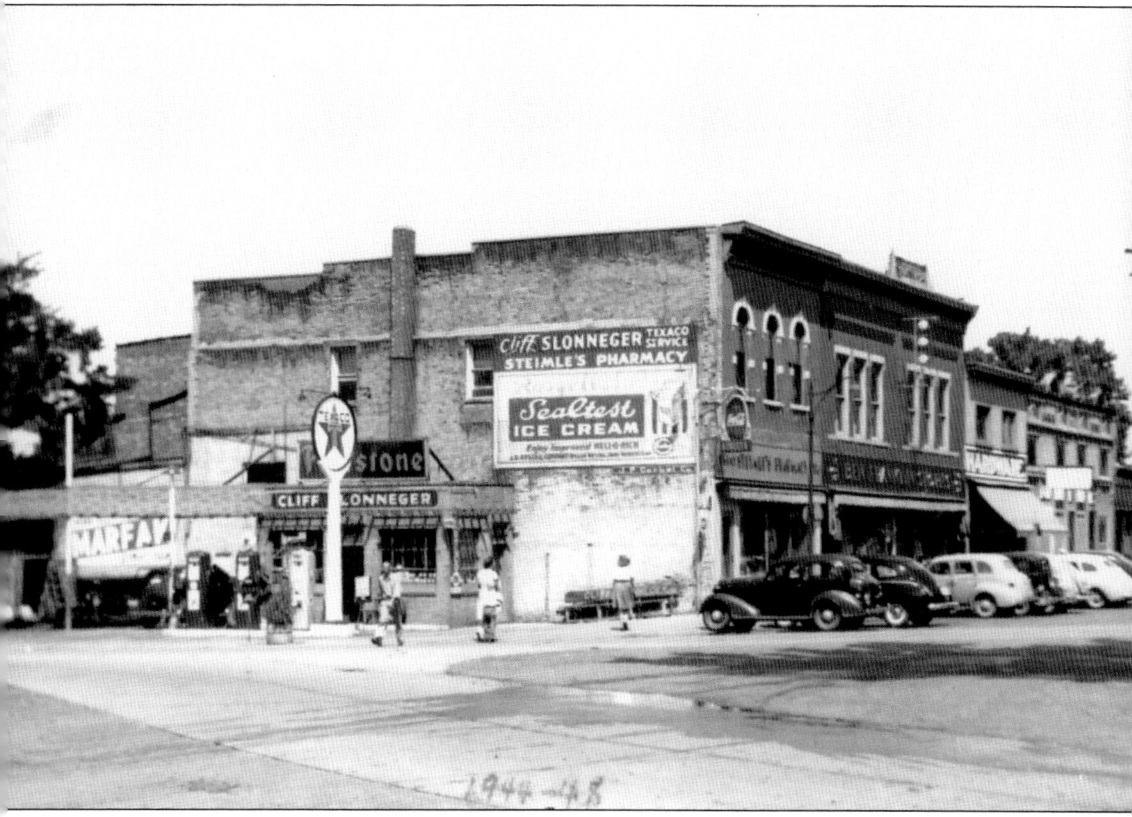

North Main Street, 1940s. Similar to the loss of the building across Peoria Street to the south, the loss of the three-story former I. Zinser Company and then Steimle Drug Store building greatly reduces the visual impact of the entry. The loss of the building gives a sense of a wider Peoria Street and the intimacy of the space is weakened. As with the opposite corner, a gas station filled the empty lot. (Courtesy of the Washington Historical Society.)

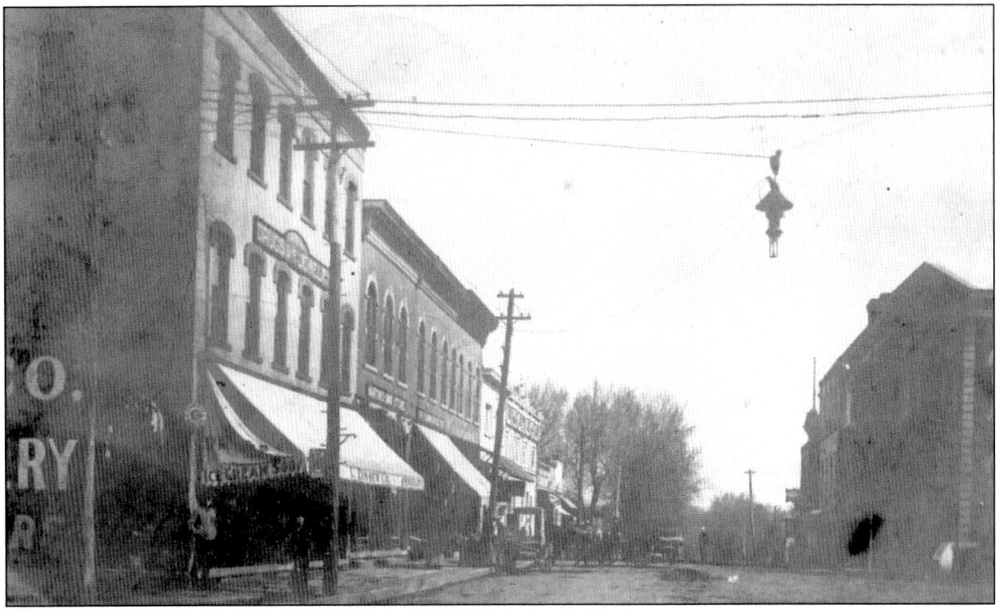

NORTH MAIN STREET, WEST SIDE. The series of taller buildings along North Main Street coupled with the Denhart Bank building across the street solidified the notion that the square was indeed a very urban space. The square gave the community an intimate, diverse, dense place in which many of the basic daily needs could be met within walking distance of one's own home in the nearby residential neighborhoods. The presence of elevated wire electric streetlights at an early time illustrates the progressiveness of the services provided within the square area. (Courtesy of the Washington Historical Society.)

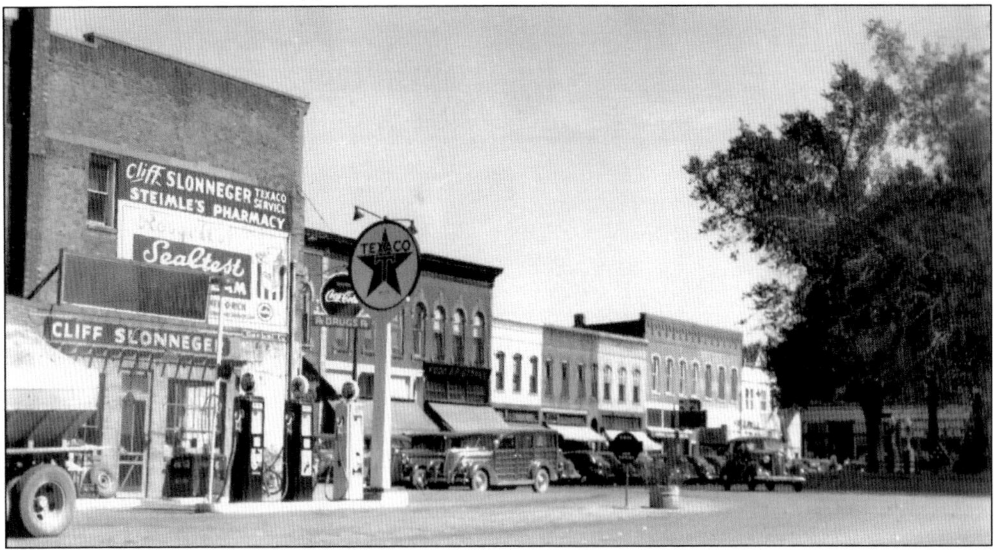

CORNER BUILDING LOST—ADVERTISING SPACE GAINED. With the removal of the three-story building and the placement of the gas station, there was a new advertising opportunity for the building next door that became the new corner structure. As with the former corner building, painted advertisements crawl up the south face, and a corner Coca-Cola blade sign extends out around the corner for eastbound Peoria Street travelers to view. (Courtesy of the Washington Historical Society.)

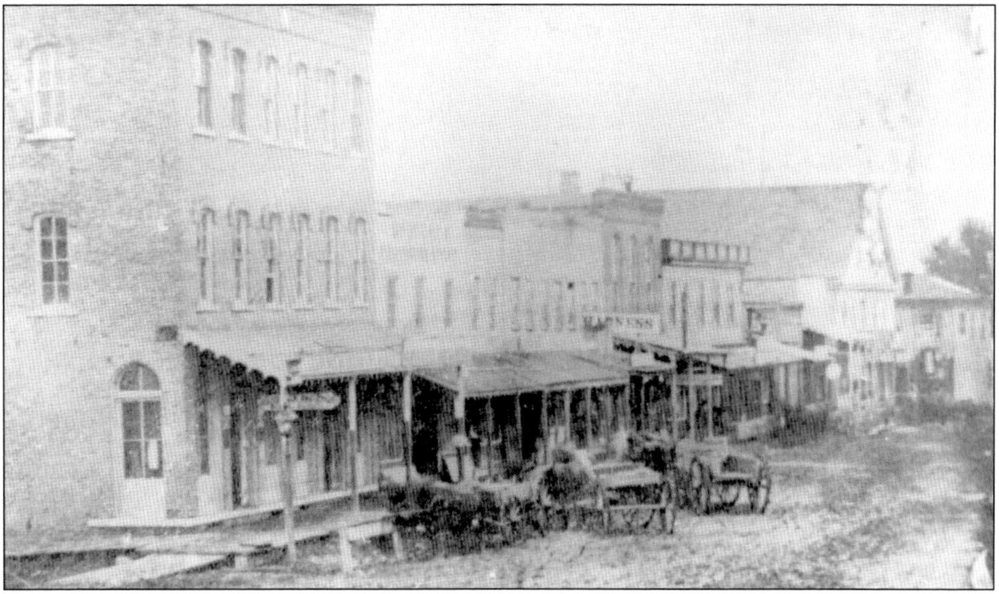

NORTH MAIN STREET, WEST SIDE, 1880S. A very early view of the corner of Peoria and Main Streets shows unpaved dirt streets, wood boardwalks in front of the commercial buildings, and horses and carts tied up directly out front. At the end of the block one can see the Sherman House, one of the earliest buildings to be located on the square.

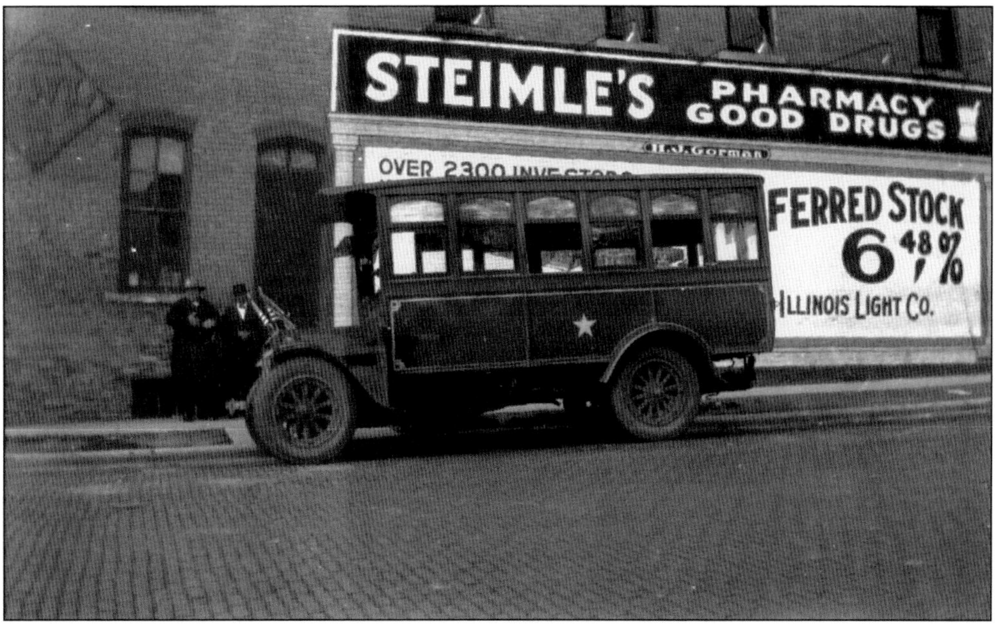

WHITE STAR BUS LINE. A White Star Bus adorned with American flags sits outside of the Steimle Drug Store on the brick street at the corner of Peoria and Main Streets. It appears the drivers are standing alongside the building waiting for passengers. The pitch of the street at this location on its approach to the square shows the topography and how elevated the square area is in relation to the surrounding terrain. (Courtesy of the Washington Historical Society.)

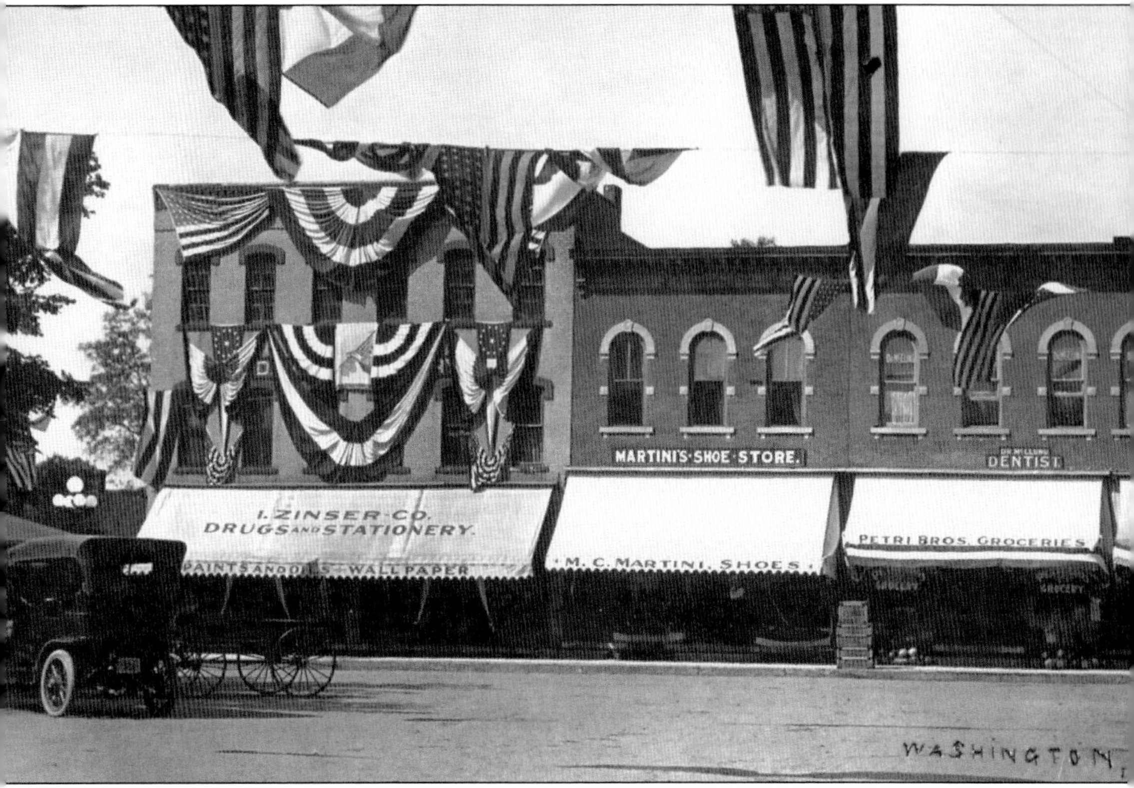

Independence Day, West Side. Another image shows the pageantry displayed on the Fourth of July across the facades of the buildings on the square. American flags and red, white, and blue bunting stretch across the square from the park space to the buildings. The buildings on the west side to the left of the I. Zinser and Company building are two-story well-proportioned brick buildings with stone window surrounds and wood cornices above. While the second floor contains residences for some and offices for others, the first-floor commercial areas play an important role on the street, inviting potential customers and filling the streetscape with activity along its extent. (Courtesy of the Washington Historical Society.)

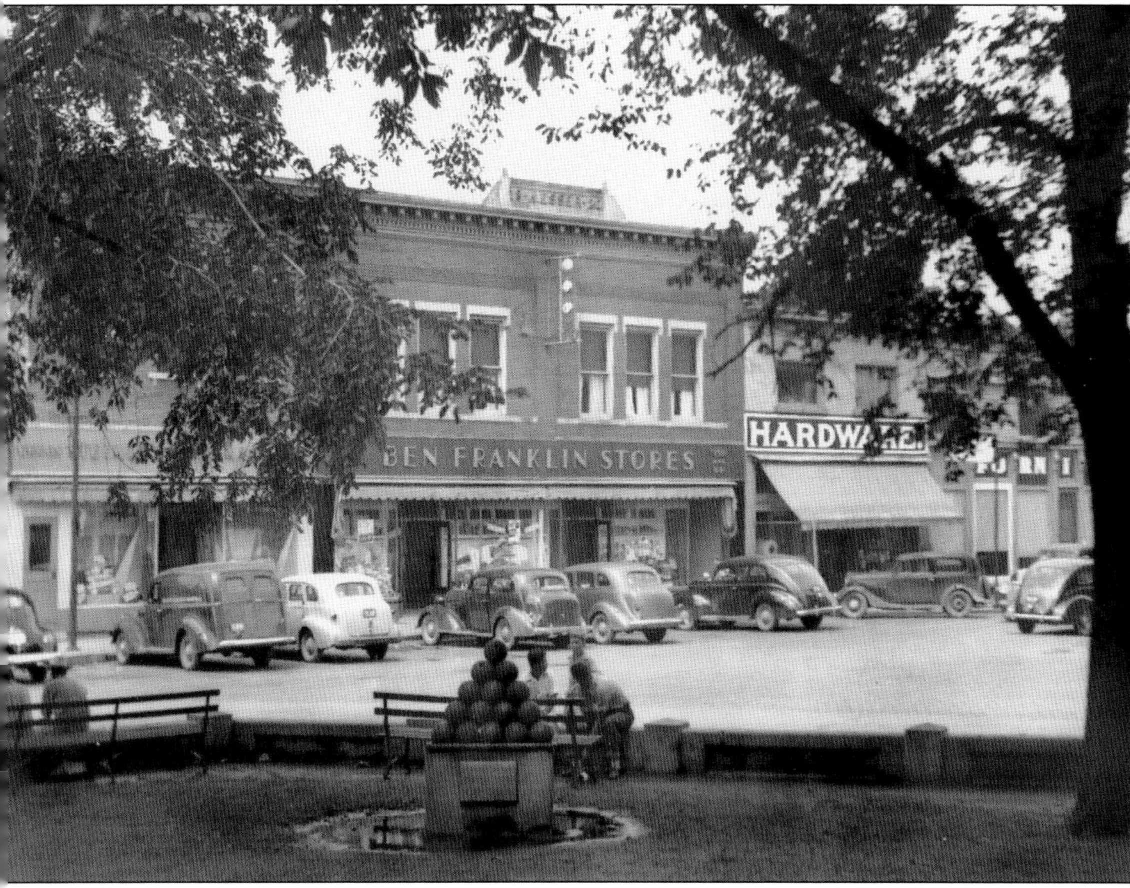

West Side, 1944. The facade of the building containing the Ben Franklin store on the west side of North Main Street had been altered. Once detailed with an Italianate design style, it was replaced by Gothic-style window treatments. This view also captures a very important memorial seen in the foreground of photograph. The stack of cannon balls on the stone pillar is in remembrance of Washingtonians who lost their lives in the Civil War. (Courtesy of the Washington Historical Society, photograph by Leo Clark.)

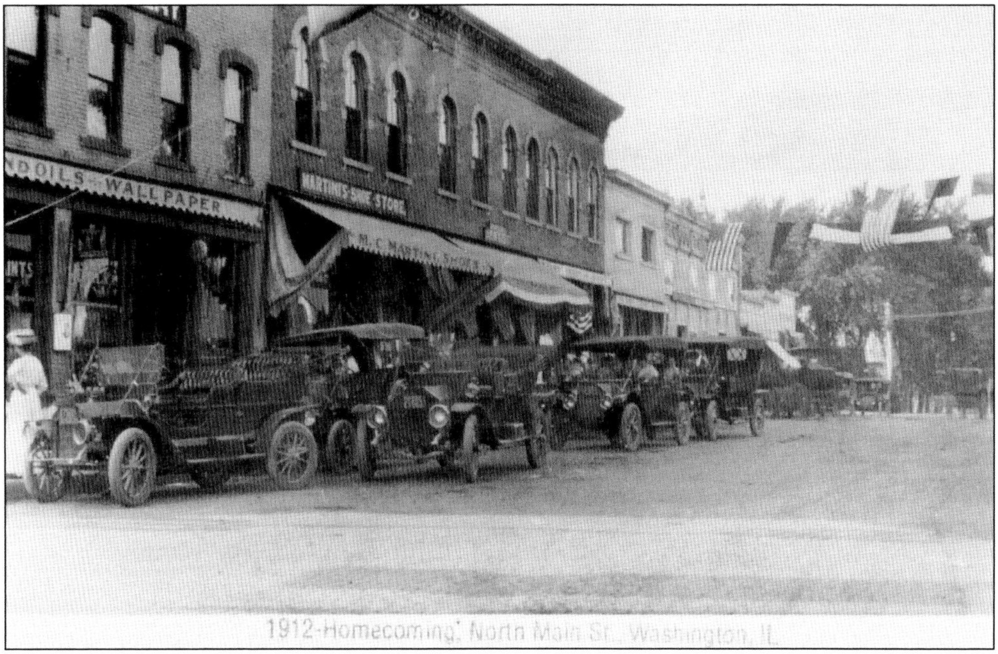

WEST SIDE HOMECOMING SCENE, 1912. Rows of automobiles park alongside the sidewalk in front of the businesses on the west side of North Main Street. Flags and banners extend across and over the brick-paved thoroughfare.

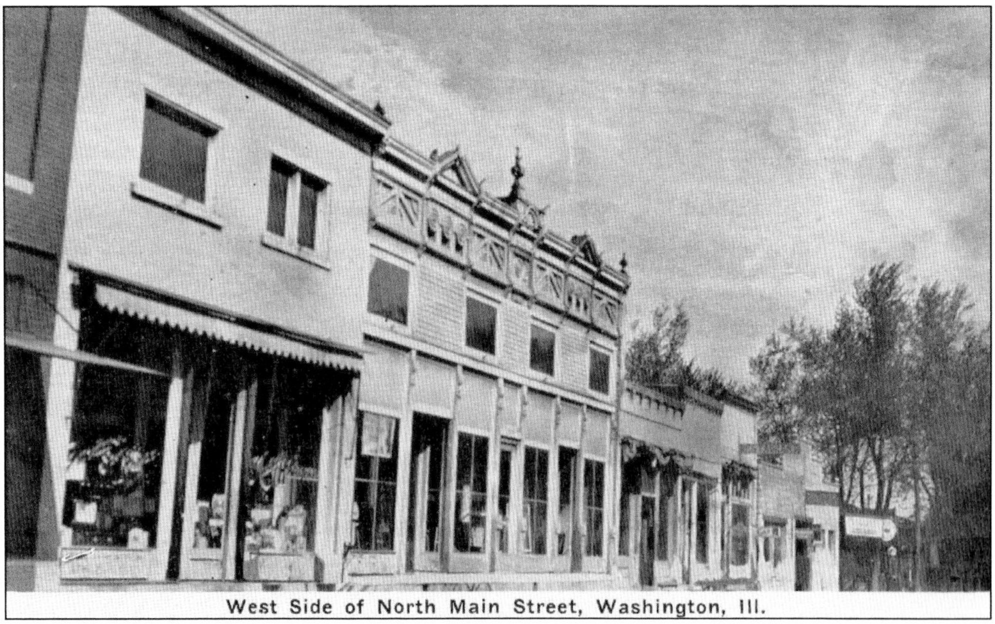

NORTH MAIN STREET, WEST SIDE. The buildings along the north end of the commercial stretch of Main Street are diverse across their facades, their height, and their overall scale. A very simple facade to the left still works as a residence or office over a commercial building but stands in stark contrast to the elaborate Victorian detailing of the building to its north. Further north is a series of one-story buildings that had as their tenants a barber, a restaurant, a bowling alley, and the location of one of the city's early fire stations.

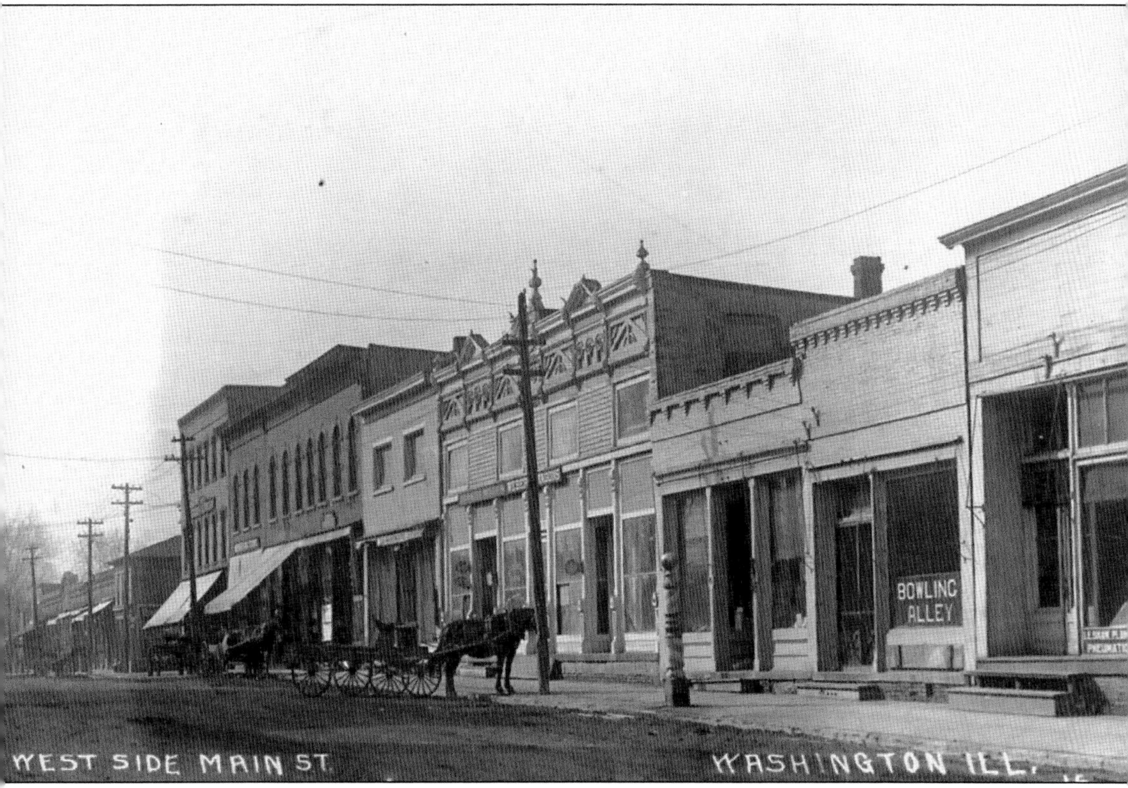

North Main Street, West Side Transition of Scales. As the street moves north the buildings begin to decrease in height, scale, and their presence along the street. As seen with the commercial buildings on South Main Street, there is a very subtle and very wonderful transition between the more urban commercial buildings that start out at three stories and work their way down to smaller one-story businesses toward the residential context that surrounds the square.

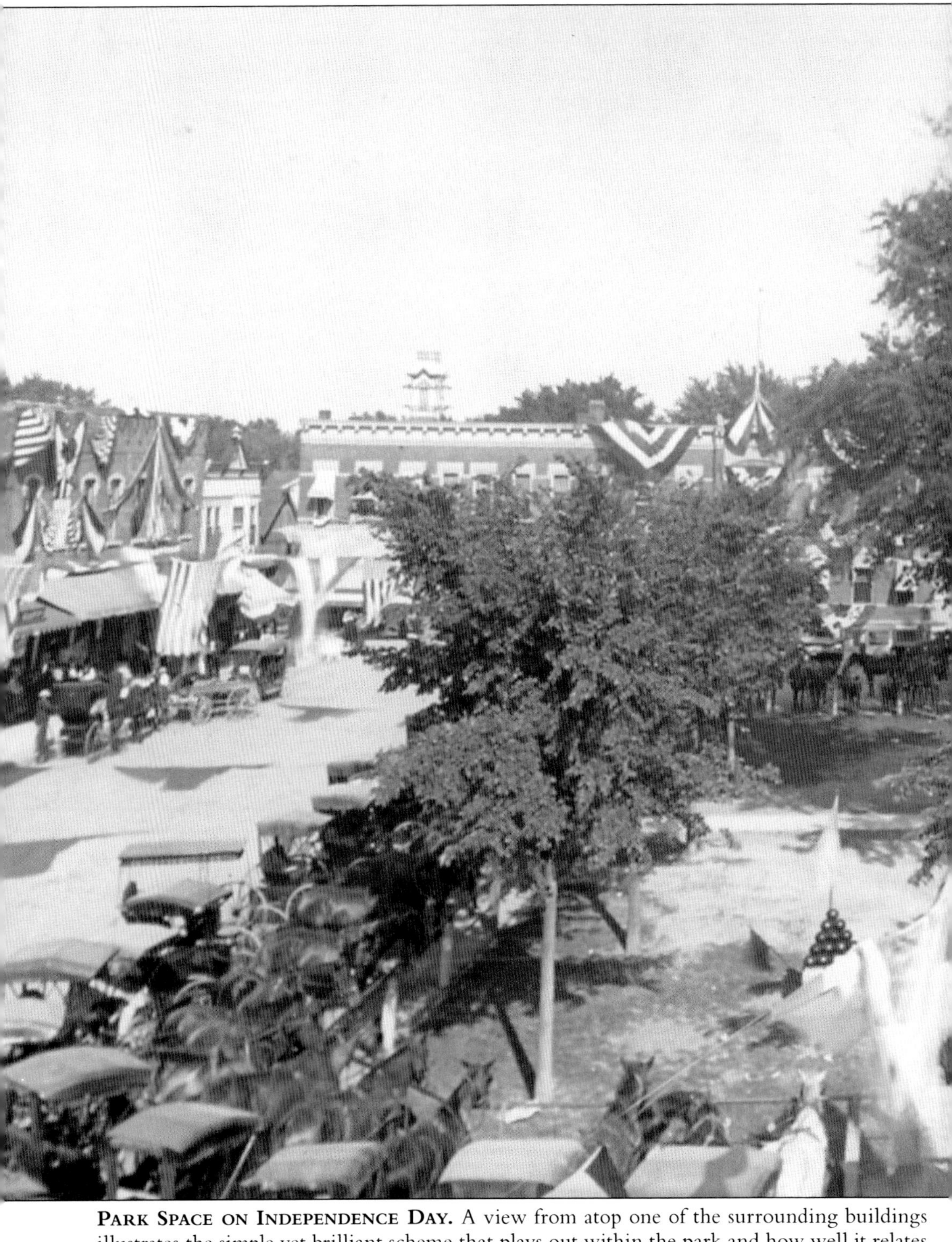

Park Space on Independence Day. A view from atop one of the surrounding buildings illustrates the simple yet brilliant scheme that plays out within the park and how well it relates to the surrounding commercial buildings. Regardless of scale, the park within Washington Square was born out of the same ideas and same principles that have created some of the world's

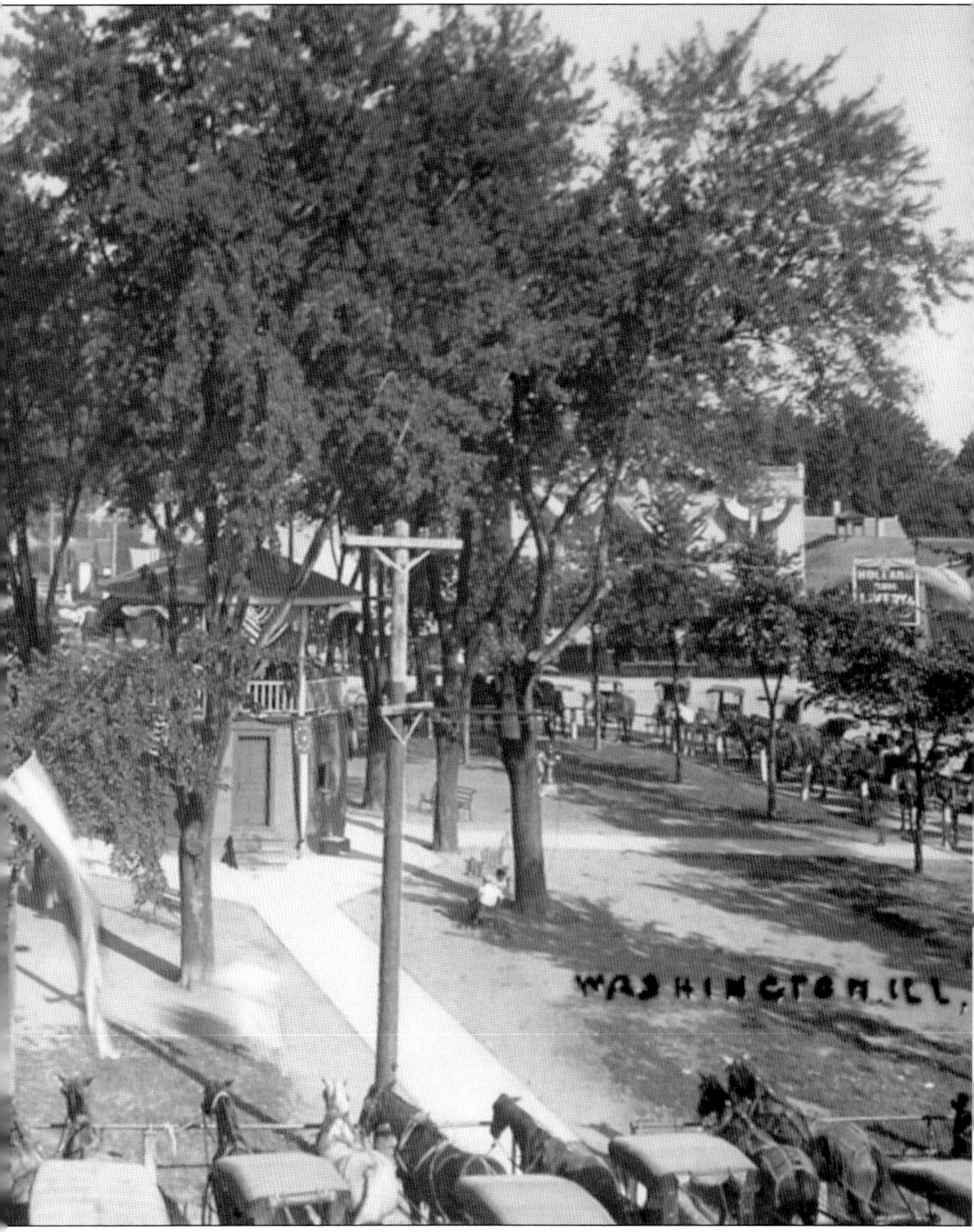

greatest public open spaces. Like Central Park in New York City and Grant Park in Chicago, the park in the square serves as a relief and calming natural oasis amid the buildings and vibrant urban character that surrounds it.

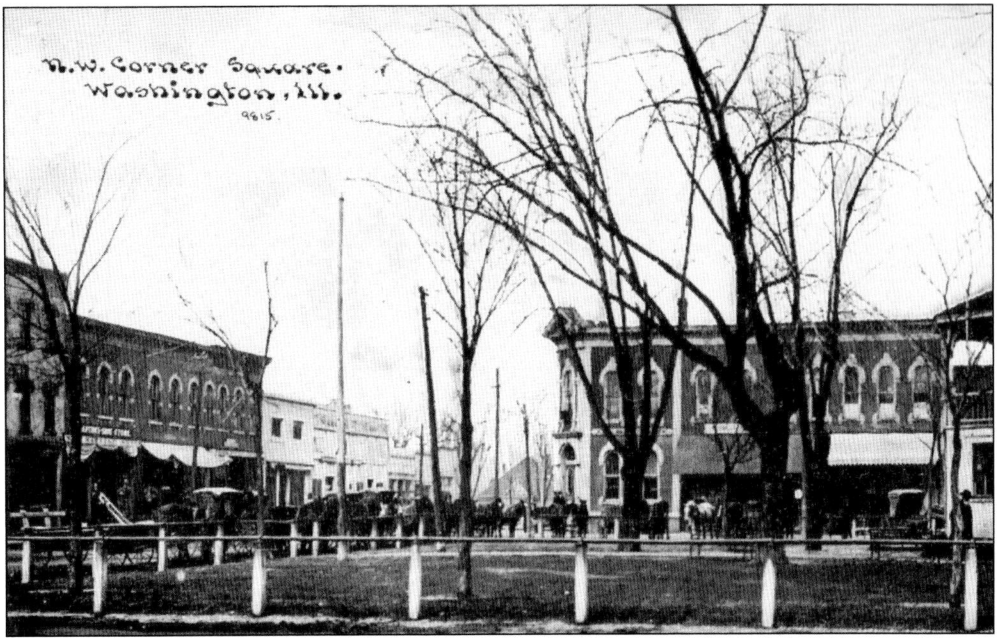

Park Space, Looking Northwest. An early view across the park to the northwest illustrates the simple and very functional nature of the open space. Hitching posts and rails surrounded the green space and were used by square visitors to tie their horses.

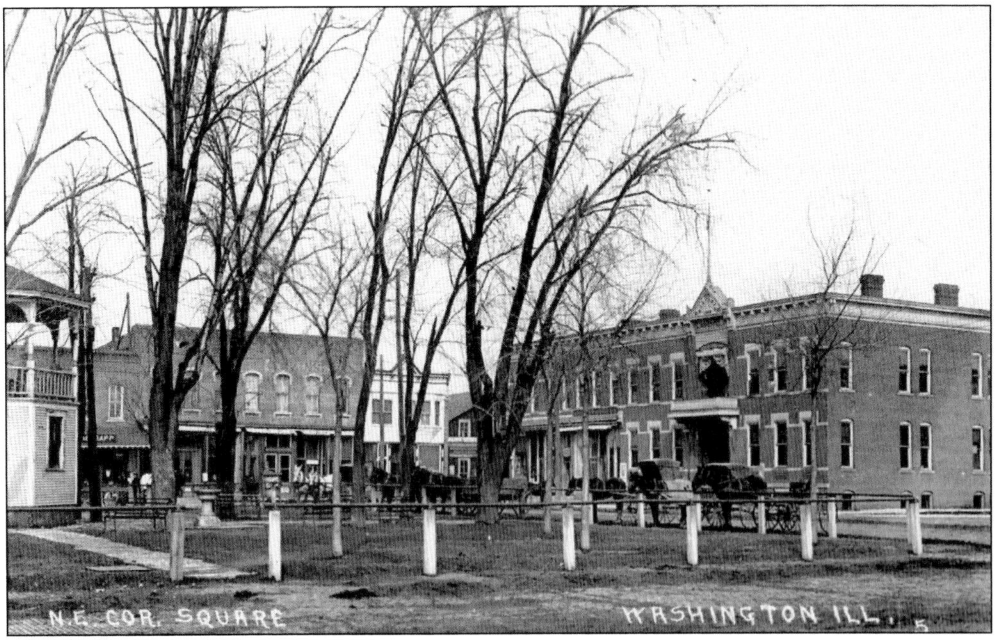

Park Space, Looking Northeast. In this image the buildings of the square can be seen looking down onto the park space as they provide enclosure around it. This enclosure creates somewhat of an outdoor room that generates an important sense of place for the park as it provides relief within the square.

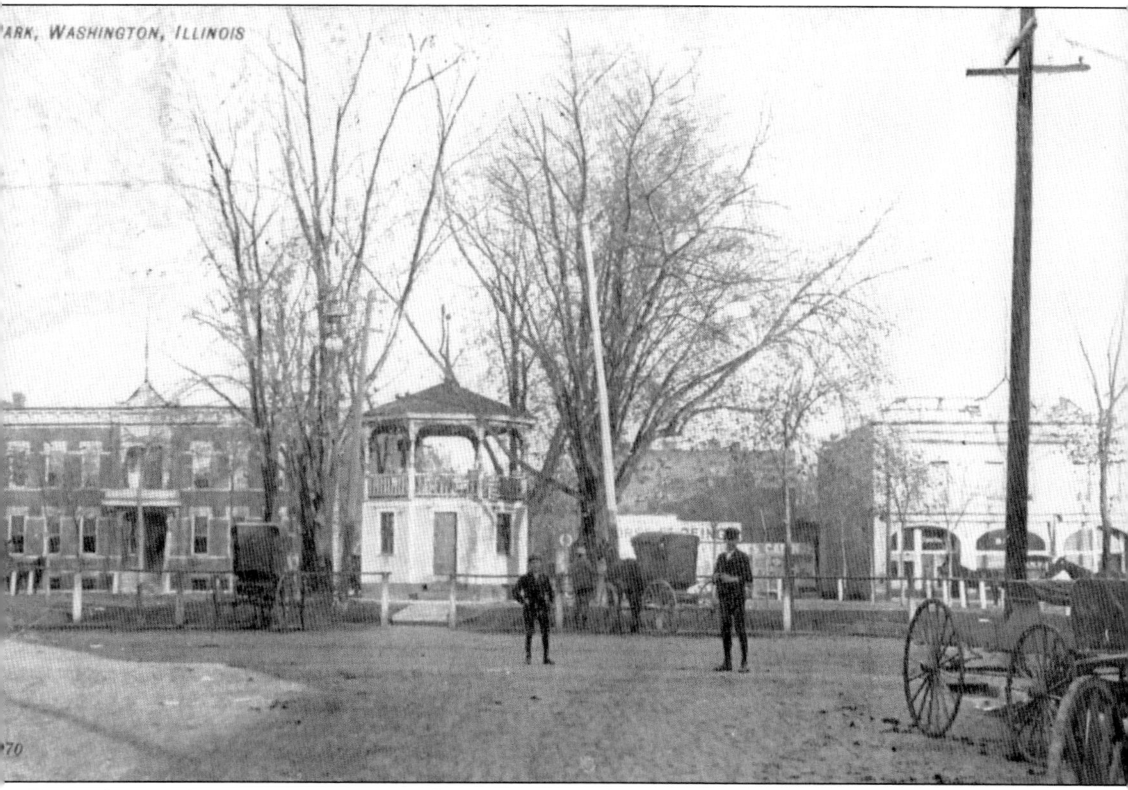

PARK SPACE, LOOKING EAST. Another important characteristic of the park was its ability to host a number of different leisurely gatherings and events. Over the shoulders of the two young men standing on the brick-paved street sits the square's bandstand. A number of different activities occurred here throughout the years, including outdoor musical performances, dances, and political speeches.

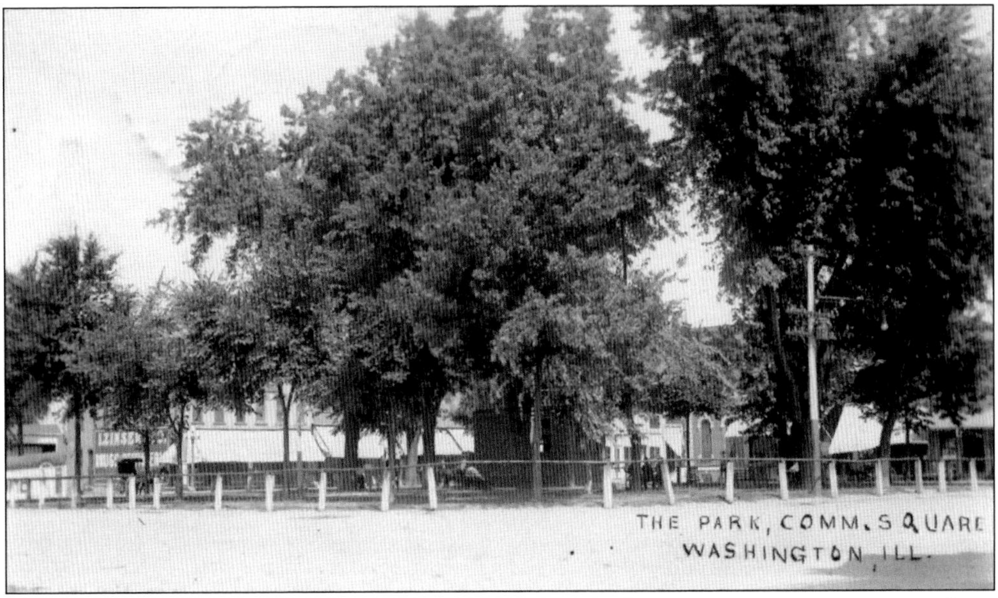

RELIEF FROM THE ELEMENTS. The park space provided relief from the sun during a time without air conditioning and refrigerated drinks and foods. Operable windows, screen doors, and shade from an awning or a tree were extremely valuable and used extensively in designing buildings and urban spaces like the square. Mature shade trees within the park provided an oasis on a hot summer day for all of those visiting. (Courtesy of the Washington Historical Society.)

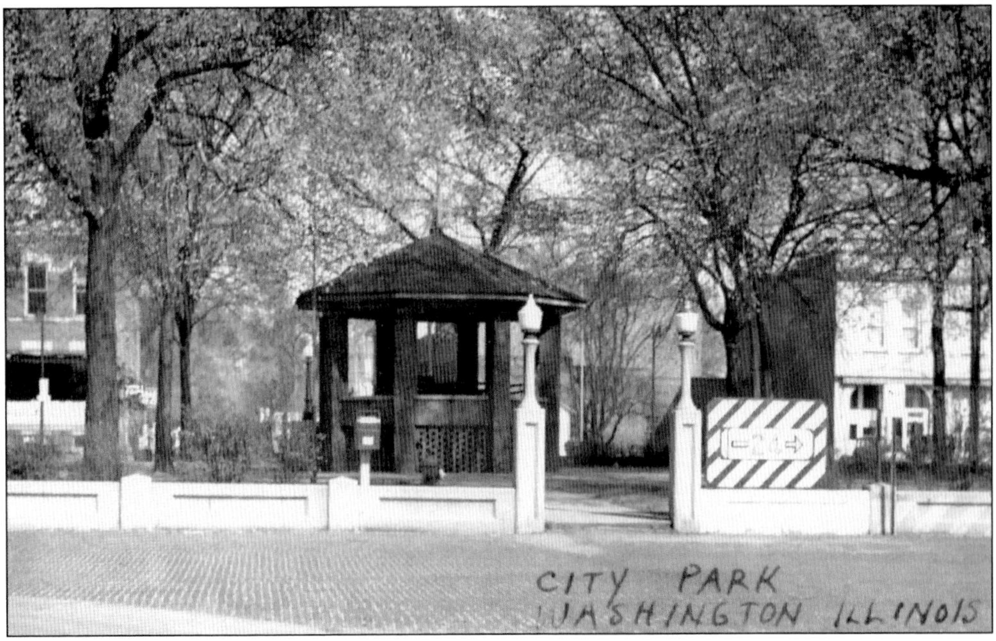

A MORE DEFINED PARK SPACE. When the streets of the square were paved in brick, the old hitching posts and rails were replaced by a new, more formal, concrete partial height retaining wall. This wall, which included hitching ties on its interior side, created for the first time the formal octagonal shape of the park. Streetlights framed the pedestrian entries into the space from each of the cardinal directions.

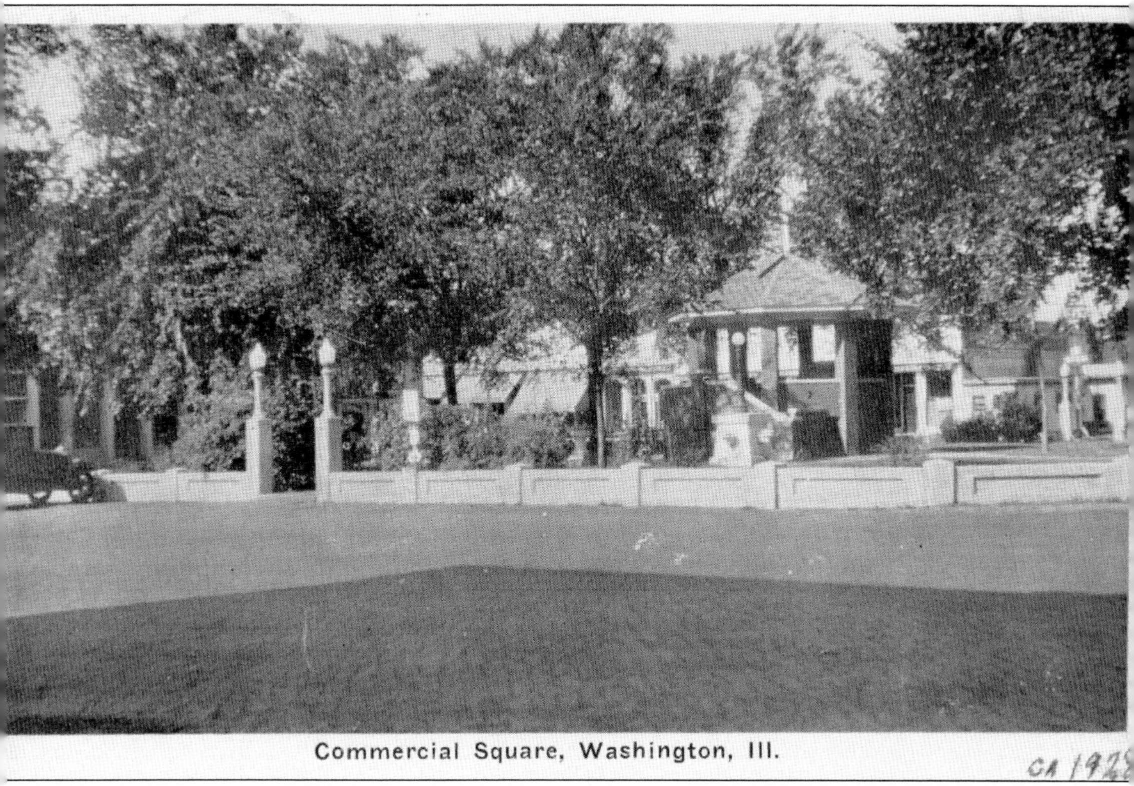

PARK SPACE, LATE 1920S. The older bandstand would also be replaced during these years by a shorter, yet sturdier version. The new open structure played the exact same role and provided a focal point within, not only the park, but the entire square. (Courtesy of the Washington Historical Society.)

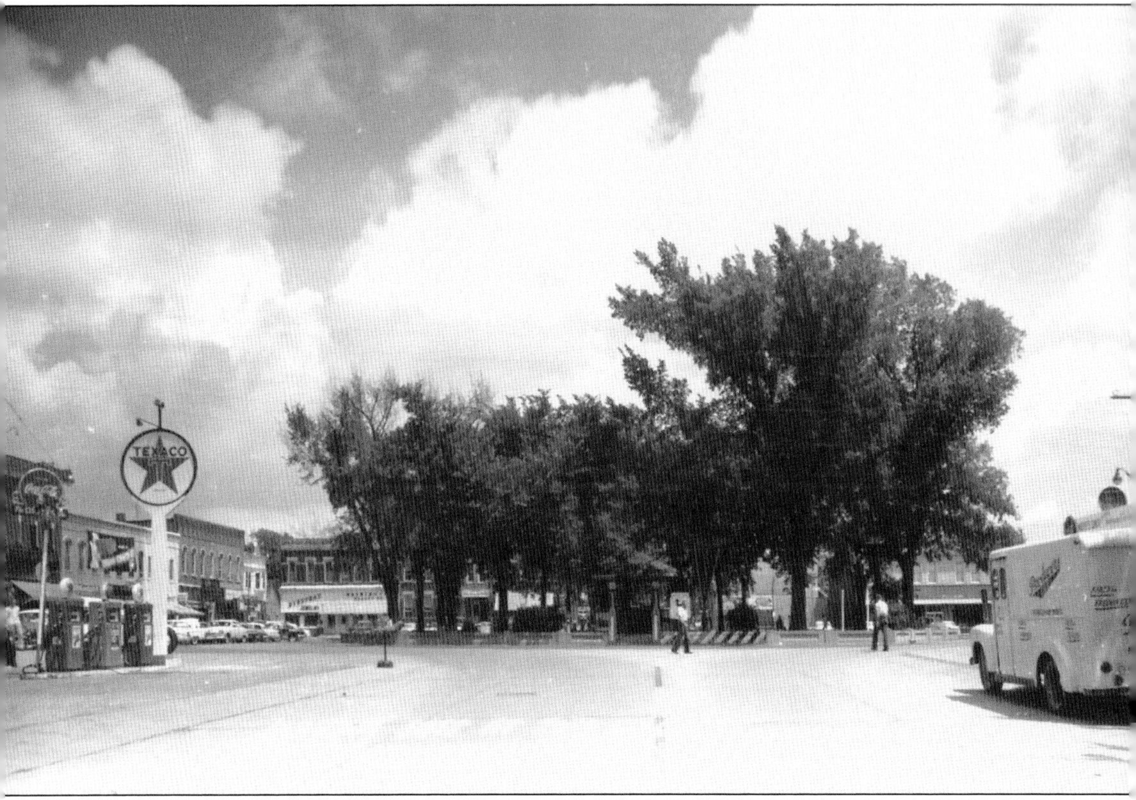

PARK SPACE AS AN ISLAND. As the automobile grew in popularity and its use was more prevalent, the characteristic of the entire square began to change, as did the park. As seen in this image from the 1950s, the park seems more like an island, and its role as an element within a vehicular roundabout, as opposed to the entire square, increased. The park and its surroundings took on a more urban structured feel.

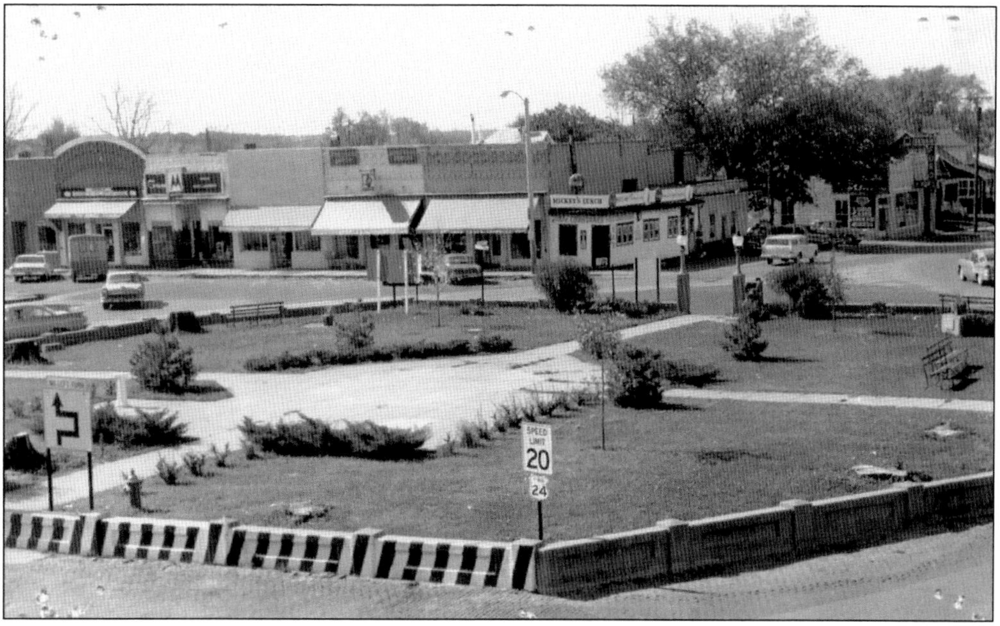

DRASTIC PARK CHANGES. Unfortunately, as time went by, things changed within the park. The bandstand was removed, and the mature shade trees were cut down. The space itself was left barren. The condition of the park and the future plans for it seem to reflect what was occurring with the buildings of the square. New ideas and trends were abruptly and drastically uprooting years of developed practice. The square would never be the same. In the image below, two men can be seen working around the fountain that replaced the square's bandstand. (Courtesy of the Washington Historical Society, photograph by Leo Clark.)

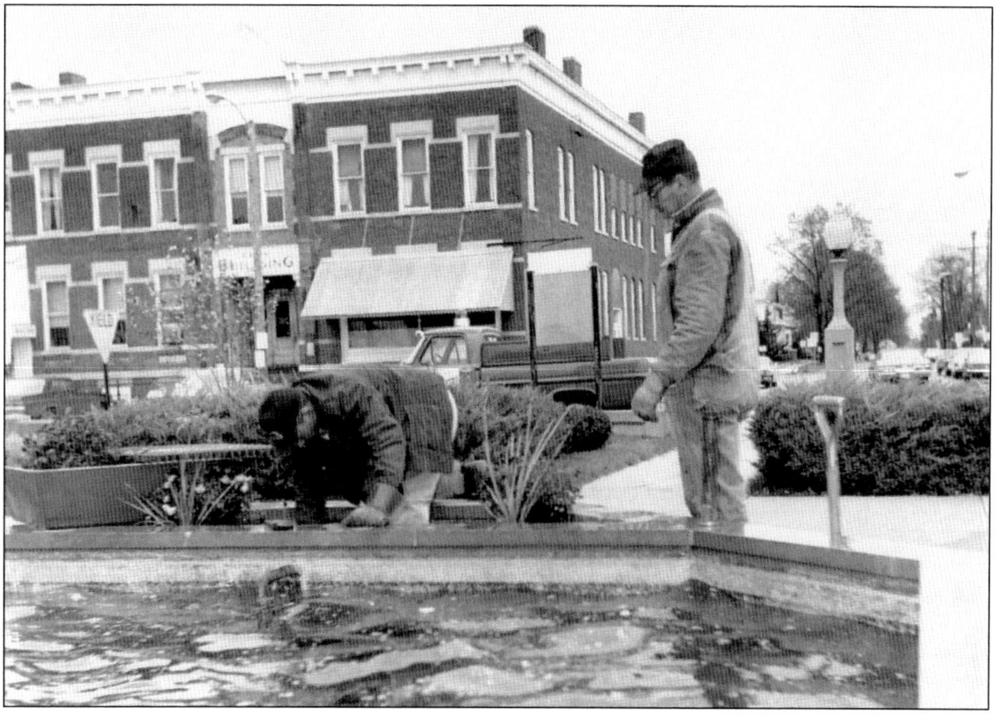

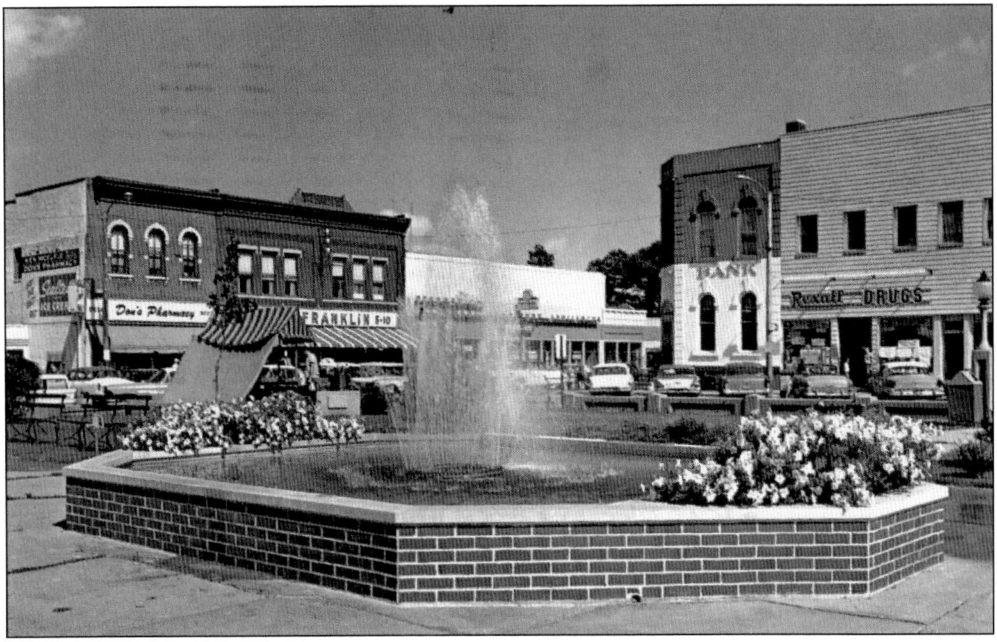

THE FOUNTAIN. In place of the bandstand, a fountain was constructed. While there was effort and consideration put into the placement of a nice design element, the change in the surroundings made a profound impact on the entire space. The changes to the buildings on the north side surrounding the park were also significant. Another view shows the scene in winter. (Below, courtesy of the Washington Historical Society, photograph by Leo Clark.)

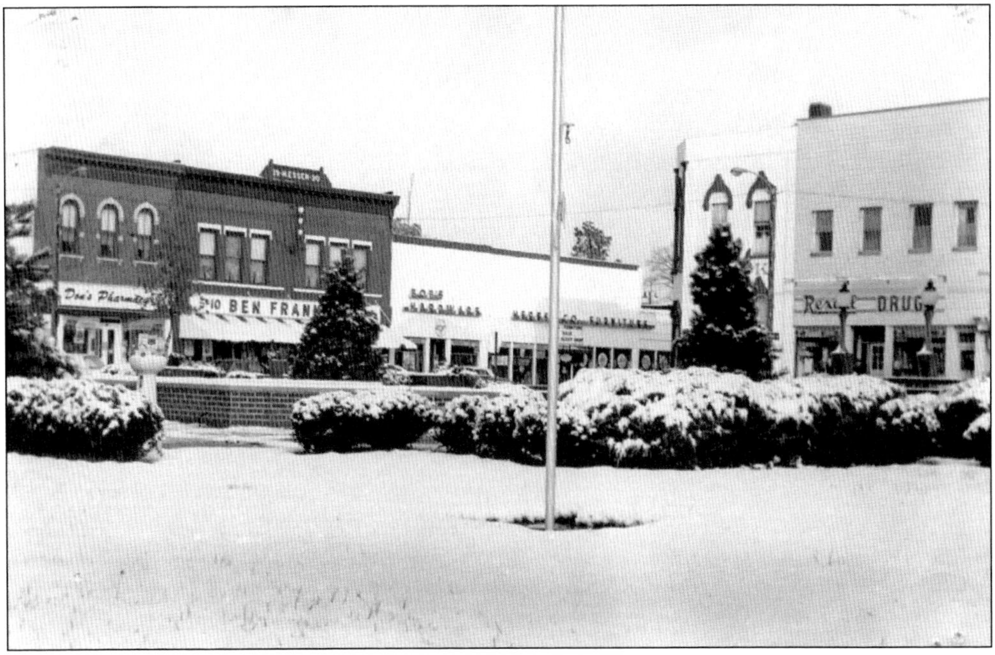

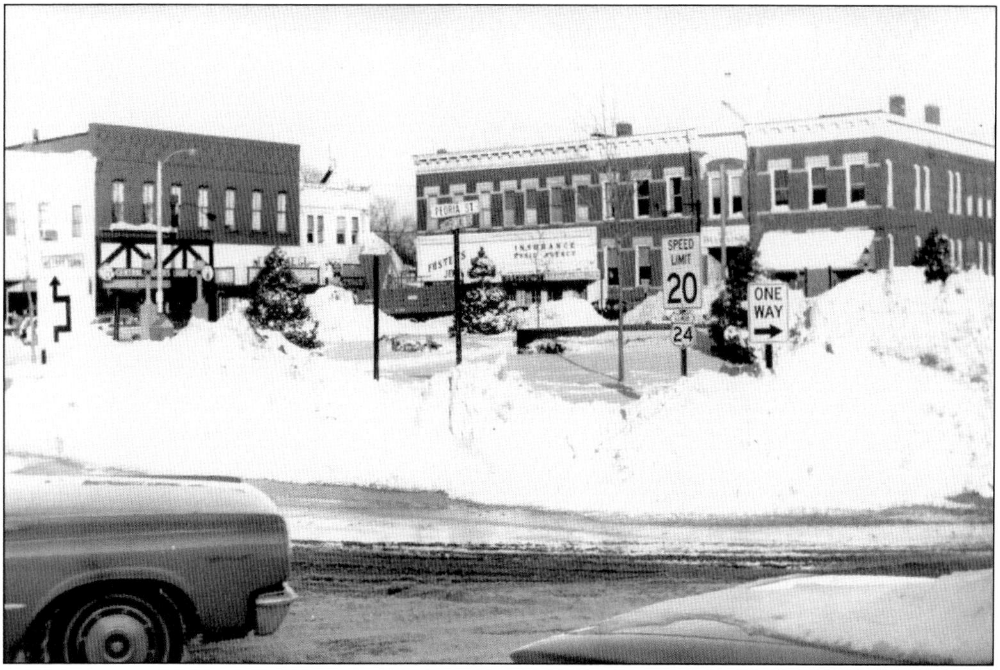

Winter Scene across the Park. The northeast corner of the square can be seen across the reworked park space covered in snow. The City Building stretch of the west side and the north side buildings still do a wonderful job of bringing very important definition and enclosure to the space. (Courtesy of the Washington Historical Society, photograph by Leo Clark.)

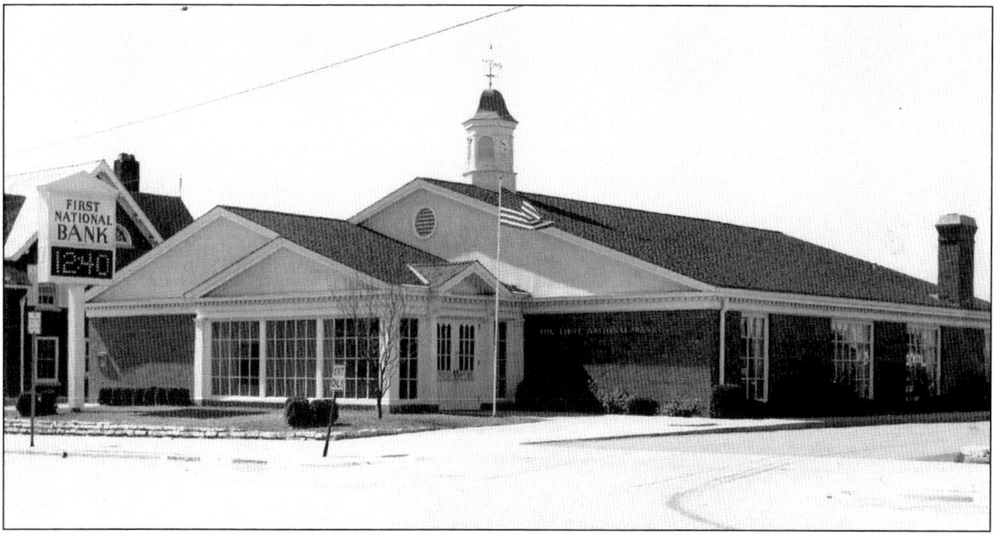

First National Bank. New development began to be seen around the square, but it was not done in a way that was complimentary to the existing elements that worked so well in the past. Instead it was planned in such a way as to suggest that the new buildings should not be considered urban at all. The large one-story bank building was set back from the street and included a significant landscape buffer. The entry was approached from the side, and there was no indication that the street and public sidewalk were fully considered. (Courtesy of the Washington Historical Society, photograph by Leo Clark.)

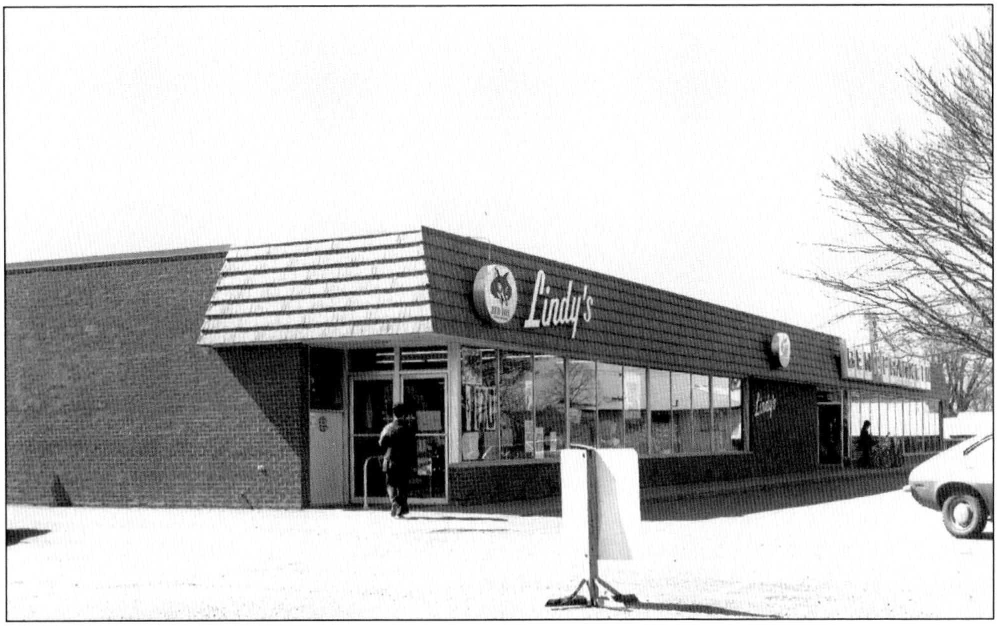

LINDY'S AND BEN FRANKLIN. The Lindy's grocery store and the Ben Franklin general store both began at locations on the square. Lindy's could be found on South Main Street while Ben Franklin could be found on North Main Street. In the 1970s, each of the stores moved to a location on the south side of Peoria Street just behind the square to the southwest. As seen best in the Ben Franklin photograph, the automobile, specifically parking, was one of the reasons for this development. This was consistent with the trend to develop strip shopping experiences that largely disregarded the idea of creating legitimate public space. (Courtesy of the Washington Historical Society, photograph by Leo Clark.)

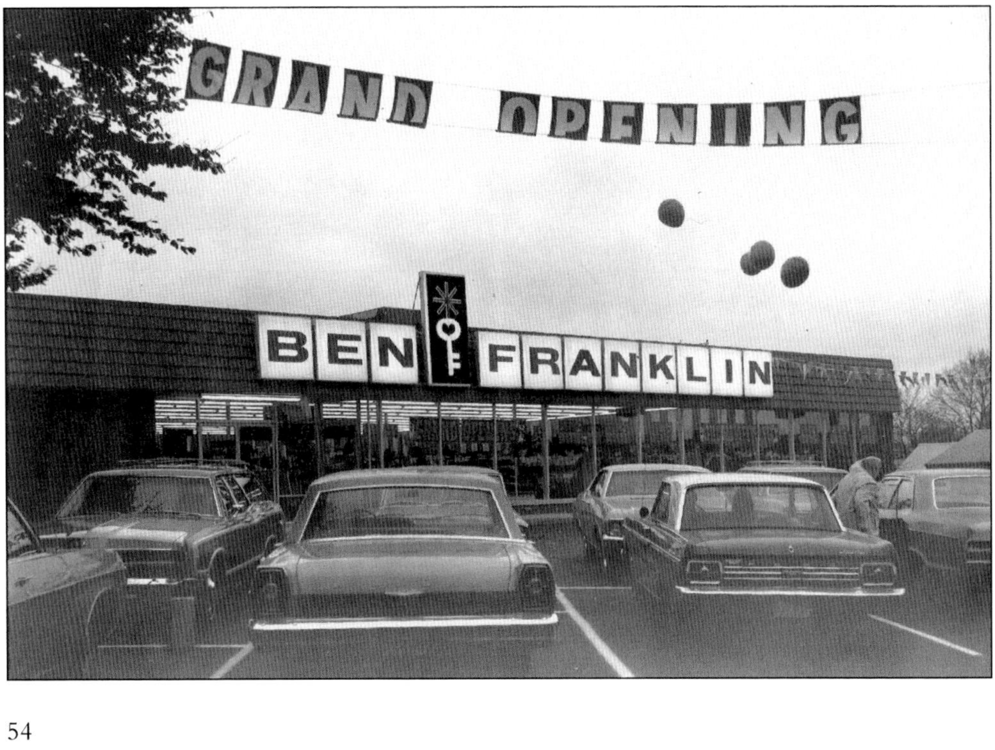

Four

THE BUSINESSES

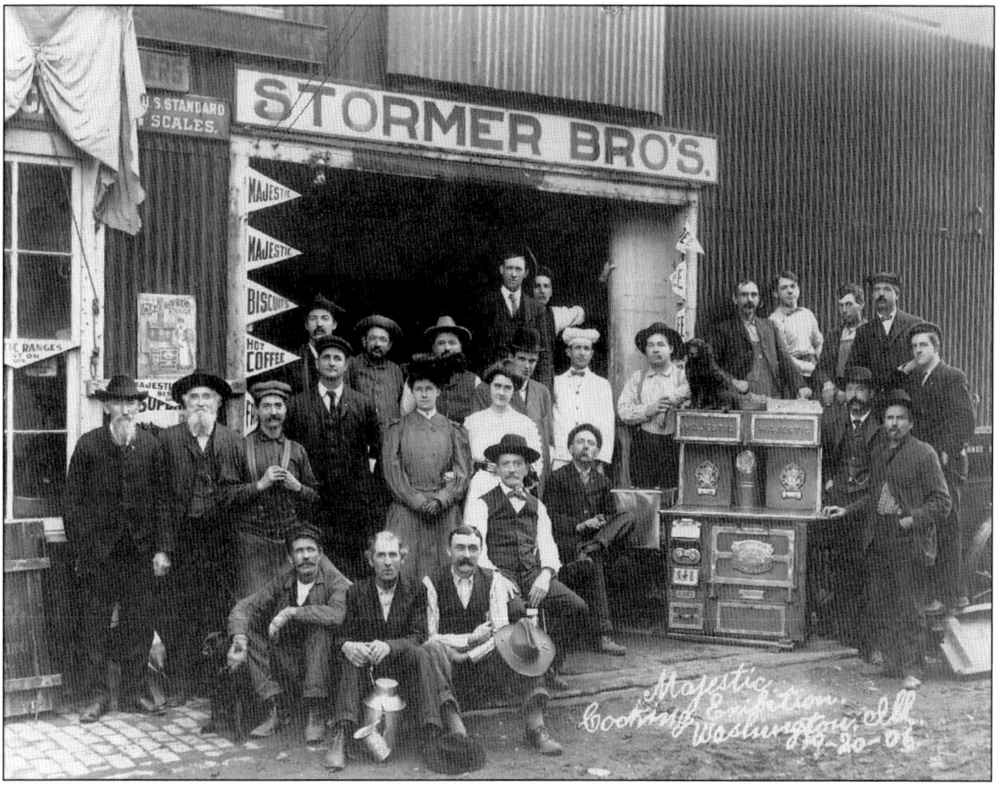

STORMER BROTHERS. Born and raised in Washington, Wilde Stormer became a successful businessman within the community during the first and second decades of the 1900s. He and his brother Dean were the proprietors of Stormer Brothers Implement Store, which was located just north of the square. Wilde also operated one of the first automobile sales agencies and would serve the community as a fireman. The group out in front of the store in 1906 is enjoying a Majestic brand cooking demonstration. (Courtesy of the Washington Historical Society.)

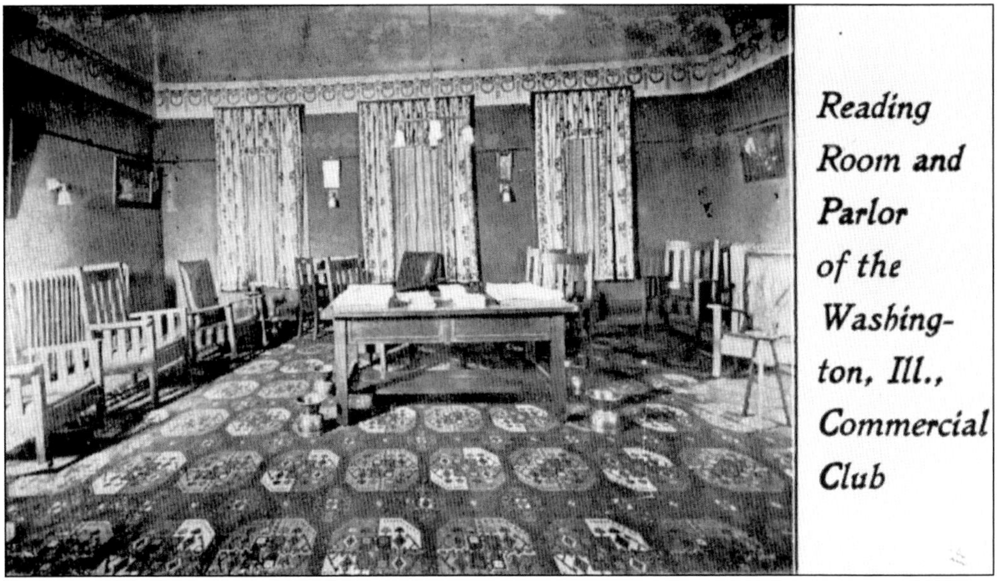

THE COMMERCIAL CLUB. Located on the second floor of a building on the south-side of the square, the Commercial Club was an organization composed of the community's wealthiest, most influential, and successful businessmen. From special events to philanthropy, the club supported the prosperous growth of Washington.

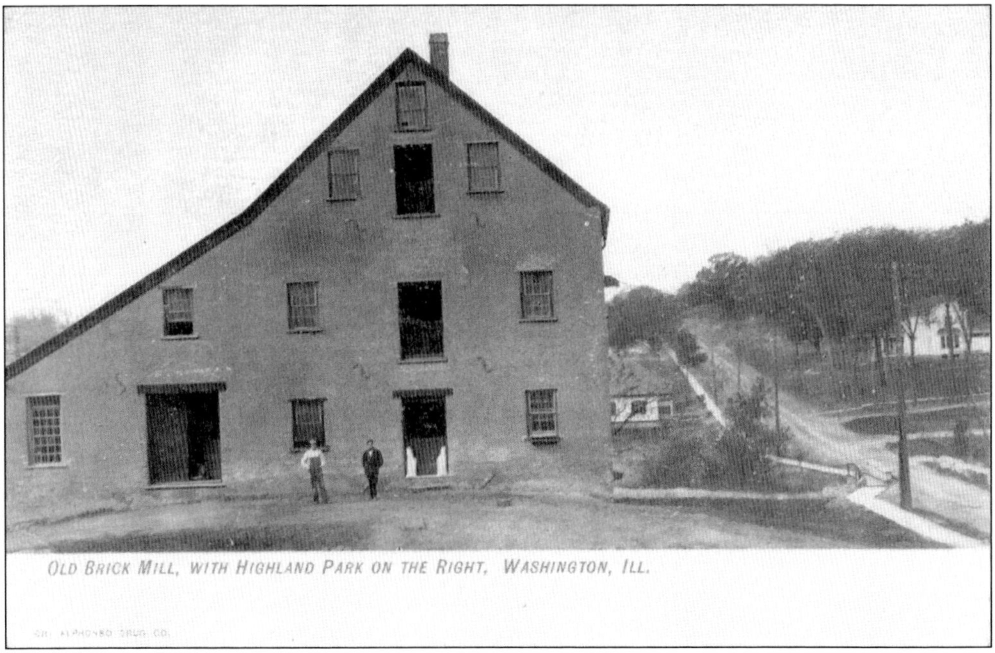

OLD BRICK MILL. Wells and John Andrews, sons of a local reverend, purchased the brick mill in 1851. Located across the road from Highland Park, this mill provided a great number of bricks to a great number of early structures throughout the community and abroad. Later on the mill would become the Washington Grain Company, located within close proximity to the Chicago and Alton Railroad.

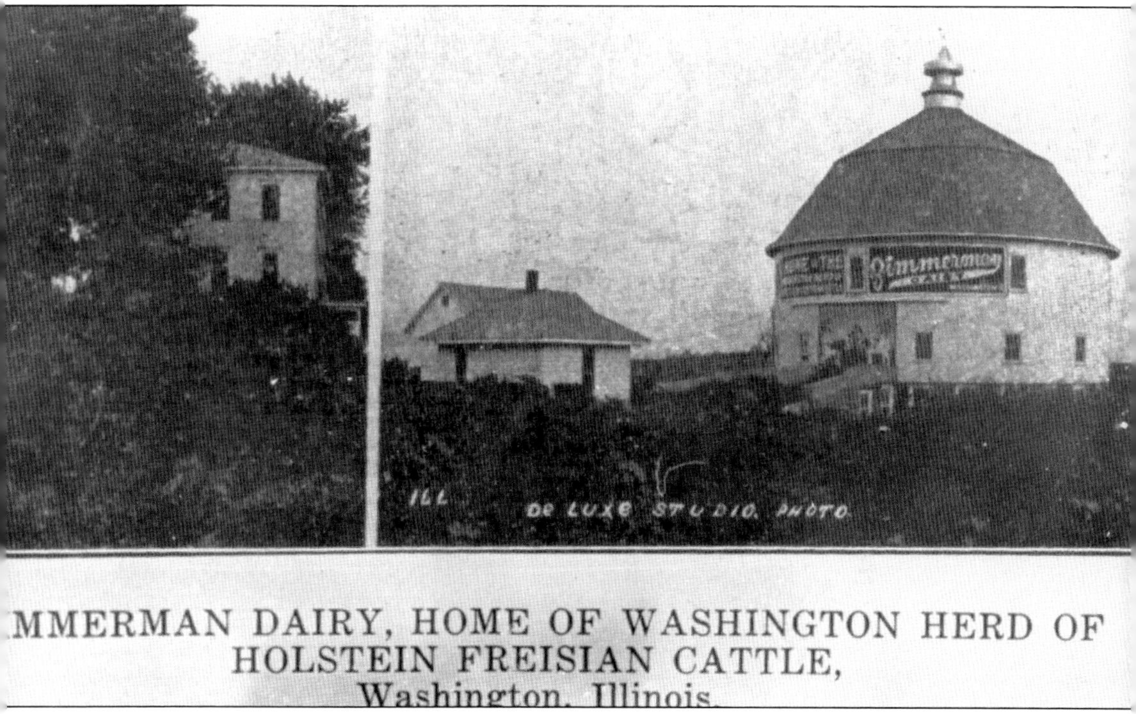

ZIMMERMAN DAIRY FARM. This successful agricultural business was well known outside of Washington. Besides the dairy business itself, the round barn, shown to the right in the image, is particularly interesting. These barns were found primarily throughout the Midwest and have become increasingly rare. Most, including the Zimmerman round barn, had wood, brick, or concrete silos in the center. The shape of the structure was intended to allow for more efficient work inside and actually strengthened the building itself. The University of Illinois was one of the early and chief developers and promoters of the round barn. Researchers at the university found that not only was the round barn a stronger structure, but it was also cheaper to build because it used less materials.

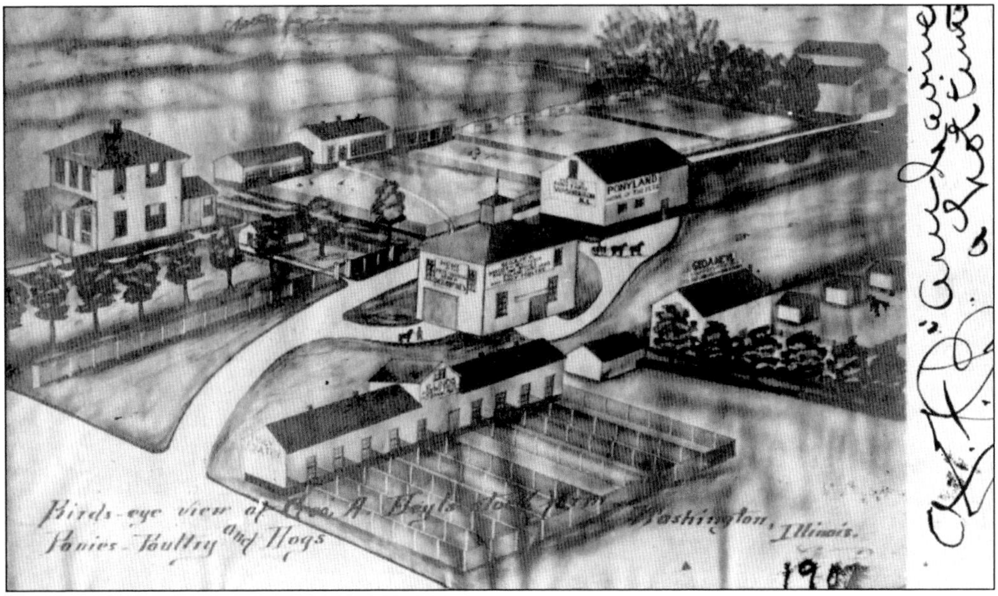

BIRD'S-EYE VIEW. An aerial rendering of the George A. Heyl stock farm in 1907 illustrates the diversity of Heyl's business operation at the time. An image like this not only shows the size of the property, but it also displays the daily operations of the business and how it worked as an organized and well-thought-out system. (Courtesy of the Washington Historical Society.)

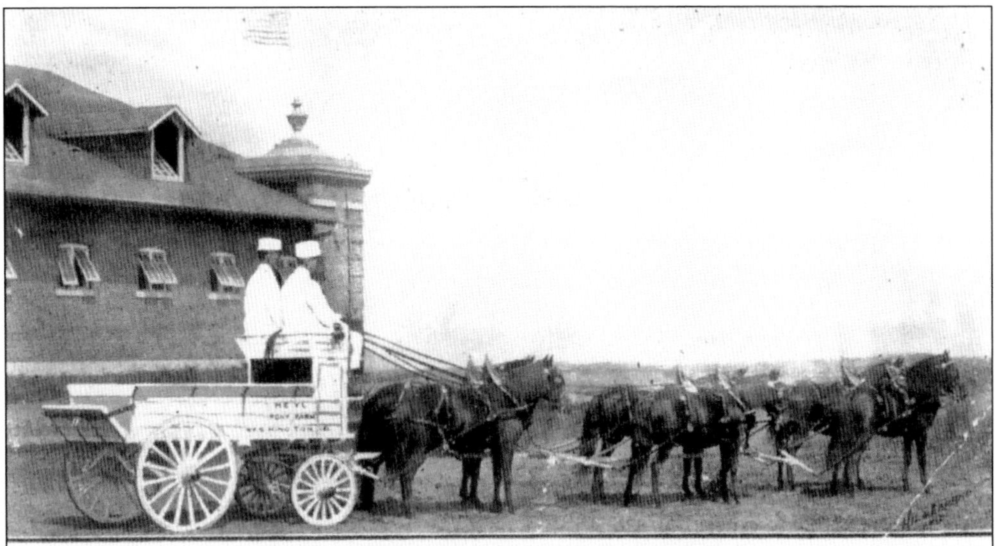

PRIZE WINNERS. Located at 81 North Main Street, the Heyl Pony Farm became a nationally recognized handler of horses and other livestock. George Heyl began his business with Shetland ponies. Sales were made all over the country and abroad, and the traffic of livestock in and out of the community was a significant reason for the existence of three prominent rail lines through the community. Heyl traveled to the St. Louis World's Fair and won grand champion for his stallion David Harum. He continued showing ponies throughout the country and continued to win awards.

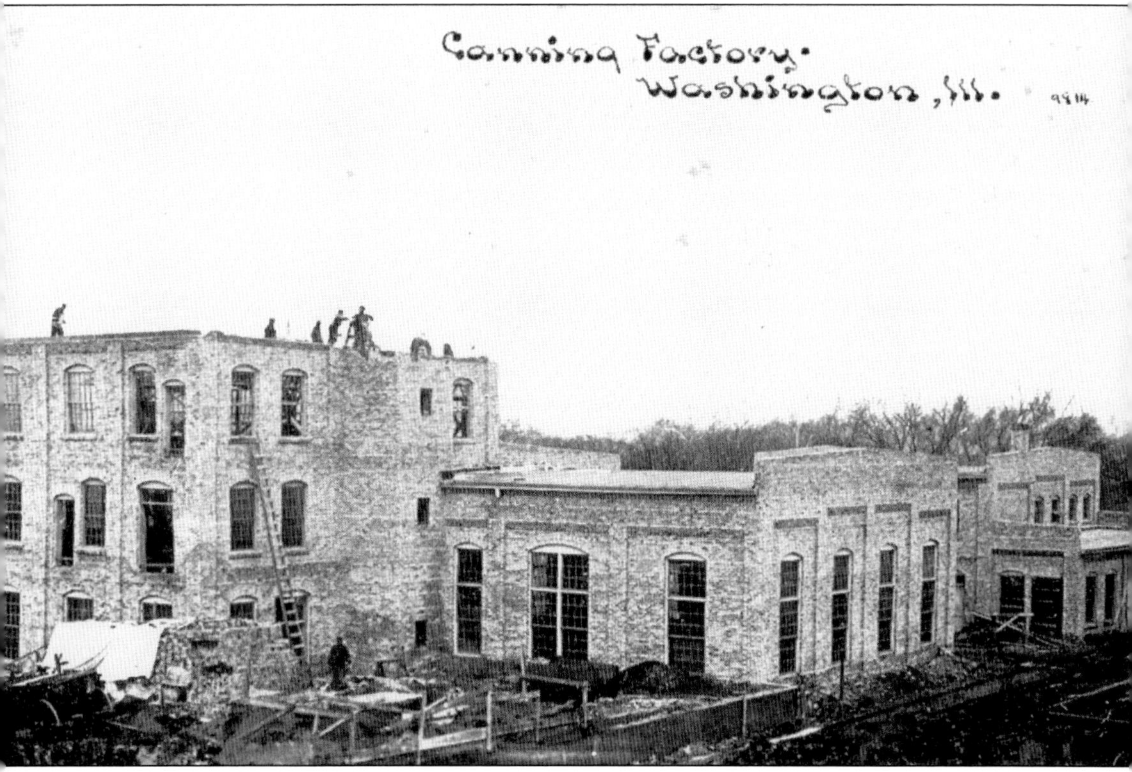

DICKINSON CANNERY CONSTRUCTION. An early-1900s view shows workers constructing the roof and other portions of what would be the Dickinson Cannery. The factory played a very large role in the community, employing hundreds at a time during the fall canning season. It also provided the community with an important manufacturing component. The cannery grounds and the brick buildings themselves were large in scale compared to the surrounding context.

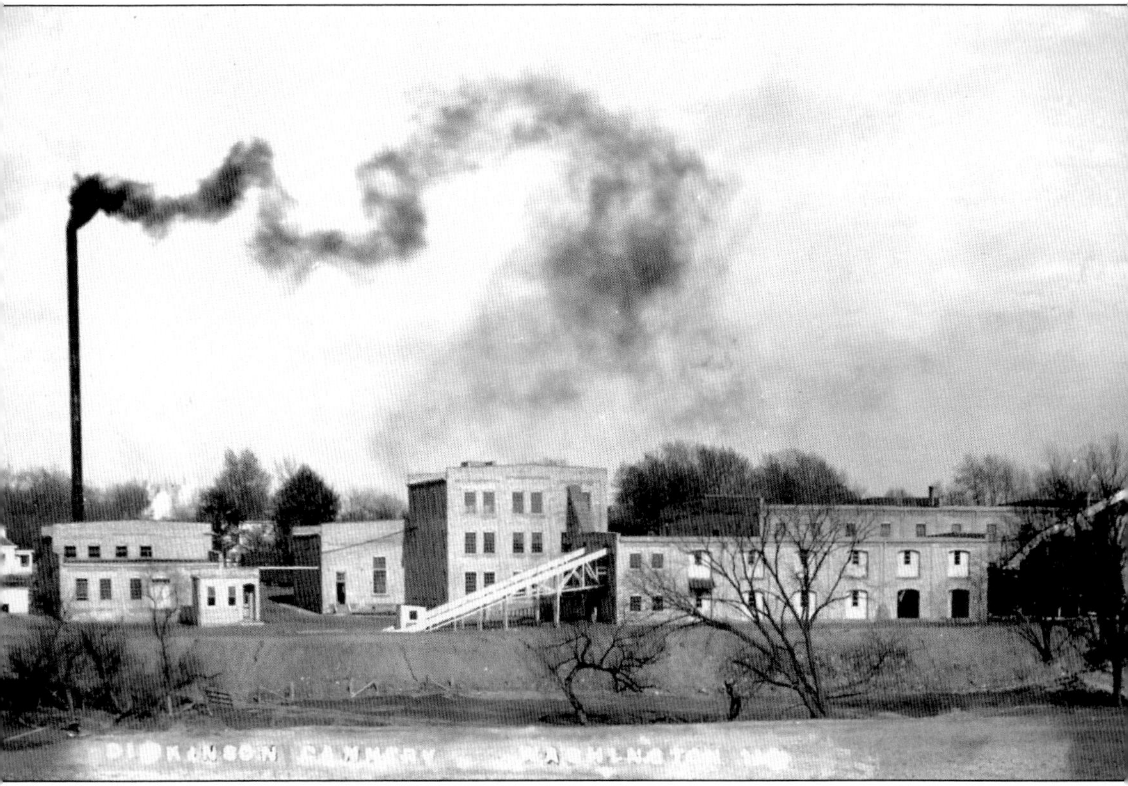

DICKINSON CANNERY. In 1929, the cannery was sold to Libby, McNeill, and Libby and it continued to grow. During World War II, German prisoners of war were held in the warehouse and were contracted to do work for the cannery itself. Army guards looked over the prisoners who were under the command of a German SS officer. The prisoners were treated well and received a number of services. The prisoners were canning goods that were actually being sent out for use by the American Red Cross and the U.S. Army. One interesting story involves the escape of a prisoner who hitchhiked and bussed his way to Chicago, where he lived undisturbed for eight years until he was arrested.

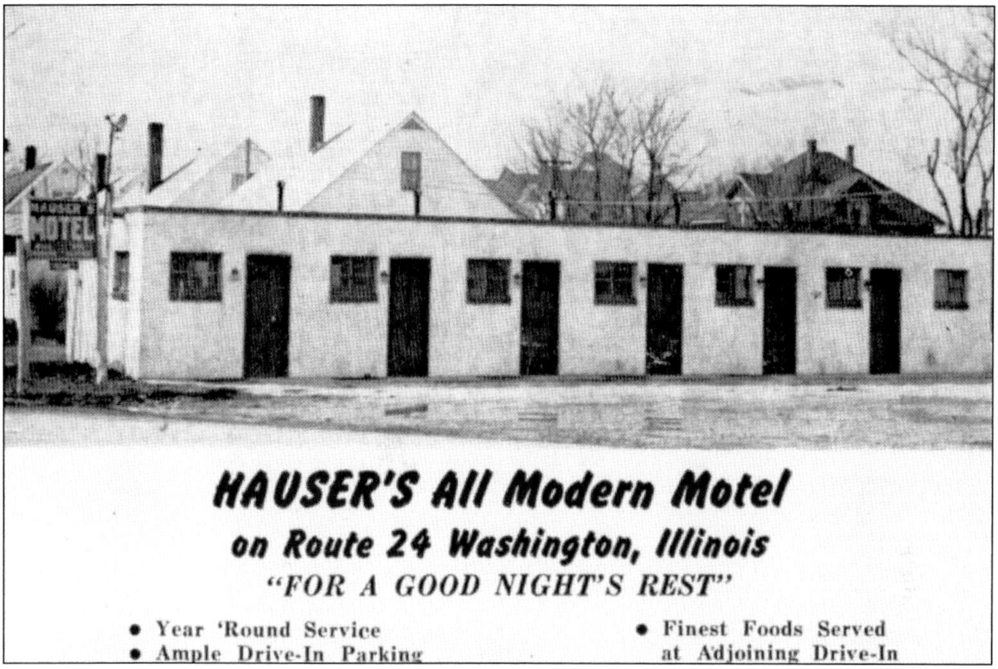

HAUSER'S MOTEL. This establishment serviced automobile travelers as they passed through Washington. Since most stays were just overnight, the accommodations did not need to be large or extravagant. The next-door drive-in provided the visitor's evening meal. The Hauser's Motel illustrated a departure from the likes of the Danforth Hotel that advertised luxury over convenience.

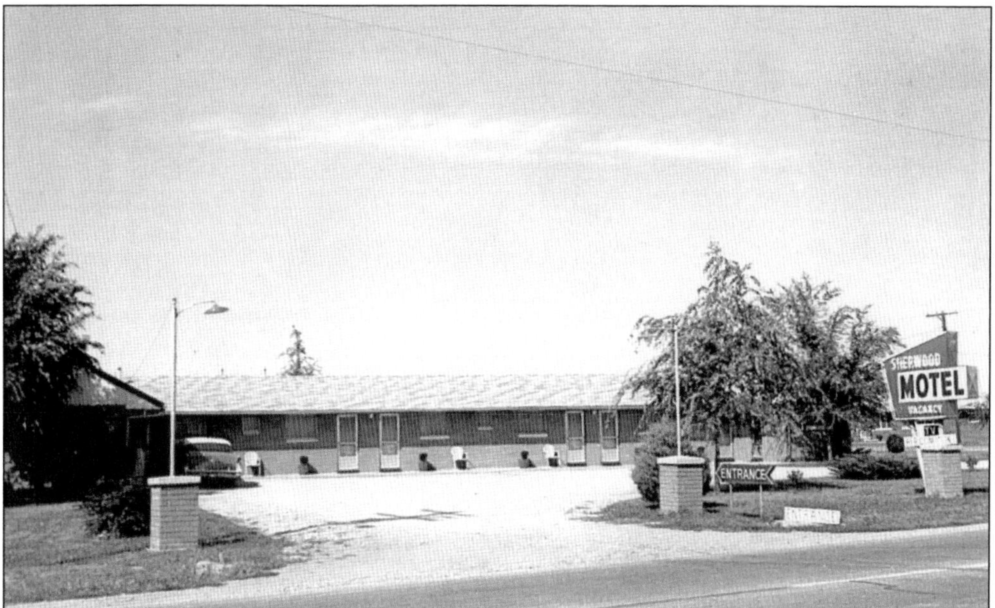

SHERWOOD MOTEL. Similar to Hauser's Motel, the Sherwood Motel was a motor court establishment geared primarily toward overnight guests traveling along Route 24. Amenities such as air-conditioning in the summer were a competitive draw for the Sherwood along with the inclusion of a television in each room.

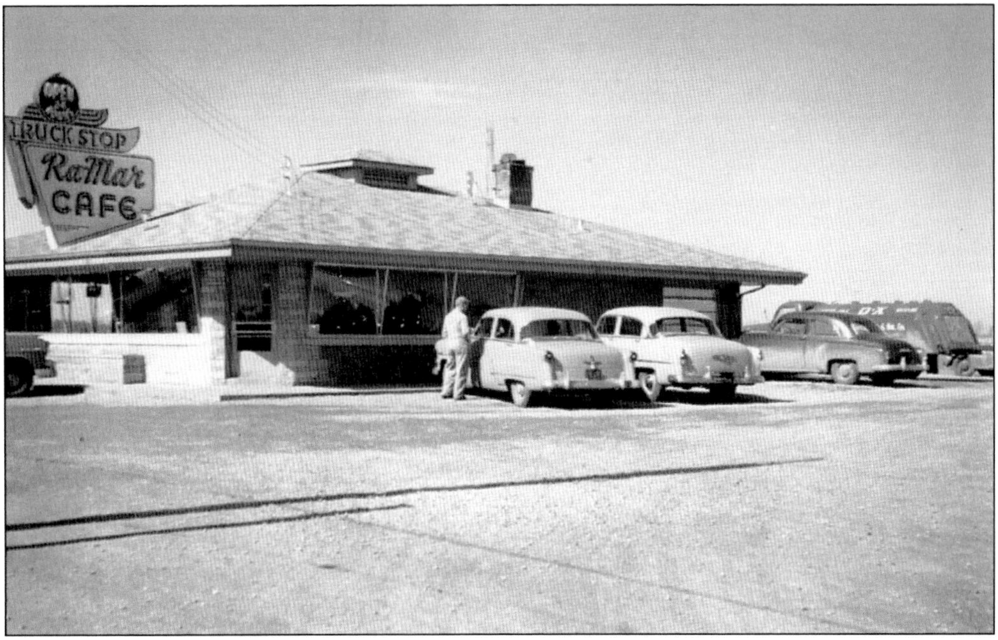

RA-MAR CAFÉ. This is a 1950s view of the 24-hour truck stop located along Route 24, which provided a place to rest and refuel for trucks headed in, out, and through the community. As the highways continued to grow throughout the country, so did the trucking business. Route 24 was heavily traveled by these trucks before highway bypasses would lead traffic completely around the community and its main east and west traveling thoroughfare.

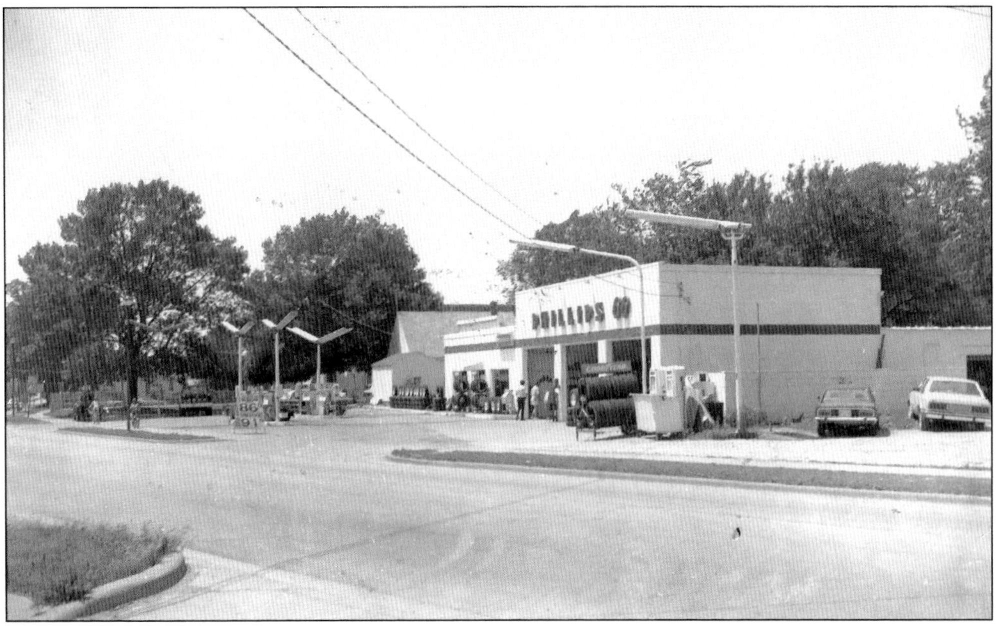

FILLING STATIONS. Travelers to, from, and about town were needing to fill up more often, and as the population of the community grew, so did the amount of automobiles and the need for more fuel. Gas filling stations that had started out in the square began to work themselves both east and west along Route 24. (Courtesy of the Washington Historical Society.)

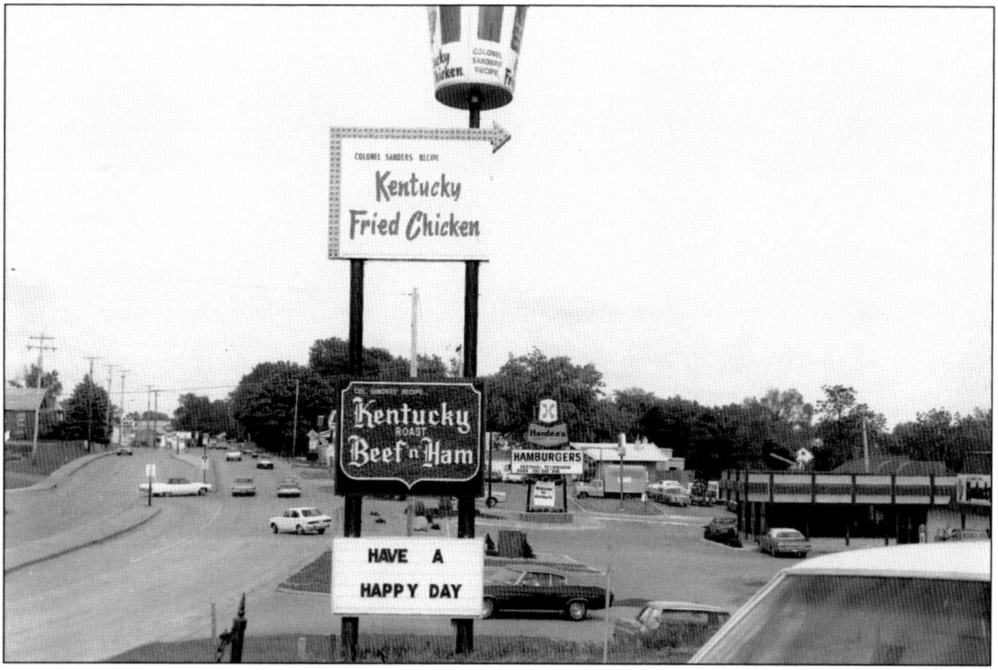

SQUARE, PART II? A view looking east along Route 24 shows a much different type of street and a much different development pattern surrounding it. Traditional development patterns would have called for another urban civic space, such as the square, to be placed here, within about a 10-minute walking distance from the last commercial center. Instead, with the dominance of the automobile, a different type of intersection was developed. Where a traffic calming device, such as the square's vehicular roundabout, could have been, this intersection will soon employ traffic signals and the like to control traffic. Commercial entities are set far back from the thoroughfare, and pedestrian sidewalks are non-existent. Large signs tower over the roadway in place of the multipurpose store awnings and blade signs. (Courtesy of the Washington Historical Society, photograph by Leo Clark.)

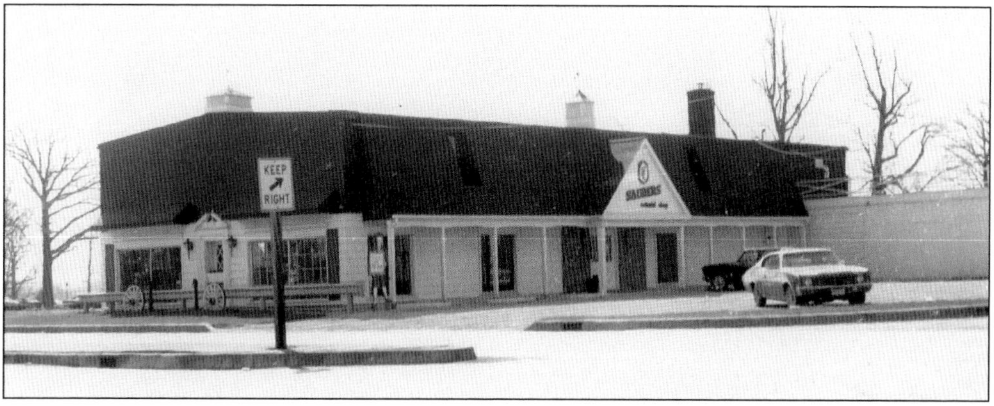

SAUDER'S FURNITURE. This commercial building shows somewhat of a transition. While the main focus of the building and its facade opens out to the parking lot, there is still a front door looking out onto the street with a number of large windows. The building itself also shows a reference to a Colonial style of design that is not a vernacular used in the area. Design references to George Washington's Mount Vernon became present at this time. (Courtesy of the Washington Historical Society, photograph by Leo Clark.)

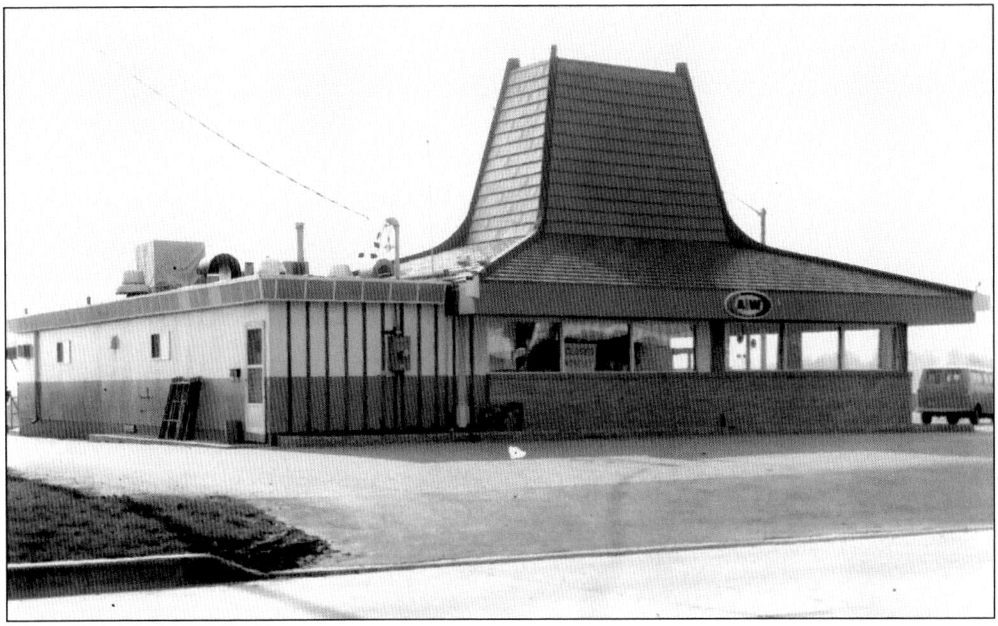

THE A&W. A stand-alone restaurant positioned well off of Route 24 also illustrates the new trend in commercial development in the community and throughout the country at the time. Traditional commercial development had given way to establishments that catered more and more to the automobile. (Courtesy of the Washington Historical Society, photograph by Leo Clark.)

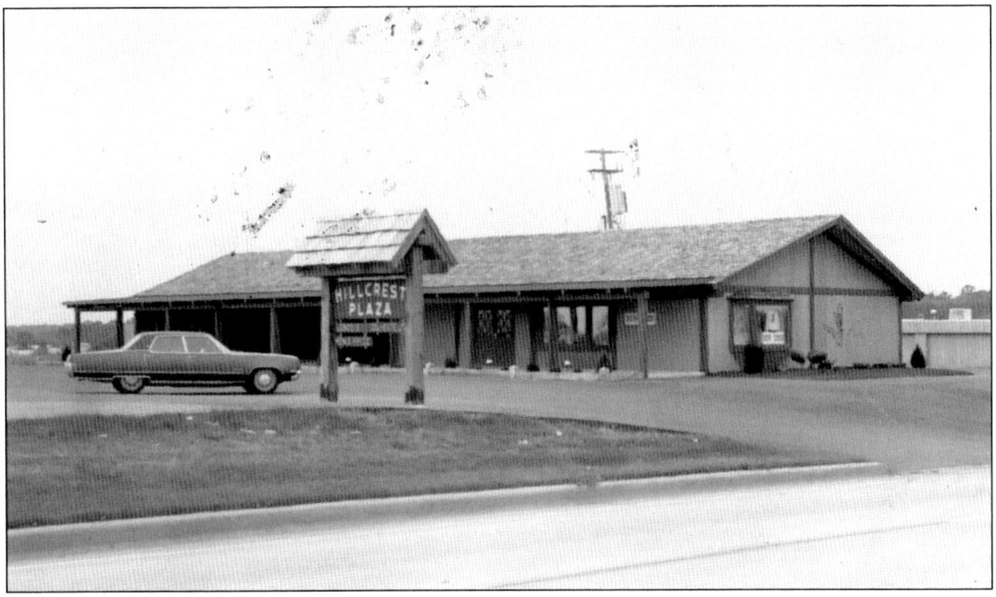

RETAIL STRIP SHOPPING. Hillcrest Plaza along Route 24 illustrates yet another structural change made to retail development. Whereas retail stores along the square opened out to their customers, the sidewalks, and the streets, developments like this literally turned away. The term *plaza* had begun to take on a very different meaning, one that was not always so welcoming to the comforts of a great open public space. (Courtesy of the Washington Historical Society, photograph by Leo Clark.)

Five

The Civic Buildings

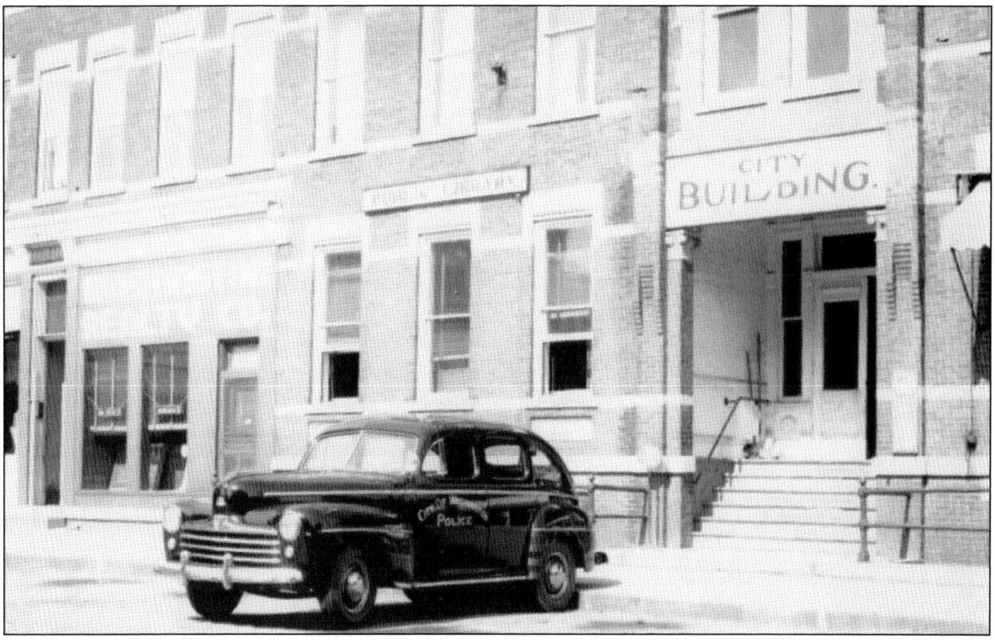

City Building, 1948. The Danforth Hotel became the City Building in 1924 when the city issued bonds for the remodeling of the building. The public library, jail, and city services were all located here. Out front sits the community's first police squad car, which was purchased that year.

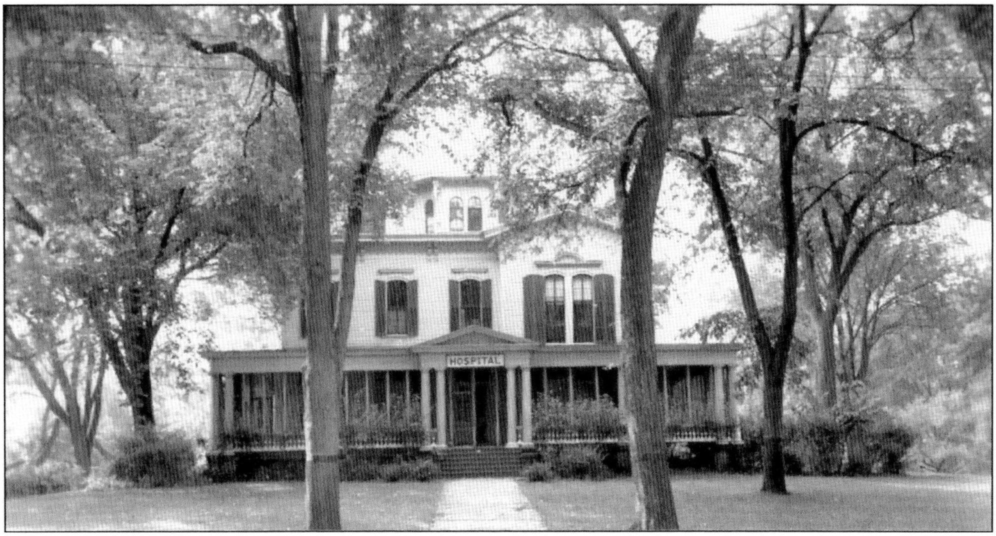

RAY LASANCE HOSPITAL. An image from the late 1940s shows the community's hospital that had moved to this location at 102 East Holland Street in May 1943. The hospital would later be renamed Washington Hospital. The building itself was formerly the home of bank and hotel owner Henry R. Danforth. It had been a hospital for only seven years before it was converted into a nursing home in November 1950. During its time as a hospital, 1,250 unique cases were handled from around the surrounding area. (Courtesy of the Washington Historical Society.)

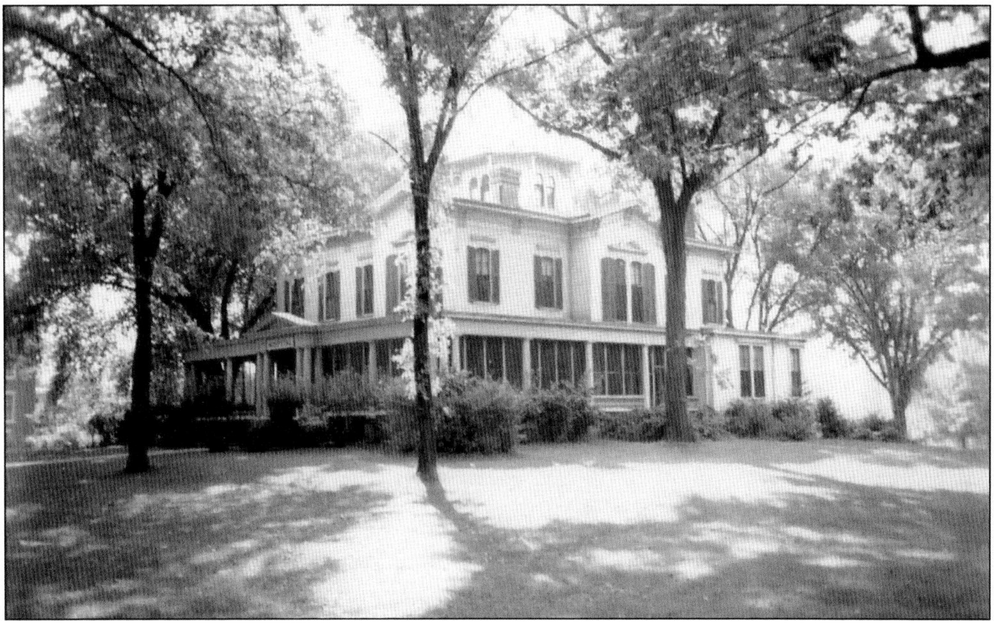

RESIDENCE TO HOSPITAL. The former residence itself is a grand and very well-articulated home with a large wrapping porch supported by a series of Doric columns. The porch entry, signified by the paired Doric columns on either side supporting a large pediment, is located at the front of the home looking out toward Holland Street. Exquisitely detailed cornice treatments, window surrounds, and protruding bays across the facade create depth and interest. A tower element atop the building adds another unique detail. The generous setback accentuates the estate feel of the property. (Courtesy of the Washington Historical Society, photograph by Leo Clark.)

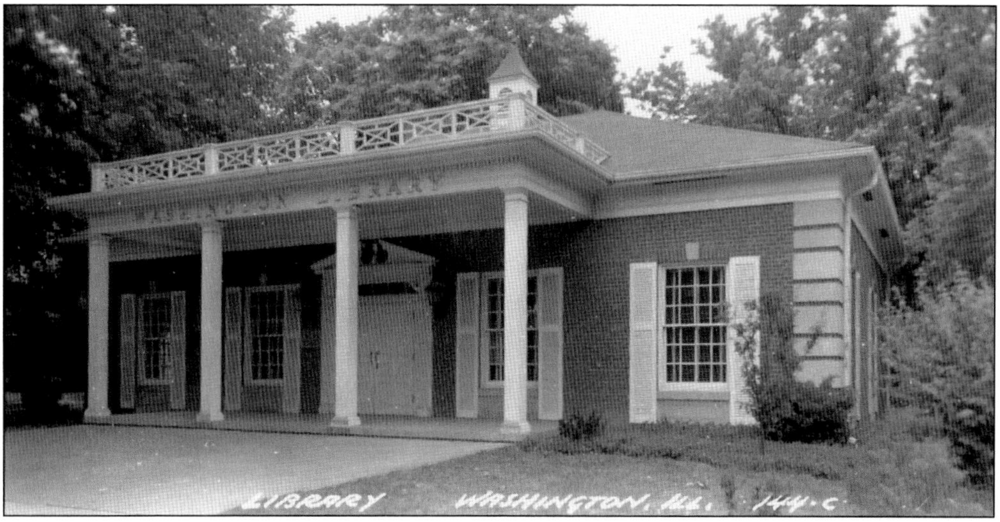

PUBLIC LIBRARY, 1950S. The first public library opened its doors on June 15, 1927, and was located within a heated and lighted room provided by the city within the City Building on the square. The library later moved to its new and present address on Walnut Street in 1950. The one-story hip-roofed building has an exterior of mostly brick and includes several Colonial-style design elements. The library's position within the residential neighborhood is an extremely important asset and provides an enriching cultural element within walking distance.

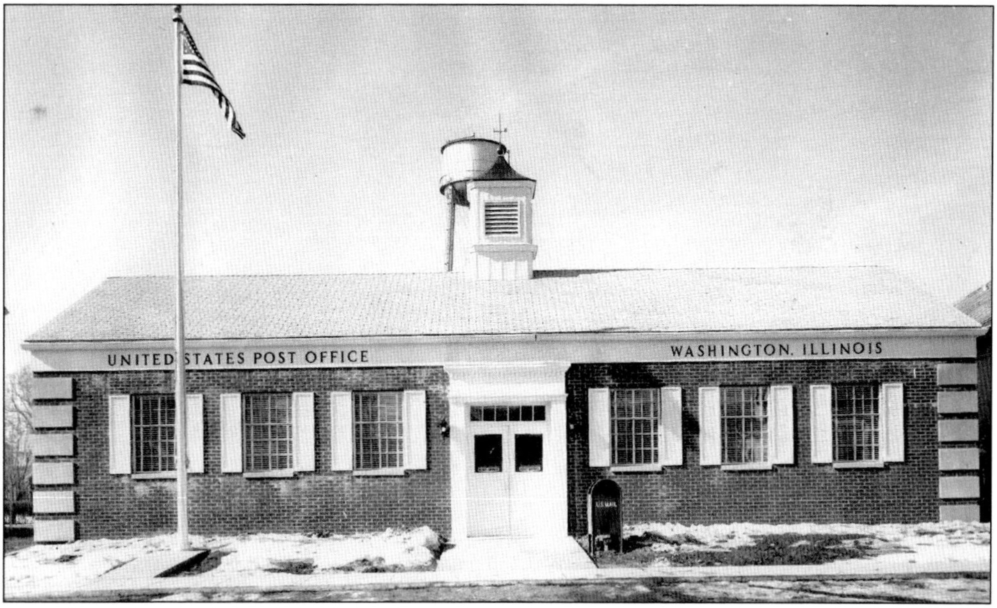

POST OFFICE. Mail first found its way into the community officially in March 1870 when Charles A. Crane became the community's postmaster. The post office found itself in a number of different locations throughout the square, but in 1962, it got its most recent home at the address of 106 South High Street. Much like the library built several years earlier, the post office was designed in a Colonial style with the exterior made up primarily of brick. As with the library, it was conveniently tucked into the neighborhood, easily walked to, and accessible to all of those within the neighborhood. (Courtesy of the Washington Historical Society, photograph by Leo Clark.)

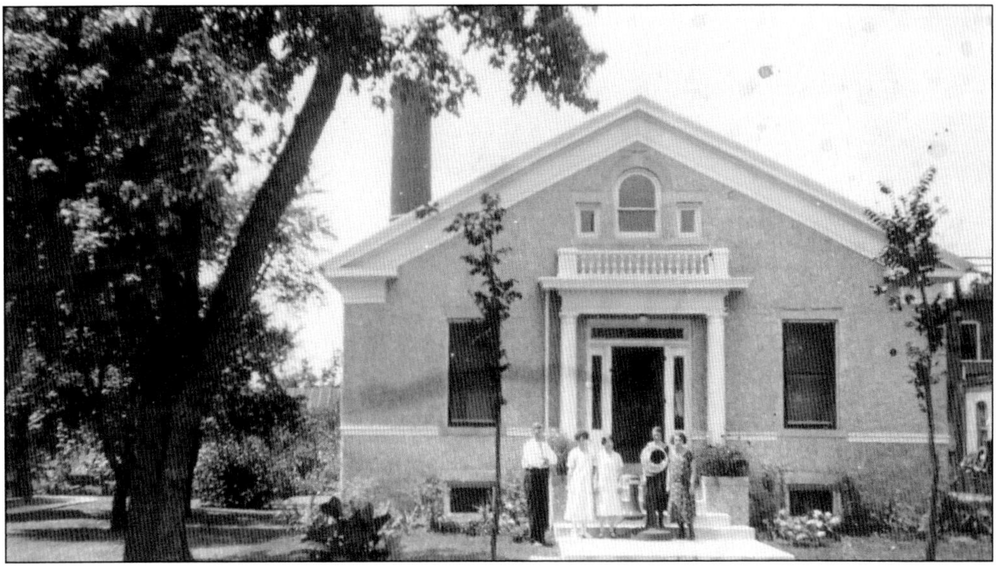

TELEPHONE SERVICE. This simple pitched-roof building was occupied by the community's earliest telephone operators. The facade is handsomely detailed with a very strong roof line and two Doric columns supporting the porch. The two-story building with basement opens out to the sidewalk and responsibly addresses the street as does the residential context surrounding it. (Courtesy of the Washington Historical Society.)

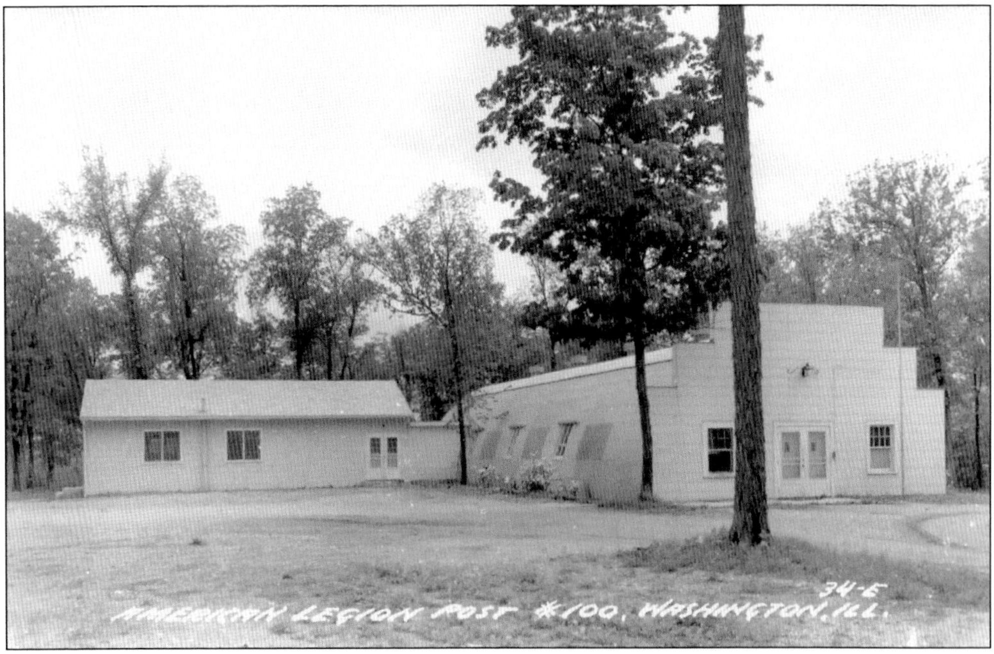

AMERICAN LEGION POST NO. 100. Organized in the spring of 1919, the Washington post began under the leadership of World War I veteran Fred Sweitzer, who became the first chairman. In its early days the group met in various places including several different rooms within the City Building until the city dedicated a room for the legion. In 1949, the land was purchased in order to build the facility shown above. The Washington post has done many wonderful things over the years for the community and its veterans.

Six

The Streets

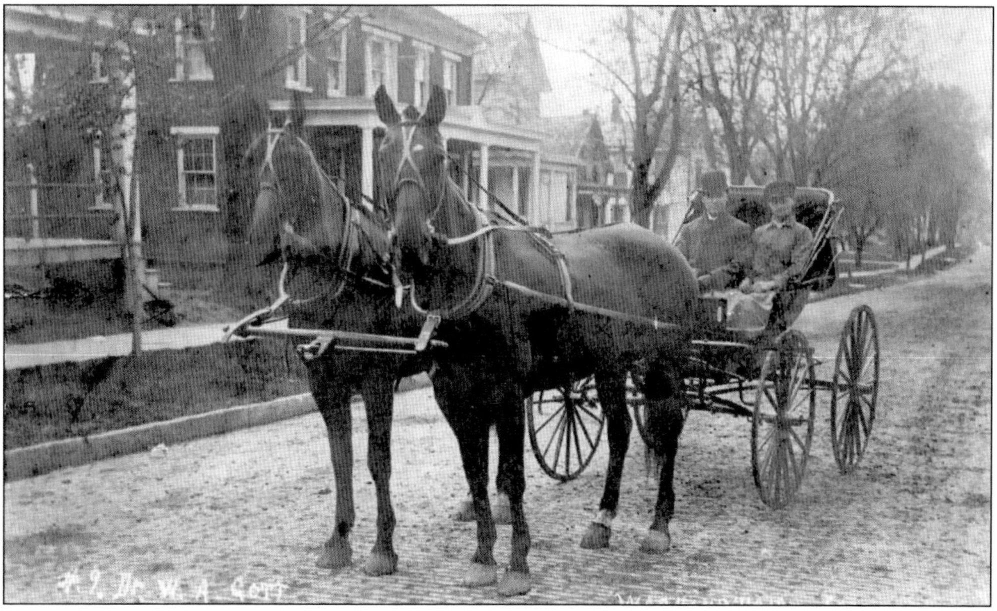

Dr. W. A. Gott Carriage. This is a typical street scene showing citizens out for a carriage ride on one of the many intimate residential streets surrounding the square. The image shows a street that is paved in brick and has a solid concrete curb, parkway, and sidewalk scheme.

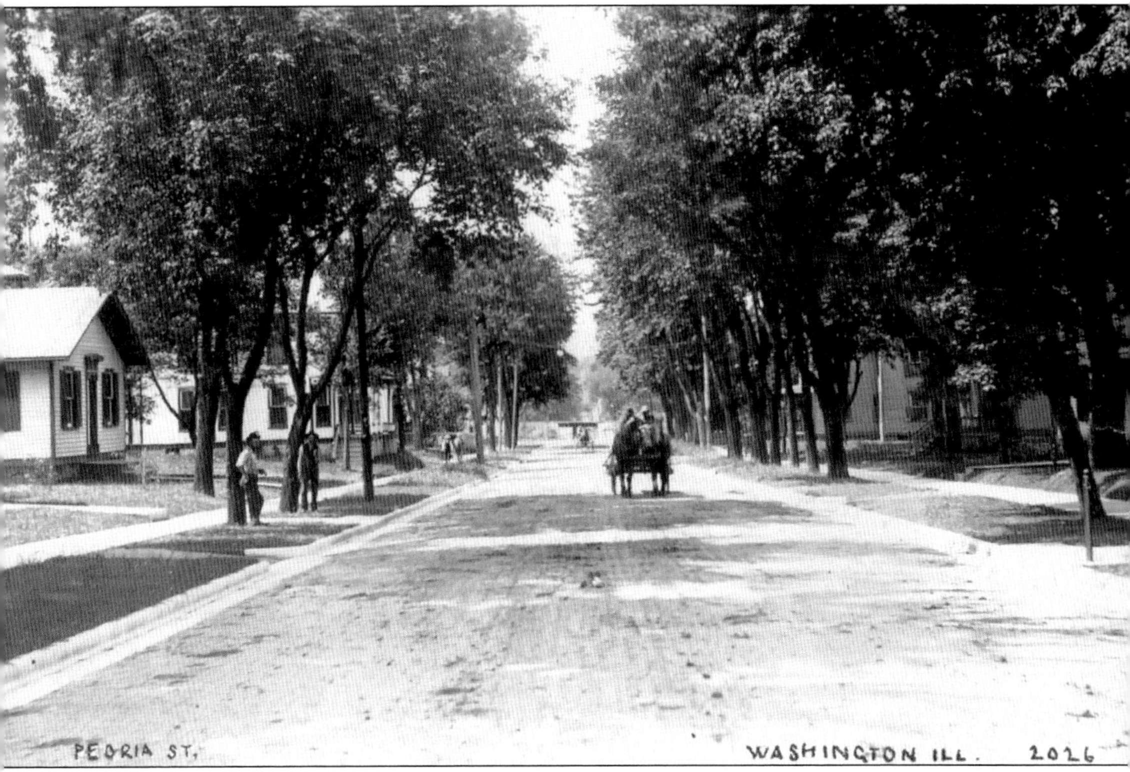

PEORIA STREET, 1907. A look west toward the railroad viaduct along Peoria Street shows the residential nature of the street as one travels away from the square. Carriage and pedestrian traffic was all that traveled along this thoroughfare in its early years. Concrete curbs, parkways, and sidewalks illustrate a diagrammatically simple yet sophisticated infrastructure system that is still the best practice today.

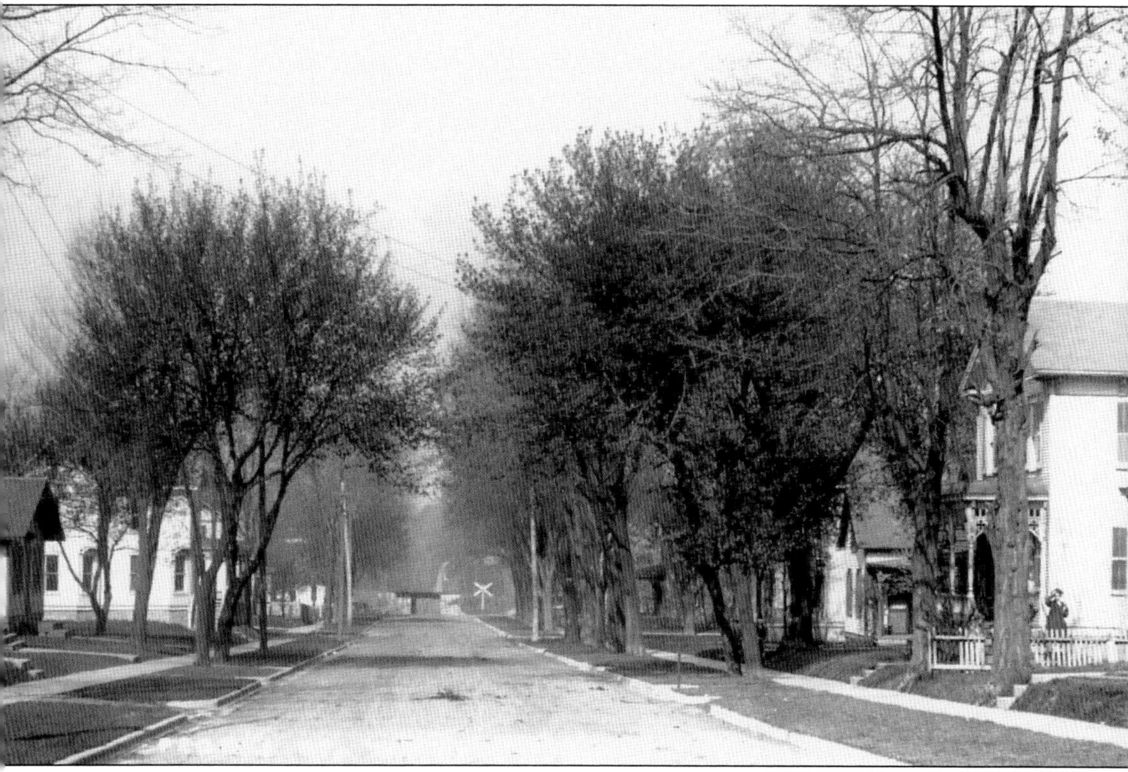

PEORIA STREET, 1914. Another view west toward the viaduct shows more of the residences lining the street. The small setbacks from the street allow the residences to play a part in providing a more enclosed and desirable streetscape. Front porches lining the sidewalk allow for friendly greetings and a more welcoming appearance that enlivens the streetscape. Trees placed within the parkway play an important role in defining the spaces as well, while providing shade on both sides of the street.

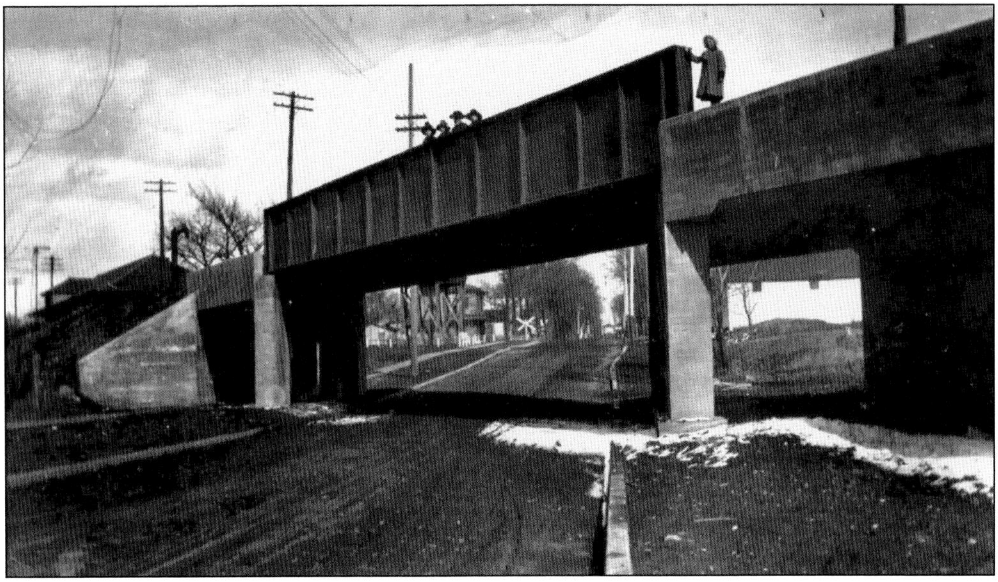

RAIL VIADUCT. Functionally the viaduct provides the means for rail traffic to travel over automobile and pedestrian traffic below. Aesthetically the viaduct frames the path along Peoria Street, which is lined by residences and businesses on into the square. The extended view of the viaduct also shows the TP&W passenger depot to the left at track level. (Courtesy of the Washington Historical Society.)

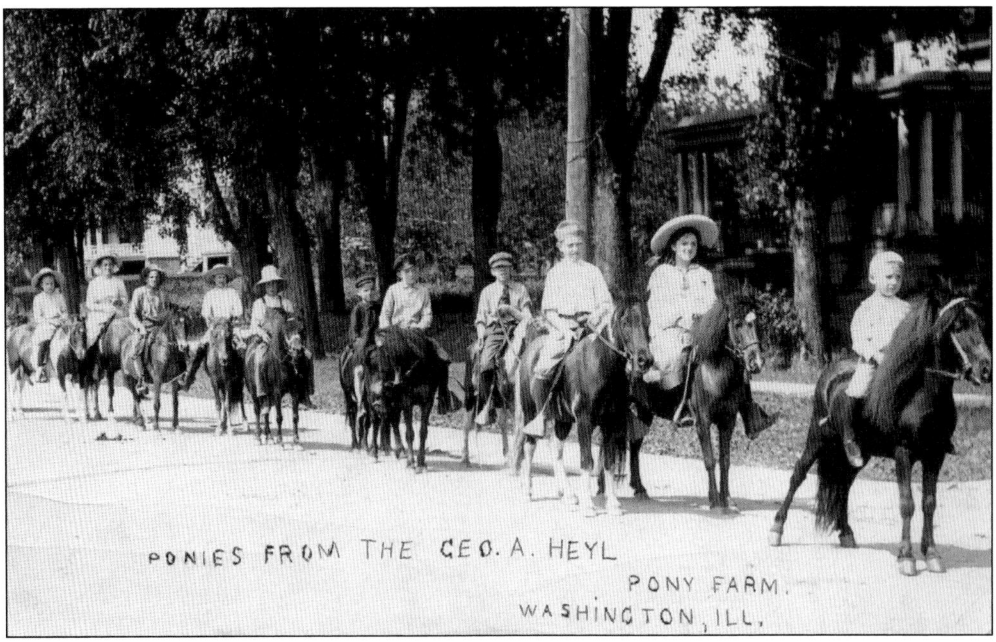

PARADE DOWN MAIN STREET. A dozen children enjoy riding along Main Street atop ponies raised at the Heyl Pony Farm. The group illustrates another great use of streets. While the flow of vehicular traffic has become the emphasis of streets today, a leisurely jaunt like this reminds one that the street should be a safe place for any number of activities, including those of the pedestrian. (Courtesy of the Washington Historical Society.)

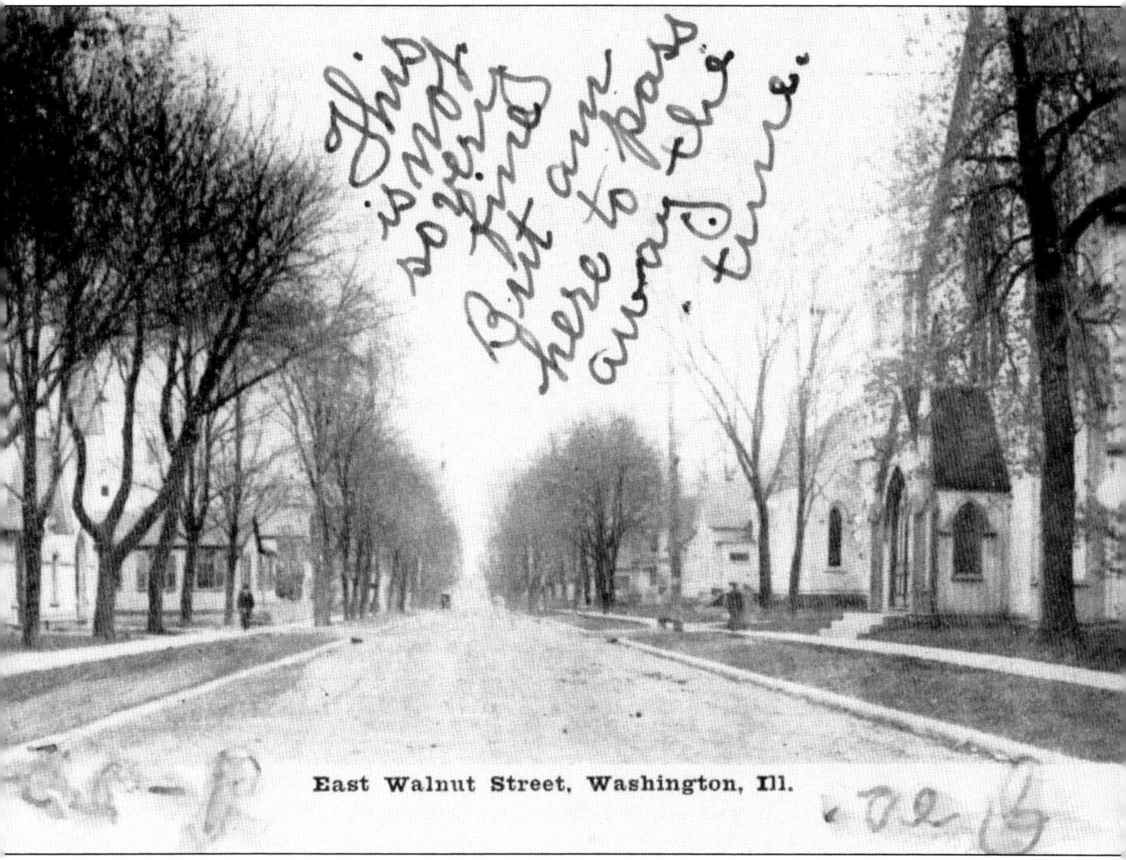

WALNUT STREET CHURCHES AND HOMES. This early view, looking down the main eastern thoroughfare originating from the square, illustrates a familiar street scene and diagram. The street is lined by a pedestrian parkway and sidewalk system along with rows of homes and churches that frame the space. In this one view, three different church buildings can be seen along and facing the street. Their presence increases the strength of the neighborhood and provides residents with a place to worship within walking distance of their homes.

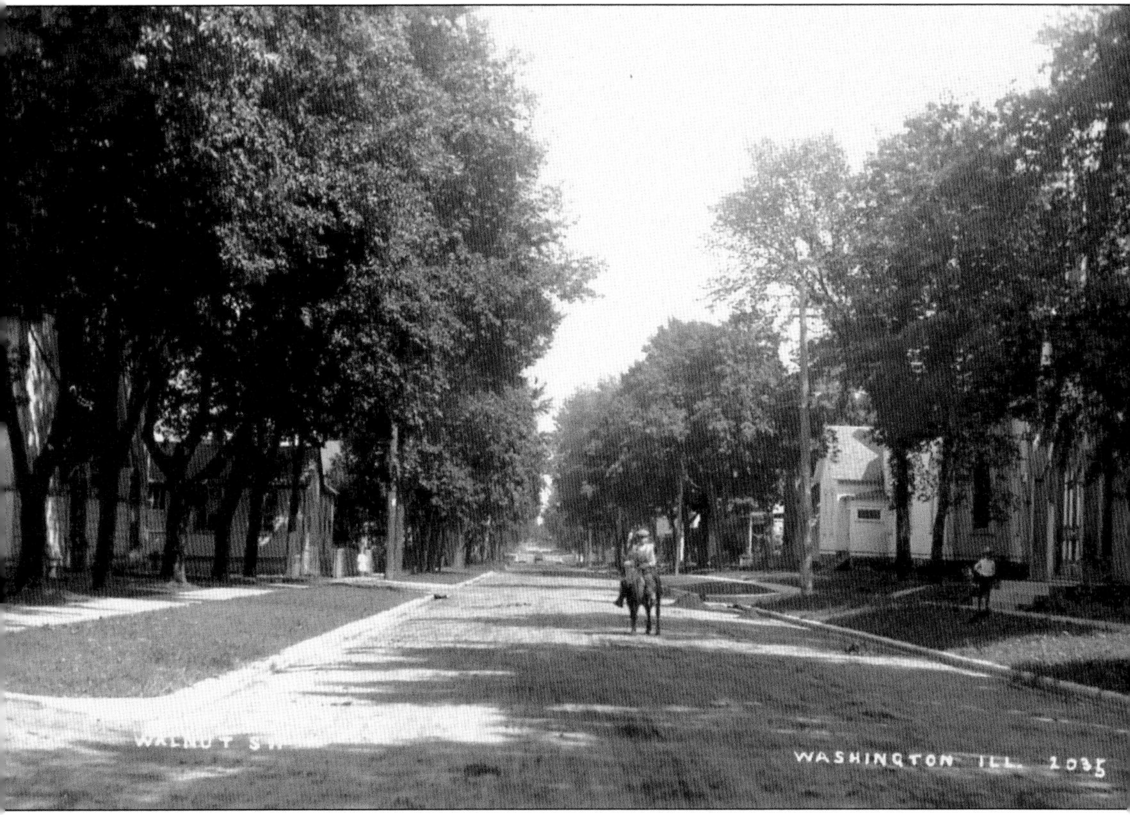

Walnut Street Enclosed Space. A later view of Walnut Street looking east shows the impact trees can make throughout neighborhood streets. The image was captured mid-year when the leaves fill the trees and make them look their fullest. The canopy of the trees along the street not only shades the residences lining the street but also the street itself and creates an enclosed space. This enclosed space strengthens the street and makes it a more comfortable space to be in.

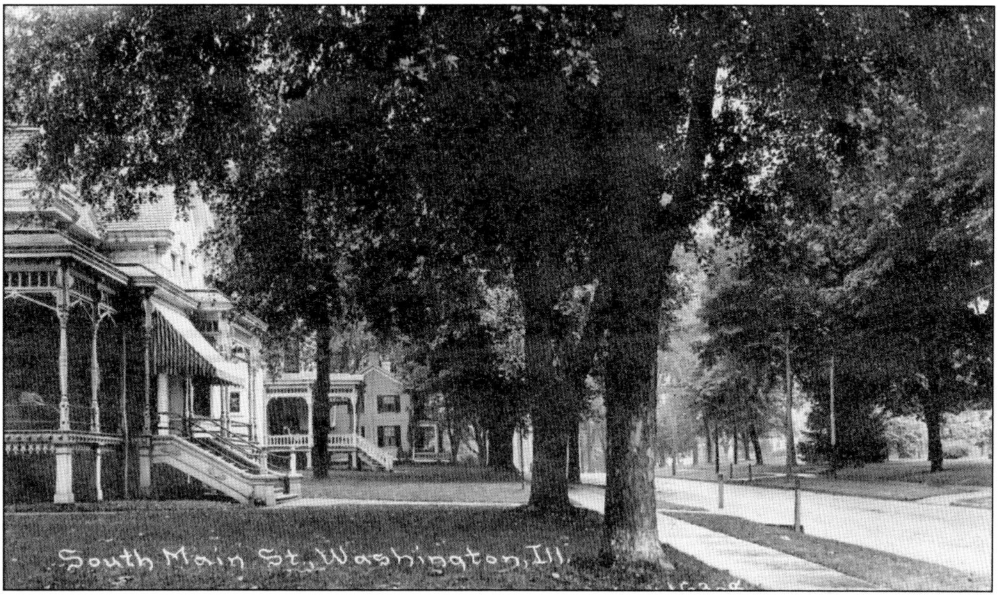

SOUTH MAIN STREET RESIDENCES. Ornate and very-well-articulated homes along South Main Street increase the depth and character of the thoroughfare, making it a very wonderful street to travel along. Celebrated front entries and porches, accessible to the public sidewalk, are not set back from the street at an exaggerated distance and create a very welcoming appearance. Mature trees placed near the street provide shade to those walking and help enclose the street itself. Parkways adjacent to the sidewalk provide a natural buffer between those walking and those traveling along Main Street itself.

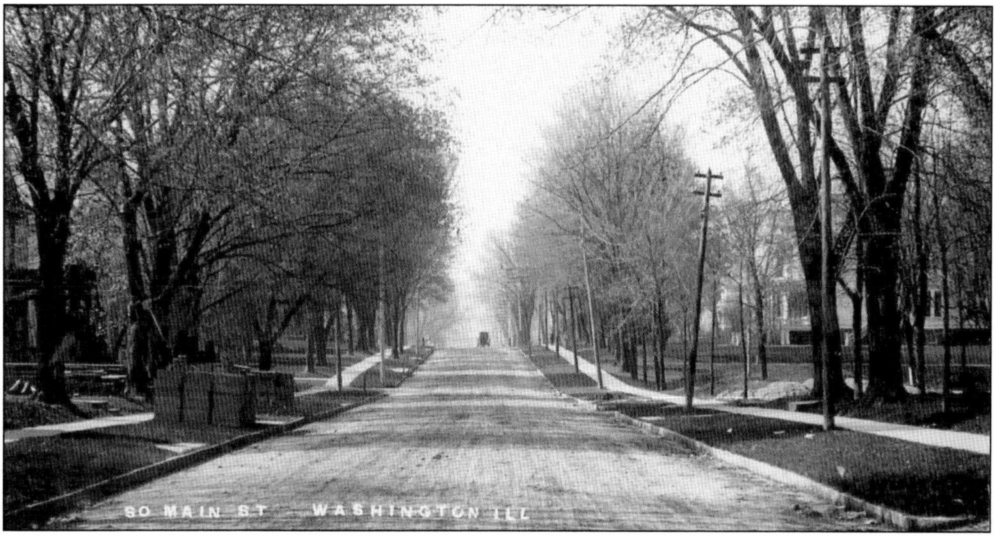

SOUTH MAIN STREET, 1911. South Main Street illustrates yet another simple yet sophisticated street plan that creates an intimate and very beautiful space. This view looking south with the square to the back shows residences lining both sides of the street, and along with mature and very beautiful street trees, they vertically frame the space. Sidewalks and parkways create the very important pedestrian realm that encourages citizens to walk the streets to and from the square as they go about their daily business. Construction materials on the side of the street hint at a new home being built.

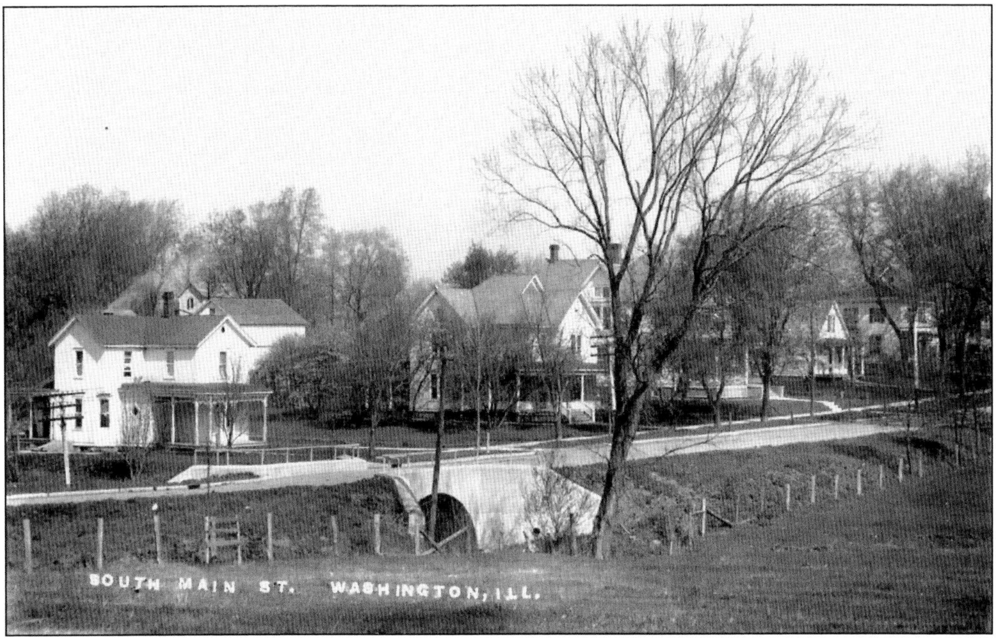

SOUTH MAIN STREET RESIDENCES AND VIADUCT. South Main Street travels over Farm Creek, a natural feature that winds throughout the community via a concrete viaduct. Farmland lies in the foreground and then meets with the increasingly residential nature of the street, including parkways and sidewalks, as it goes north toward the square.

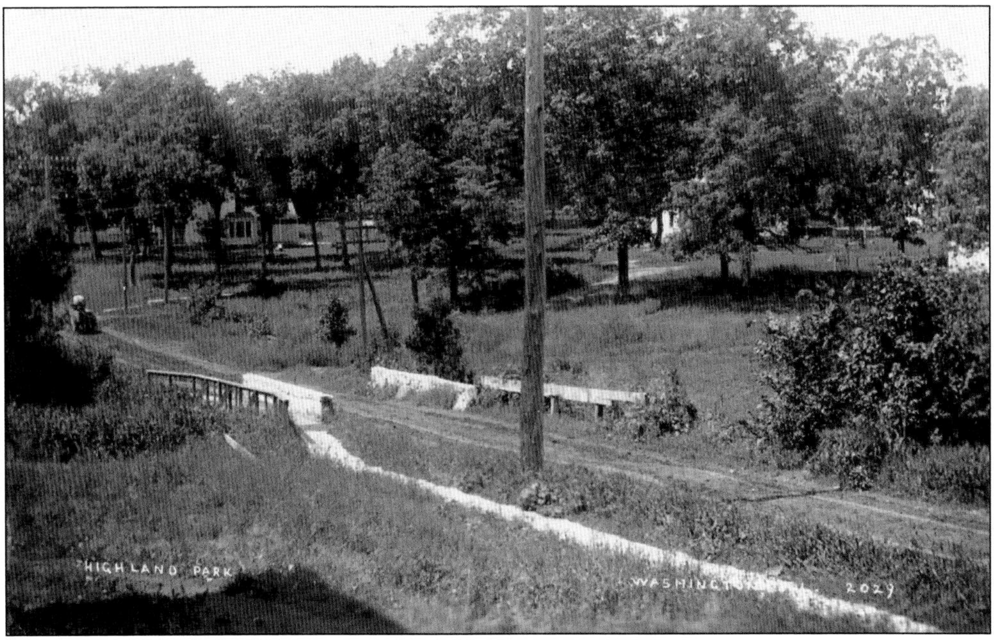

HIGHLAND PARK, NATURAL PATH. In contrast to the articulated paved streetscapes originating from the square, this path through Highland Park illustrates a more rural and natural path for carriages to travel. A stone bridge spans Farm Creek allowing both vehicles and pedestrians to cross. A gravel path in the foreground provides citizens on foot a more defined and cleaner path alongside the road.

Seven

The Homes

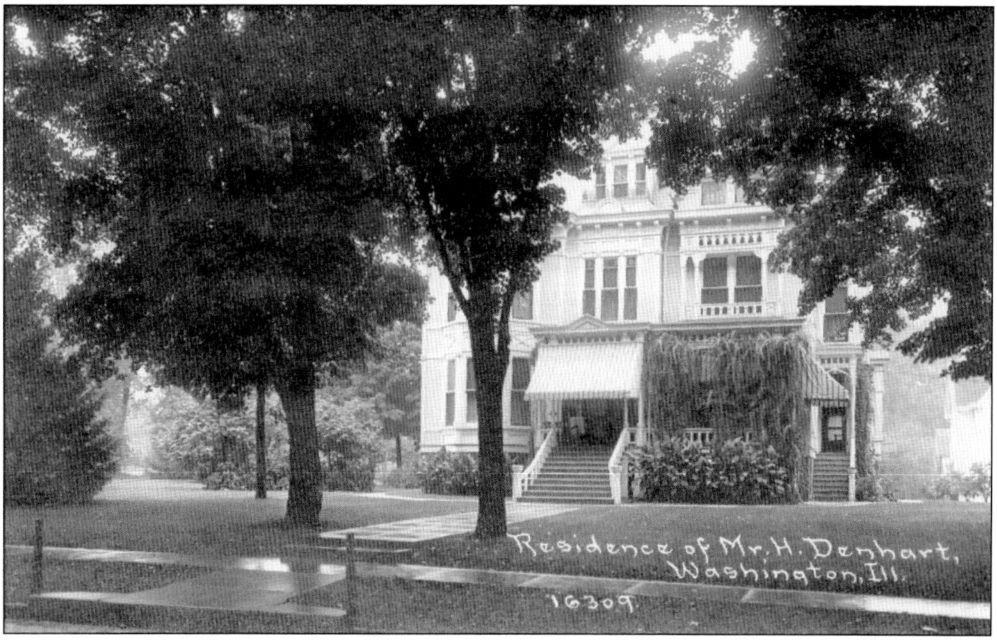

Residence of Mr. H. Denhart. A view across South Main Street after a daytime rain shower shows the beauty of the home's exterior. Lush landscaping adds to the inviting nature of the front porch, which opens up to a front walk framed by large trees that travel out to the public sidewalk and street. The coach house for the residence can just barely be seen to the right. Such a structure, pulled away from the house, alleviates the need for any attached garage that detracts from the beauty of the home.

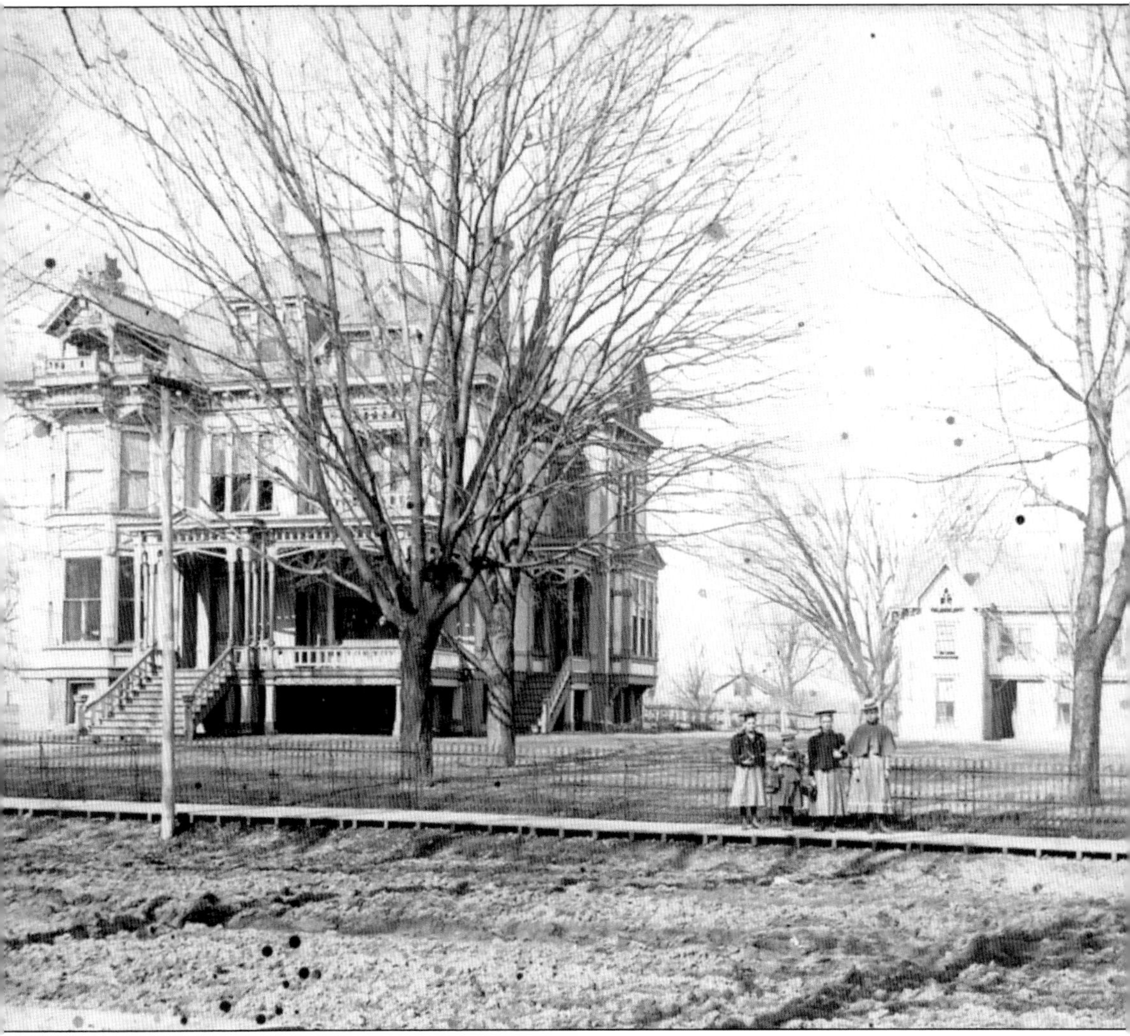

Dirt Street. This late-1800s photograph illustrates the difficult terrain that existed on even the most heavily traveled roads. The simple iron fence surrounds and defines the Denhart property. Four young ladies stand alongside the boardwalk on the west side of South Main Street. (Courtesy of the Washington Historical Society.)

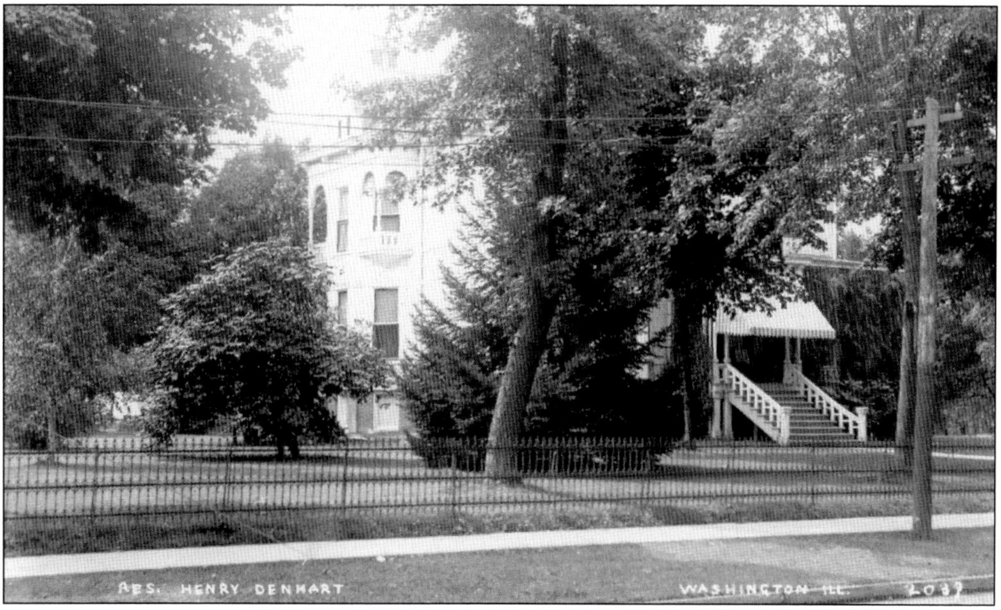

Residential Street Wall. Yet another view of the Denhart residence illustrates not only a look at the wonderful Victorian detailing of the bay on the southern side of the home, but also a look at the wonderfully detailed iron fence along the sidewalk in front of the residence. Fences or street walls are intended for security or privacy, but they also lend yet another interesting element to the streetscape and street section.

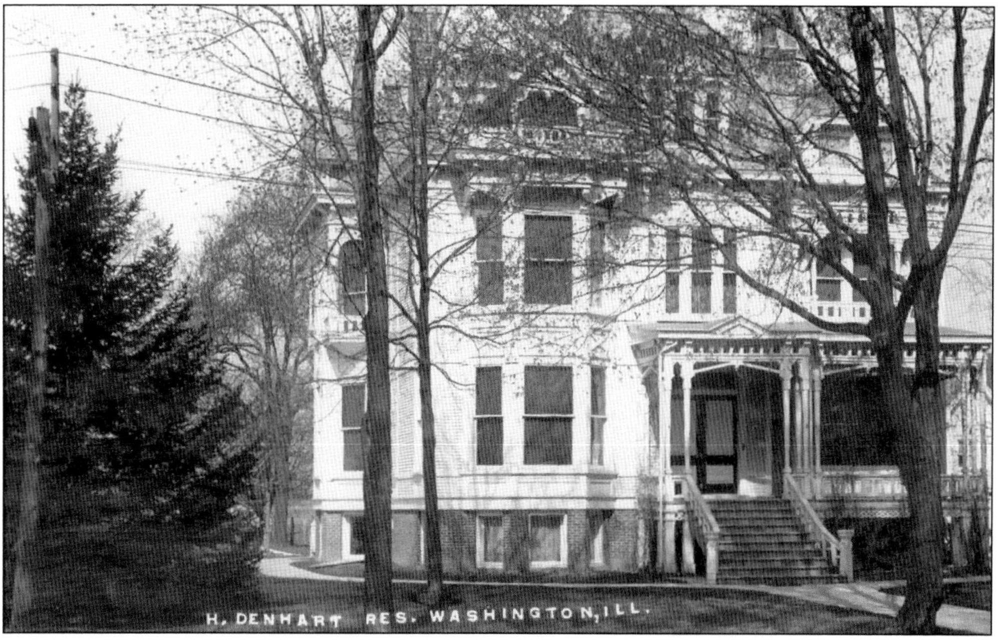

H. Denhart Residence, 1911. This home was built and owned by well-known local banker Henry Denhart. The wonderfully well-articulated Victorian frame home has a brick masonry foundation. The generous front porch, adorned with Victorian ornament, celebrates the entry to the home beautifully. A number of bays and projections accompany detailed woodwork window surrounds and ornamentation to compose a very successful front elevation.

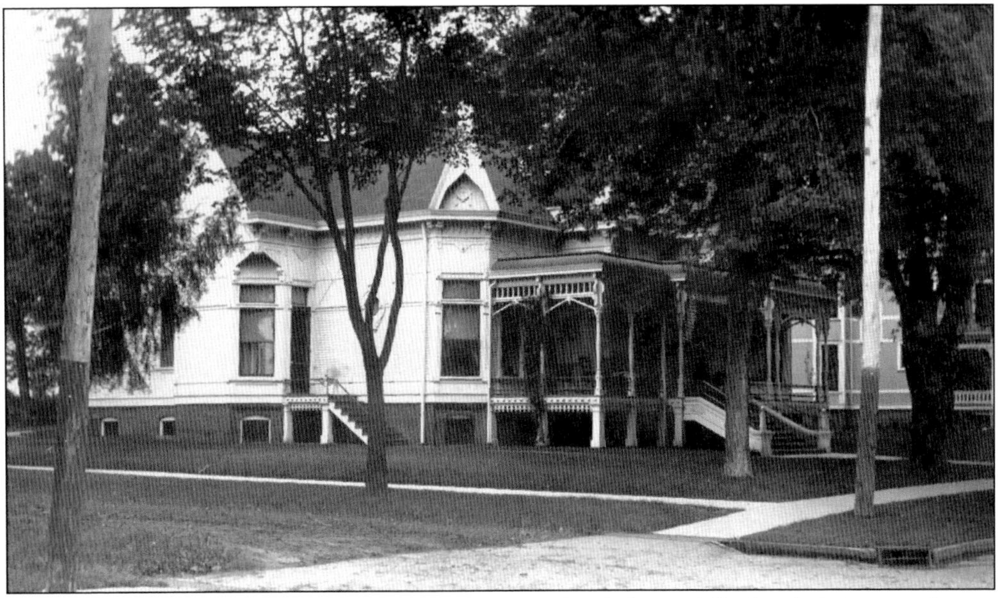

GEORGE STIMSON RESIDENCE. This is another example of a beautifully detailed Victorian home. The ornamentation across the porch is extremely well detailed. The porch opens out in grand fashion onto public space. The dirt road that interrupts the sidewalk shown in the foreground would become Catherine Street. The two utility poles on either side of the road illustrate the growing luxury of telephone and electrical service throughout the community. The original owner, George Stimson, was a banker with the A. G. Danforth Bank and Company and served the city through two terms as an alderman.

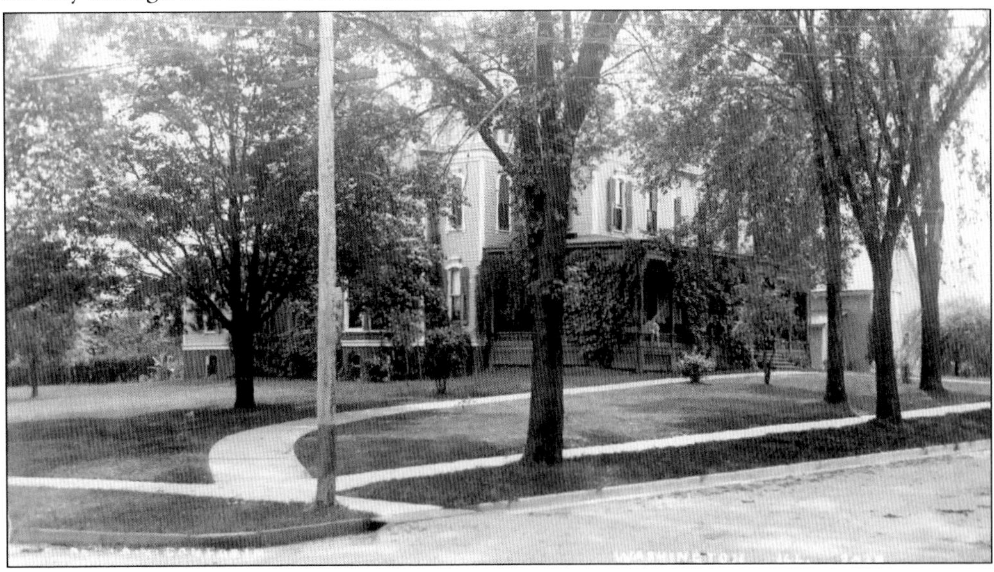

DANFORTH RESIDENCE. A large two-story wood-sided home located at 106 West Holland Street and along the brick-paved South Main Street is pushed back off the corner. The porch, being enjoyed by a young person sitting on the railing, is covered with foliage and opens toward the street. A front walk connects the home with the sidewalk to the front as well as to the corner. Through the trees a tower element can be seen, allowing the residents to enjoy views across the community above the tops of the surrounding homes.

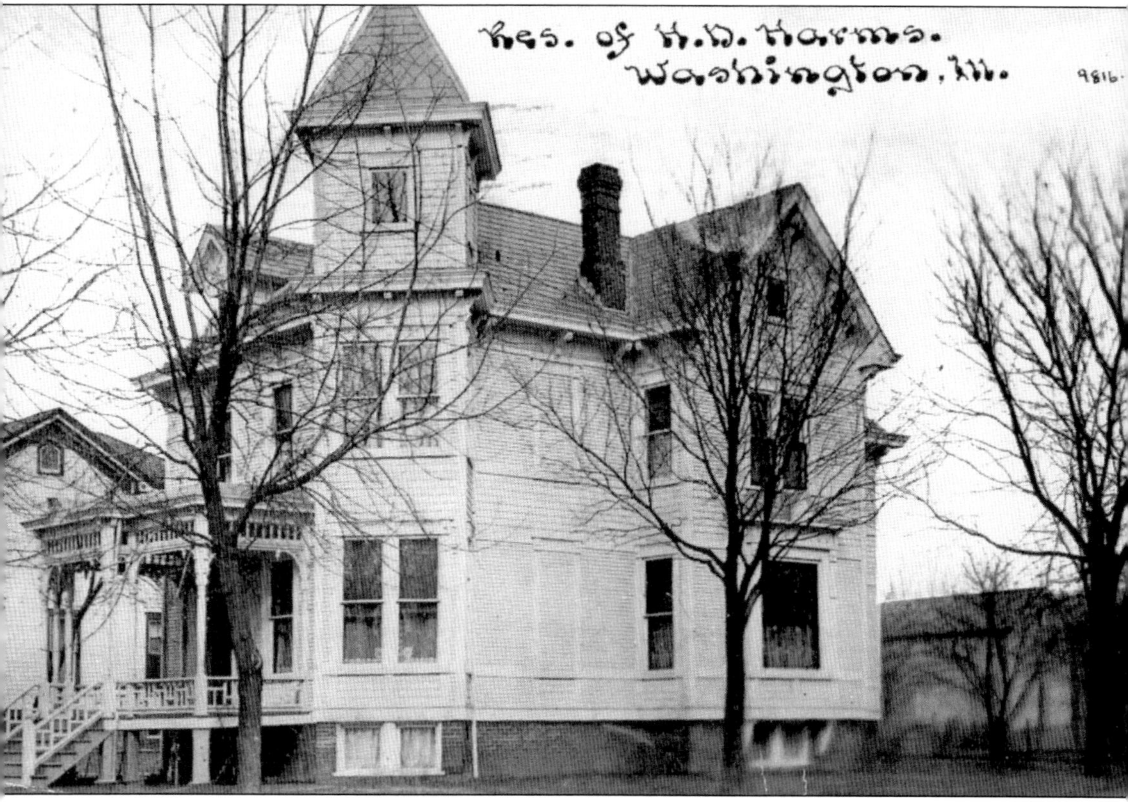

H. D. Harms Residence, 1912. A handsome frame-built, brick masonry foundation Victorian residence can be found at 127 South Main Street. The porch is finely detailed and opens out to South Main Street welcoming guests and those passing by while providing an open outdoor space for the home owner to enjoy. The rotated corner bay and tower element face directly out to the intersection of South Main and Catherine Streets, adding another interesting feature to the home.

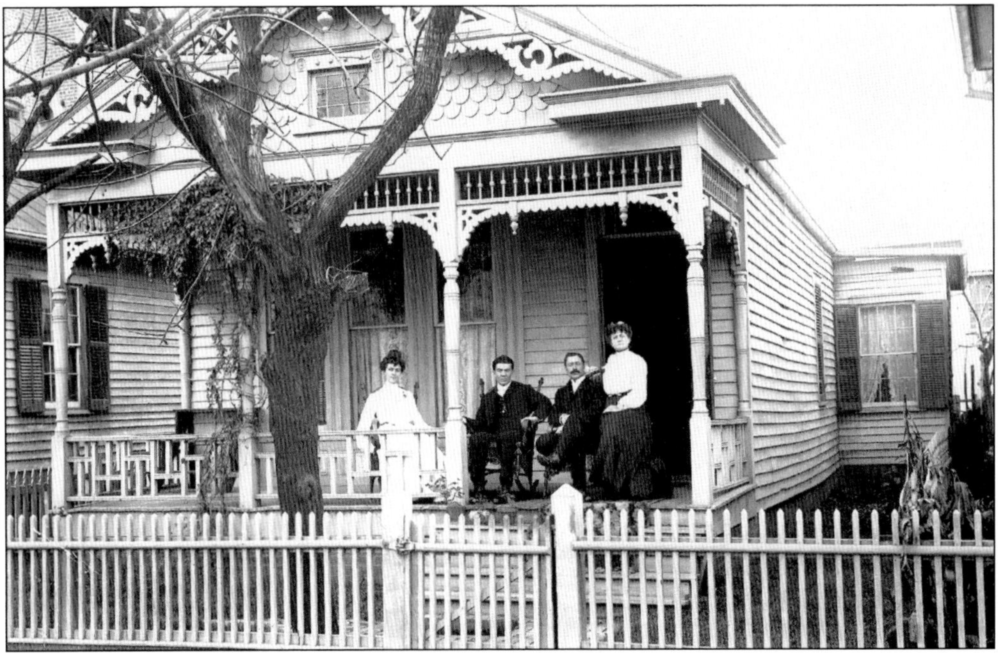

LAVISH VICTORIAN DETAILS. A very proud family can be seen outside on their porch posing in front of their home. This elaborately detailed one-story Victorian-style home is constructed of wood and is generously decorated with ornamentation across the front elevation. The home itself is located close to the public sidewalk, and a white picket fence provides enclosure and safety while giving definition to the streetscape. Notice the close proximity to the neighboring home and the interesting composition made up by the railing of the porch. (Courtesy of the Washington Historical Society.)

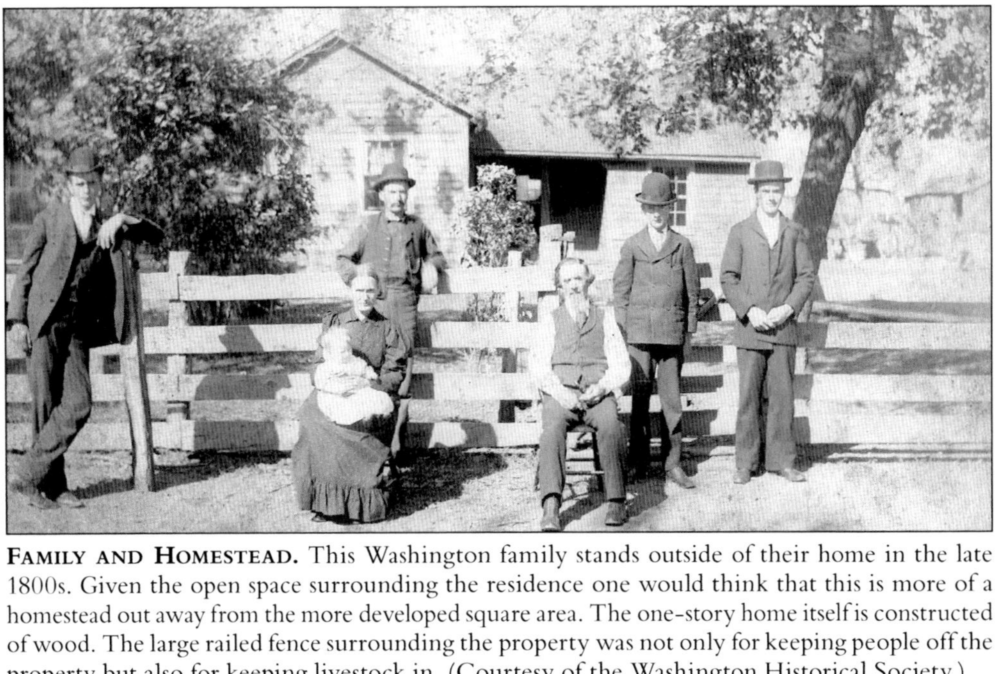

FAMILY AND HOMESTEAD. This Washington family stands outside of their home in the late 1800s. Given the open space surrounding the residence one would think that this is more of a homestead out away from the more developed square area. The one-story home itself is constructed of wood. The large railed fence surrounding the property was not only for keeping people off the property but also for keeping livestock in. (Courtesy of the Washington Historical Society.)

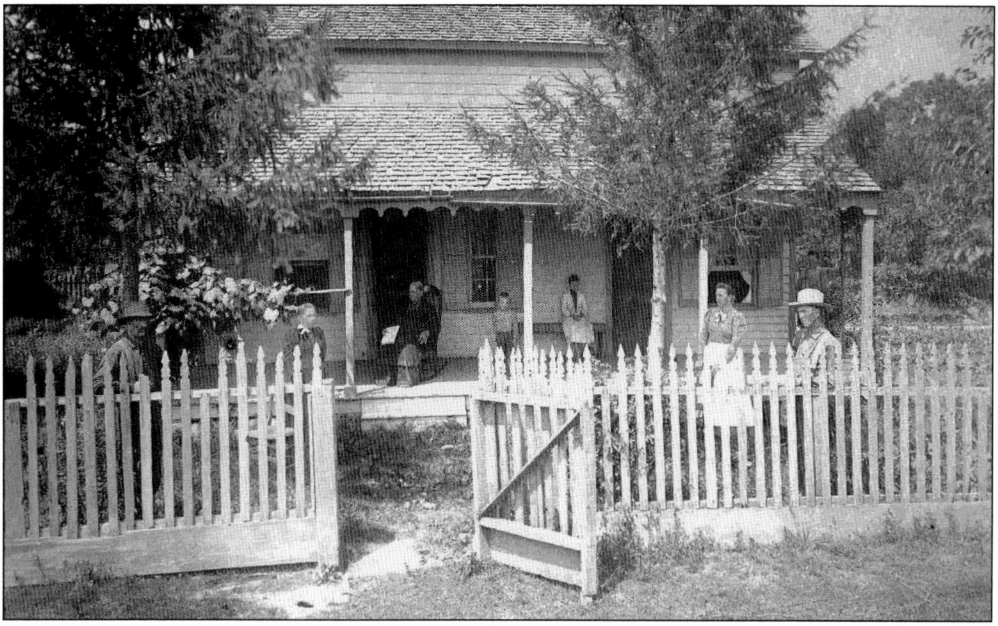

FAMILY, HOMESTEAD, AND PORCH. This late-1800s photograph shows a family in front of their modest wood constructed home. In this view, like many other homes shown, the front porch is an extremely important place for a family to use as an outdoor place to meet, relax, and communicate with each other. (Courtesy of the Washington Historical Society.)

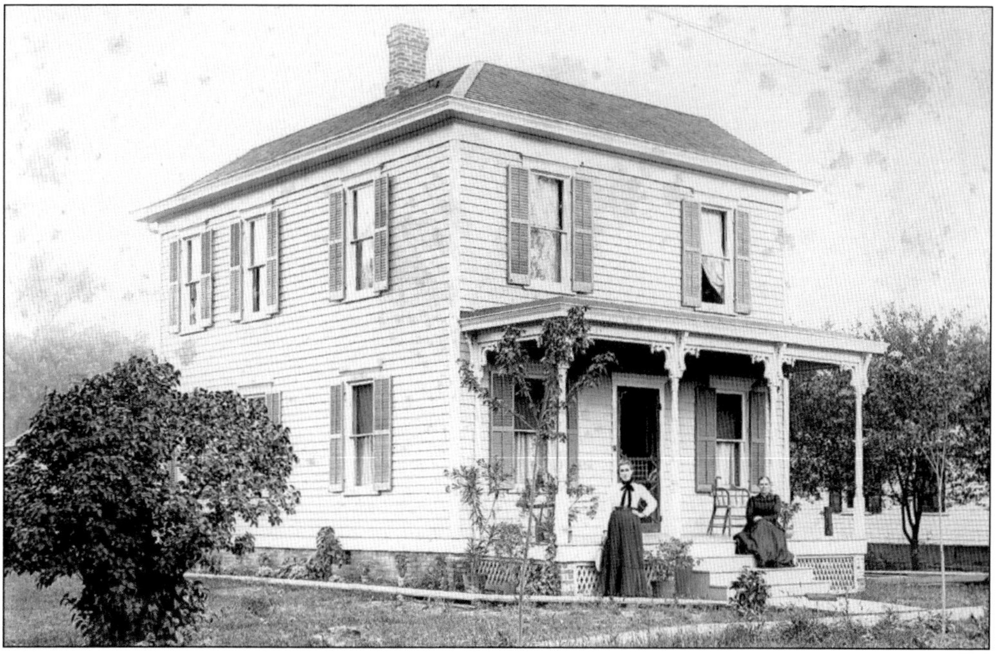

SIMPLE AND PROPER. Another late-1800s photograph shows two ladies in front of their home. A wood plank sidewalk goes past the home, and a walk juts out and meets the steps of the front porch, which is supported by four decorated Victorian columns. Shutters adorn the windows and work functionally as well as aesthetically in providing the facades with another level of detail. (Courtesy of the Washington Historical Society.)

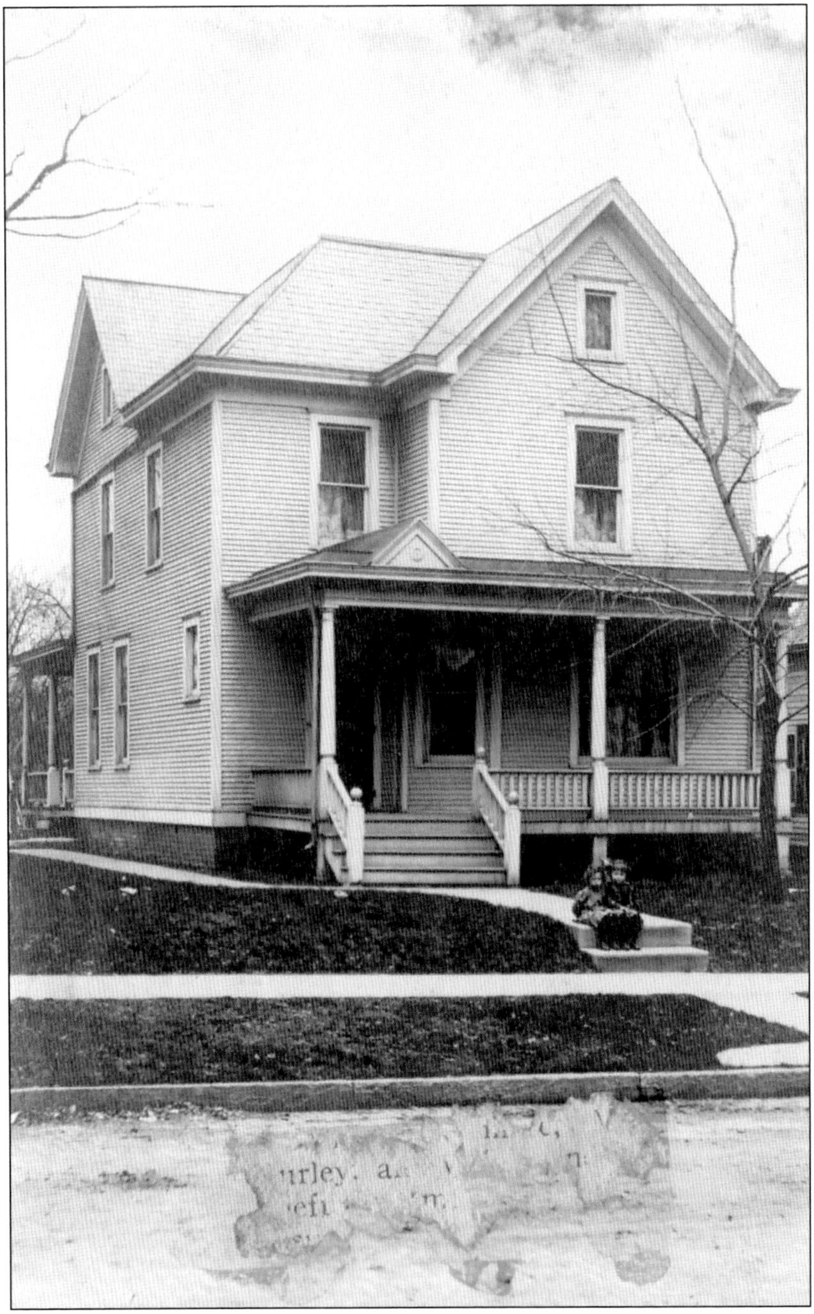

Mrs. E. Reich Residence. This particular home, located on 121 South Main Street is a wonderful example of how a typical residence should be composed and aligned along the street. The home itself is a well-proportioned wood-frame structure with a brick masonry foundation. Large inviting windows look out onto the street. A generous covered porch is handsomely detailed and provides an outdoor room for those who enjoy it. The porch also acts as a smooth transition between private and public space. The children on the steps outside of the home exhibit how well this scheme works as they enjoy watching the life of the community pass by. (Courtesy of the Washington Historical Society.)

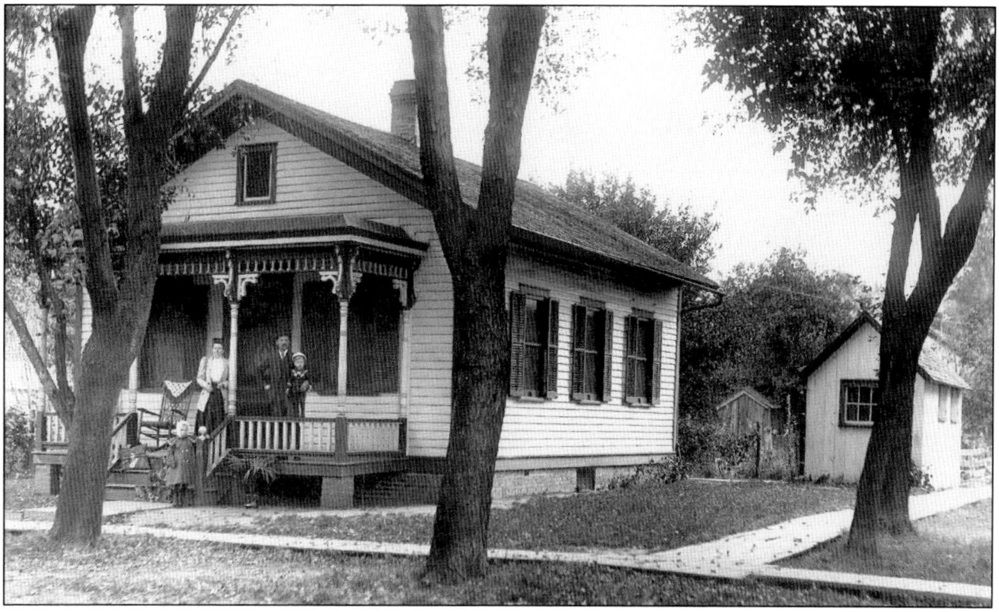

AN INTIMATE COTTAGE. A young family poses outside on their porch for this early photograph. A detailed and very welcoming front porch leads out to a boardwalk sidewalk. Mature trees line the road in what would become the parkway after the path was paved. An auxiliary structure lies along another walk to the back of the property alongside what looks like a small garden. (Courtesy of the Washington Historical Society.)

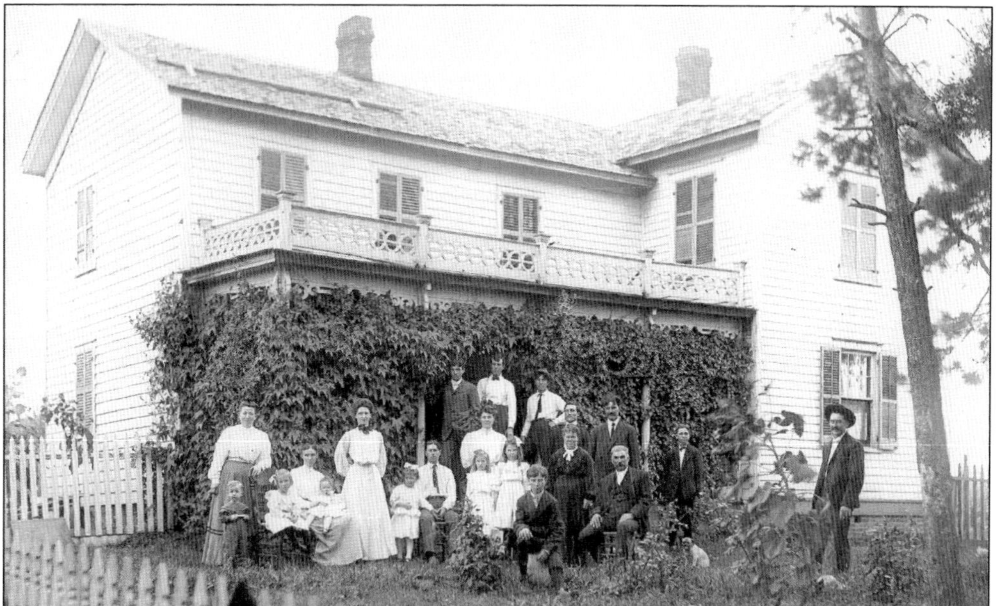

IVY COVERED PORCH. This early group photograph shows a family in front of their home. The residence has an L-shaped plan with a large porch and second-story balcony space. The porch is covered by layers of ivy vines and other foliage, adding to the interest of the elevation and providing shelter and privacy while using the space. Amid the elders and their children sits a small dog enjoying the occasion. (Courtesy of the Washington Historical Society.)

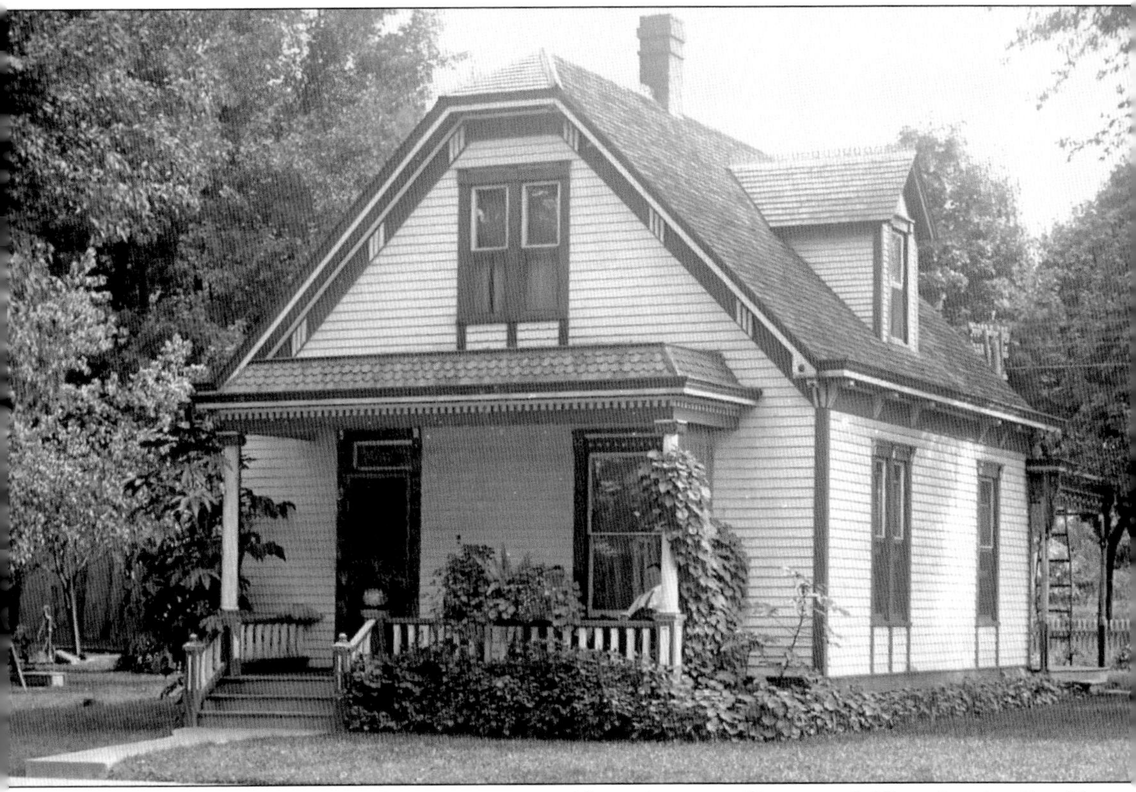

VICTORIAN COTTAGE. This picturesque residence is very well executed. Victorian details add a sense that there was a great deal of care that went into the design and construction. Ornamental and very functional cresting lines the peaks of the roof. Fine window surrounds add a layer of detail to the wood-sided home. Residents are relieved by cool breezes on the front porch or even the back porch on a warm summer day. The house lies close to the street, and the walk from the porch leads to the sidewalk. Lush landscaping adds to the inviting nature of the home. (Courtesy of the Washington Historical Society.)

Eight

The Churches

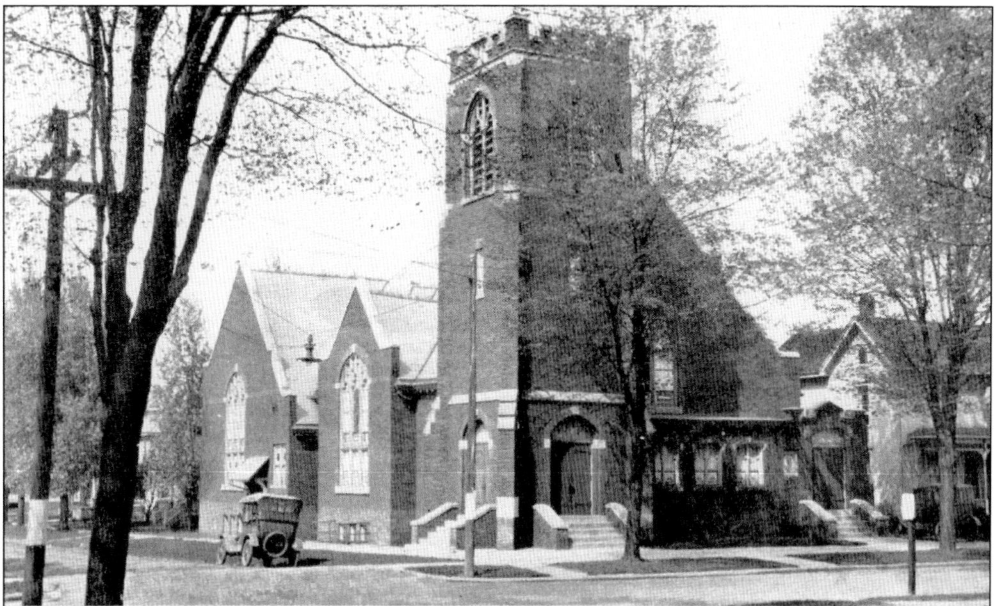

Evangelical Church. Like many churches throughout the community, the Evangelical church went through many changes and iterations during its early years. The congregation first met in a log church built during the 1850s. After that they moved into a second, much larger building in 1882. By the early 1900s, growth of the church forced yet another construction project, and in 1911, the building shown was dedicated. Interestingly the new building was constructed with and around the old building, which had been moved to the new site.

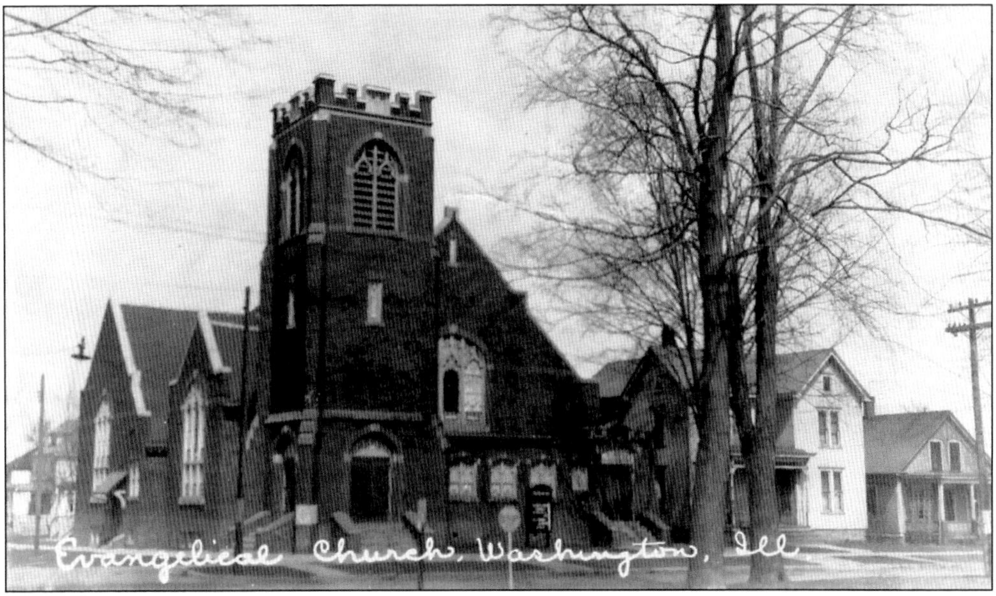

EVANGELICAL CHURCH, NEIGHBORS. The main entries of the church opened out onto Walnut and Elm Streets. The building itself was set back off the street only slightly, but the overall massing and scale of the structure did not overwhelm nearby residences. The steeple rose up past a steeply pitched roof. (Courtesy of the Washington Historical Society.)

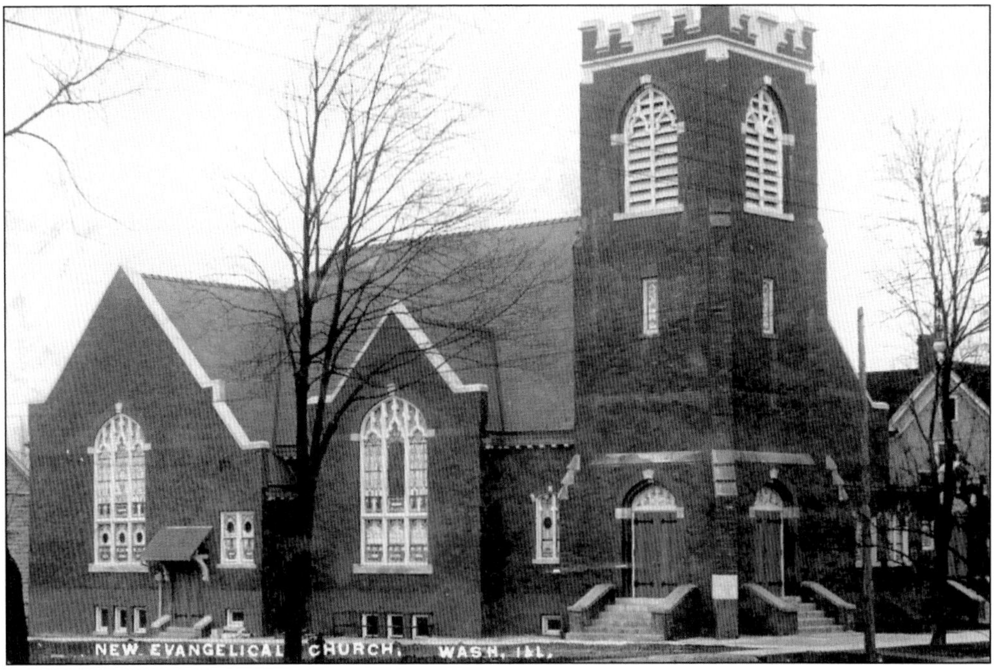

EVANGELICAL CHURCH, ARCHITECTURAL STYLE. The building was designed in the Gothic Revival style and was composed primarily of brick with stone details. Large and intricately detailed windows adorned each of the street-facing elevations. The windows featured a perpendicular or rectilinear style of tracery that held in place a number of beautiful stained-glass window panes. Brick Tudor arches surrounded the window openings and included a keystone and stone support.

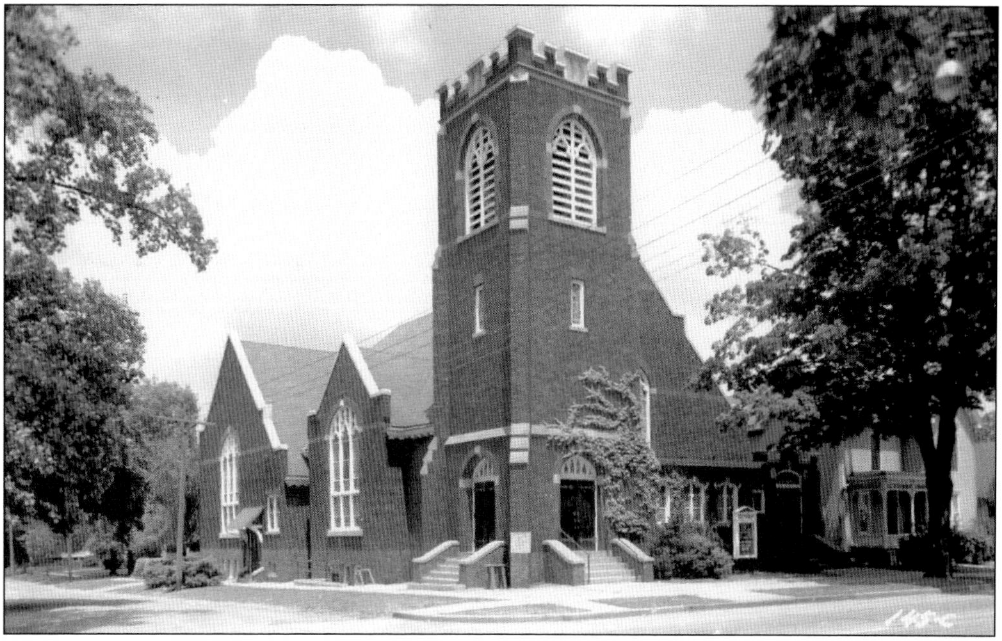

CHURCH MERGER. In 1968, the Evangelical United Brethren Church merged with the Methodist church, and thus, this congregation would now be known as the Evangelical United Methodist Church. Sadly this building no longer stands. It was indeed one of the city's finest structures, rivaling the well-articulated nature of the Lutheran church.

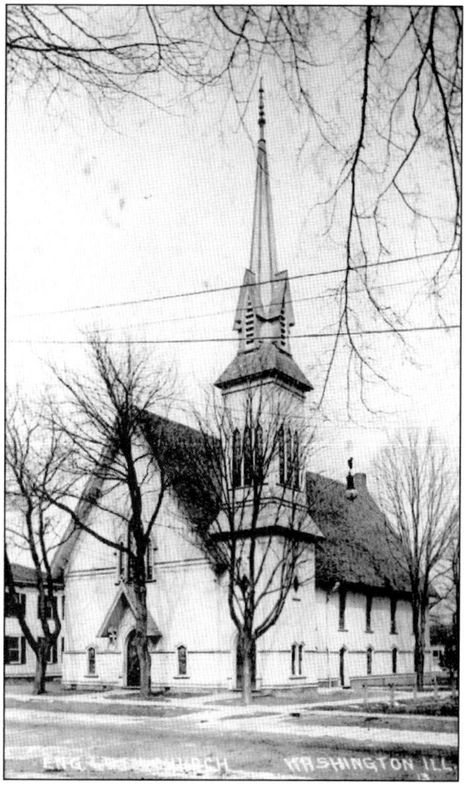

ENGLISH LUTHERAN CHURCH. On the corner of Elm and Walnut Streets, the first church building of the Lutheran Church was constructed at the cost of $6,000 and was dedicated on August 26, 1877. The building itself was of wood construction. The exterior of this church is an extremely well-proportioned composition. A pitched entry awning shelters one of the front entries. The other falls at the base of the building's steeple. Rotated window openings above the steeple entry add interest and lead up to the roofline of the nave or main worship space, which makes up the primary mass of the building. The steeple continues up to a trio of three window openings and then up to the louvered spire reaching up into the sky.

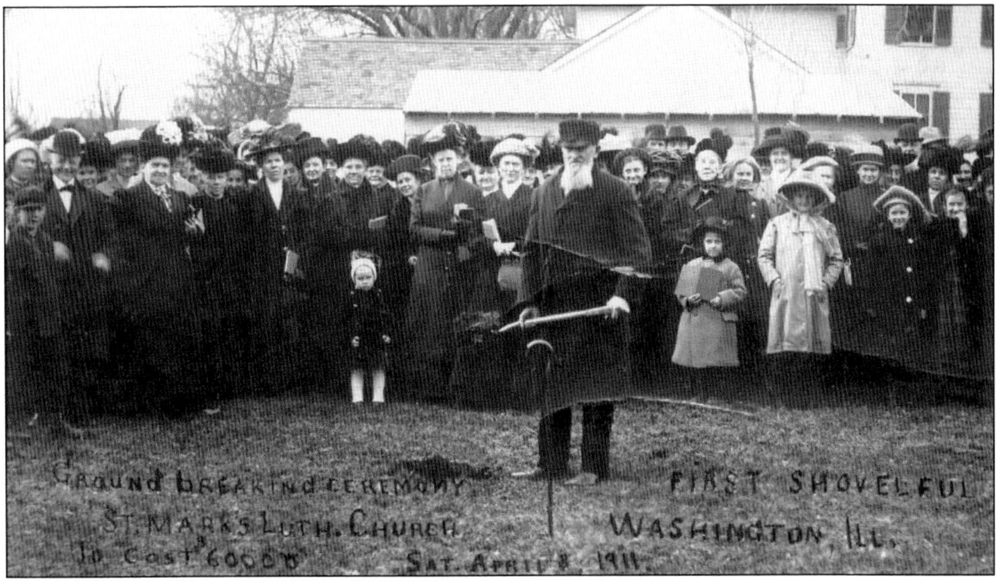

St. Mark's Evangelical Lutheran Church, Groundbreaking. The first shovelful is presented in front of a crowd of churchgoers at the groundbreaking ceremony on April 8, 1911, for the new church. Well-known citizen Henry Denhart provided a significant donation for the construction of the church. After the groundbreaking ceremony, the cornerstone was laid in June of that same year and was dedicated in September. As the image indicates, the cost of construction was to be $60,000. (Courtesy of the Washington Historical Society.)

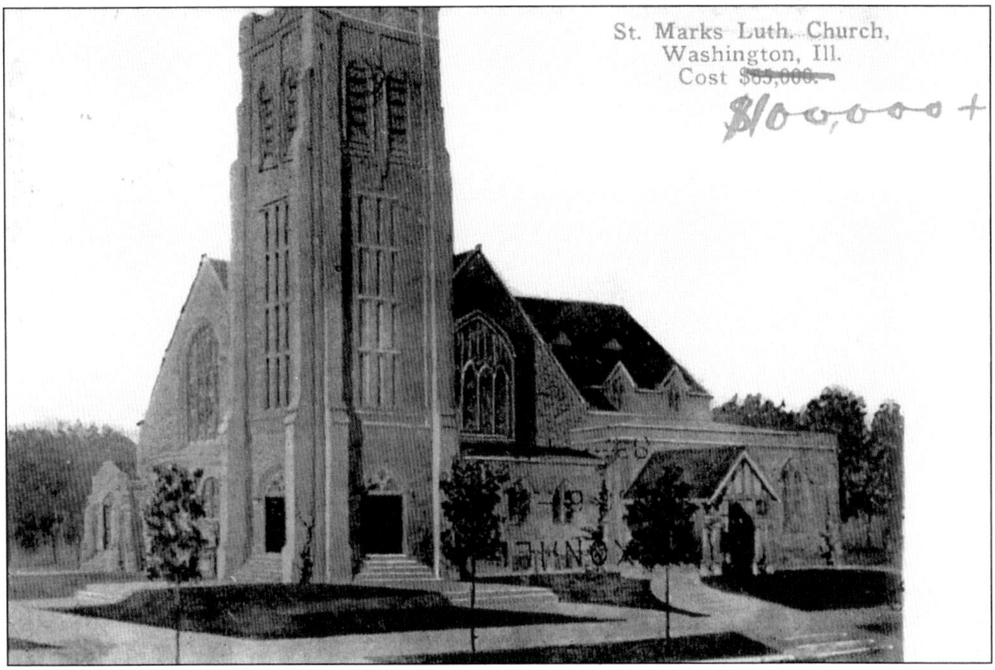

St. Mark's Evangelical Lutheran Church, Constructed. This is one of the most beautiful churches in the community located along South Main Street just south of the square. As noted on the previous image, the total cost of construction was $60,000, but a previous owner of this image seems to disagree and puts the total closer to $100,000 or more.

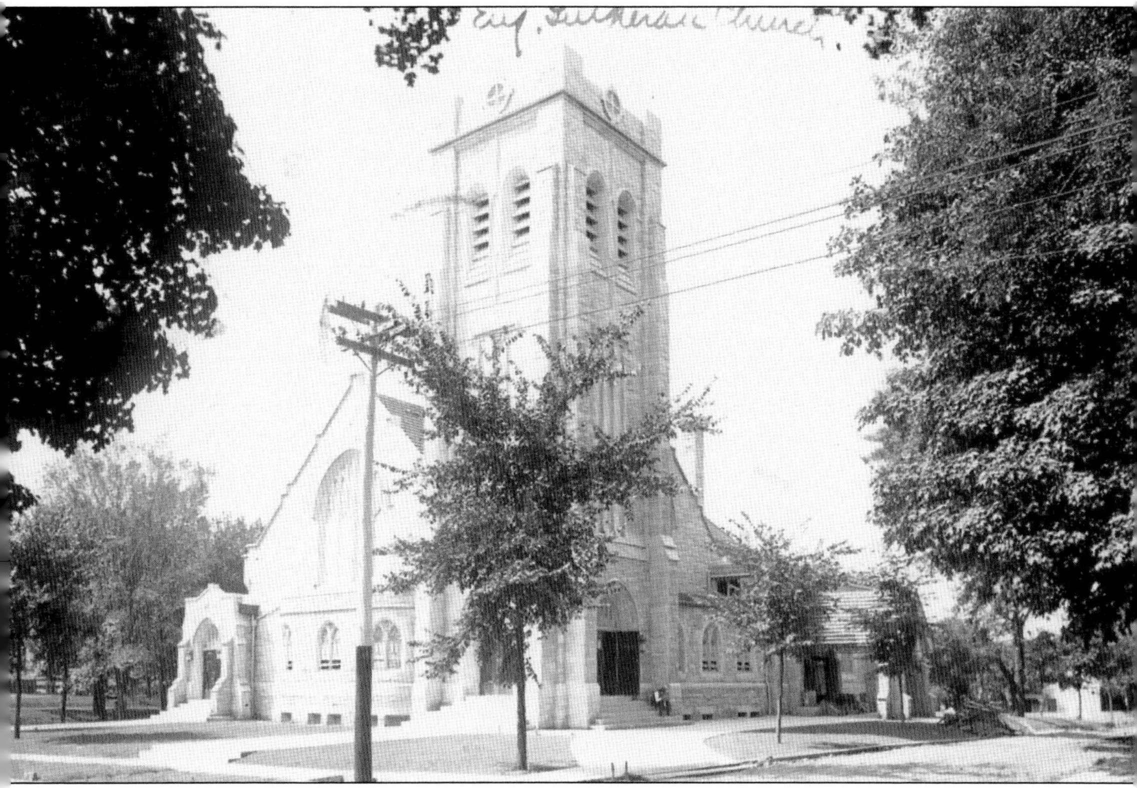

ST. MARK'S EVANGELICAL LUTHERAN CHURCH SITE. Adjacent to the Henry Denhart residence on South Main Street, the church is set back from the street at a distance similar to that of the surrounding residential context. Several entries open to the streetscape and have walks leading to the public sidewalks. To the north of the building exists a porte cochere and drive where churchgoers can be dropped off.

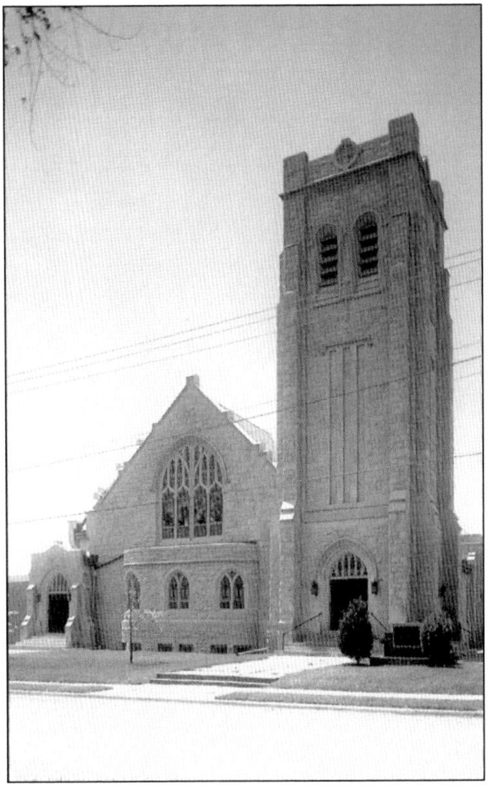

ST. MARK'S EVANGELICAL LUTHERAN CHURCH, STYLE. The exterior of the church is composed primarily of rusticated stone and Gothic Revival was the chosen style. Several detailed stained-glass windows look out onto South Main Street. The steeple rises up with a number of buttresses like pilaster details fronting the corners. Louvered openings at the top allow the sounds of the bell to resonate out. The top of the steeple is squared off and does not have a spire like its predecessor.

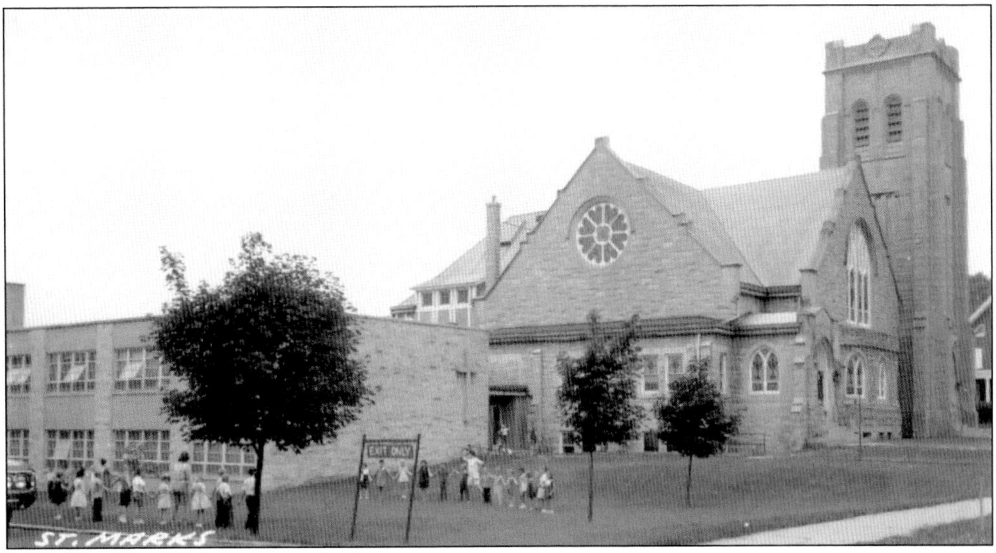

ST. MARK'S EVANGELICAL LUTHERAN CHURCH ADDITIONS. Through the years, additions were made to many of the churches throughout the community, especially for educational purposes. At St. Mark's, such an addition was made to the southern portion of the building. Although not in the same style, similar materials at a similar scale were used to minimize the aesthetic impact of the new building addition. From this view, one can also see the beautiful wheel window on the southern face of the original building. A wheel window is a kind of rose window that has distinctly radiating mullions amid the stained glass as opposed to just tracery.

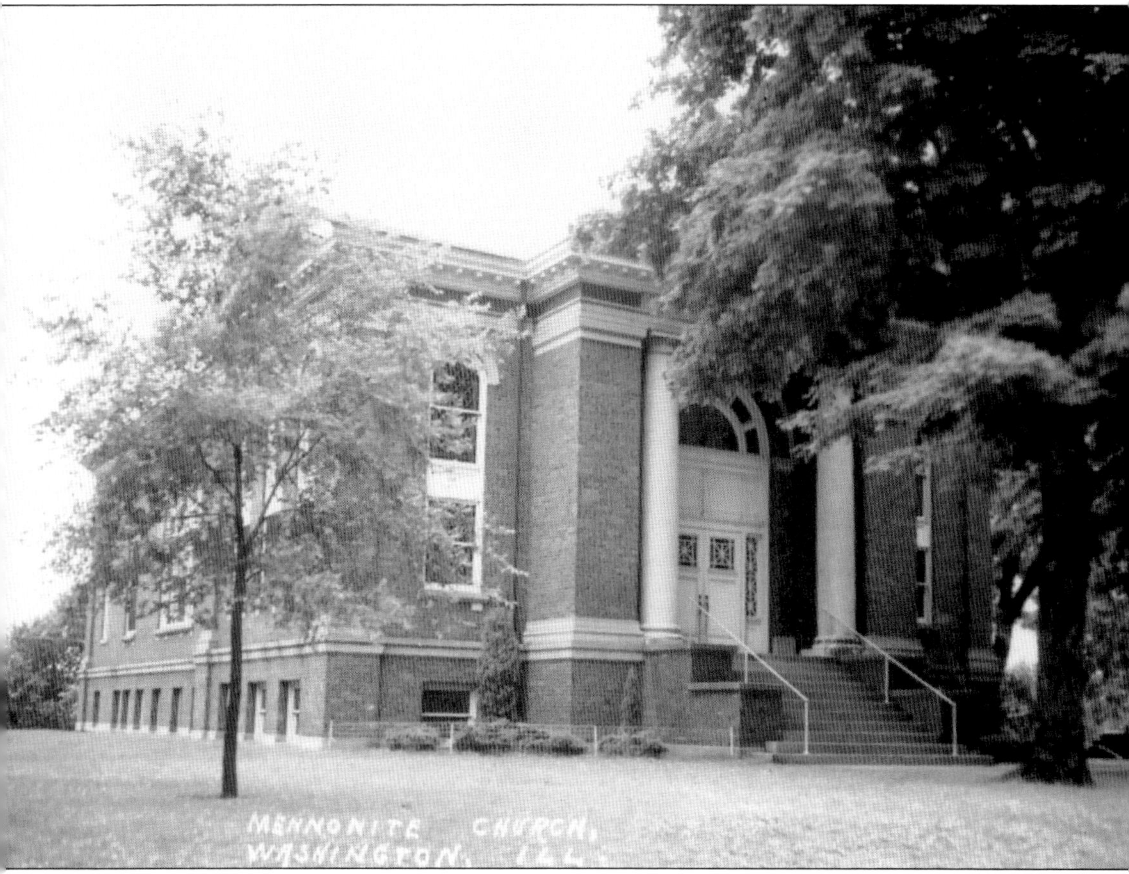

CALVARY MENNONITE CHURCH. The original church was built in 1869 and was named the East Washington Church. After a period in the 1890s of significant growth, a South Washington Church was born. In 1925, the church constructed a new building on East Jefferson Street. Since then, additions have been made to the main building.

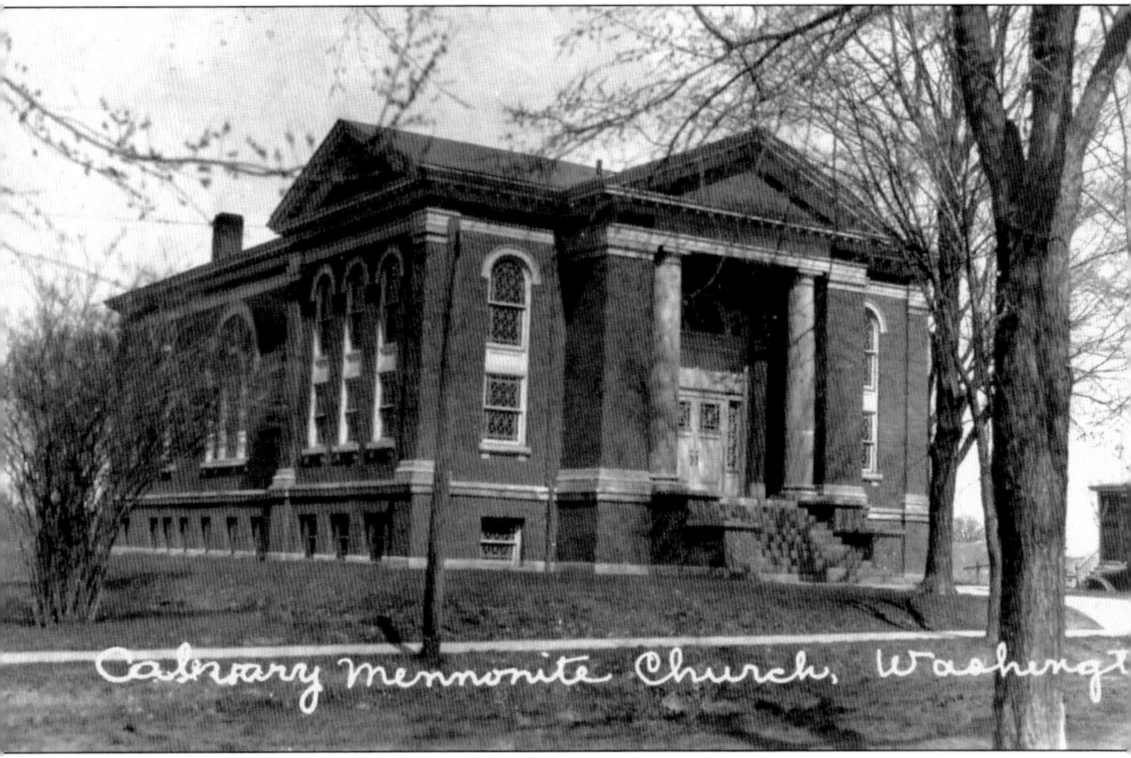

CLASSICAL REVIVAL. The Calvary Mennonite Church, composed primarily of brick and stone, is one of the few examples of the classical revival architectural style found within the community. Two-story stone simplified Doric or Tuscan-order columns make up the distyle culmination that frames the portico area of the main entry and supports the pediment. Roman arches surround the tops of each of the top-story window openings. (Courtesy of the Washington Historical Society.)

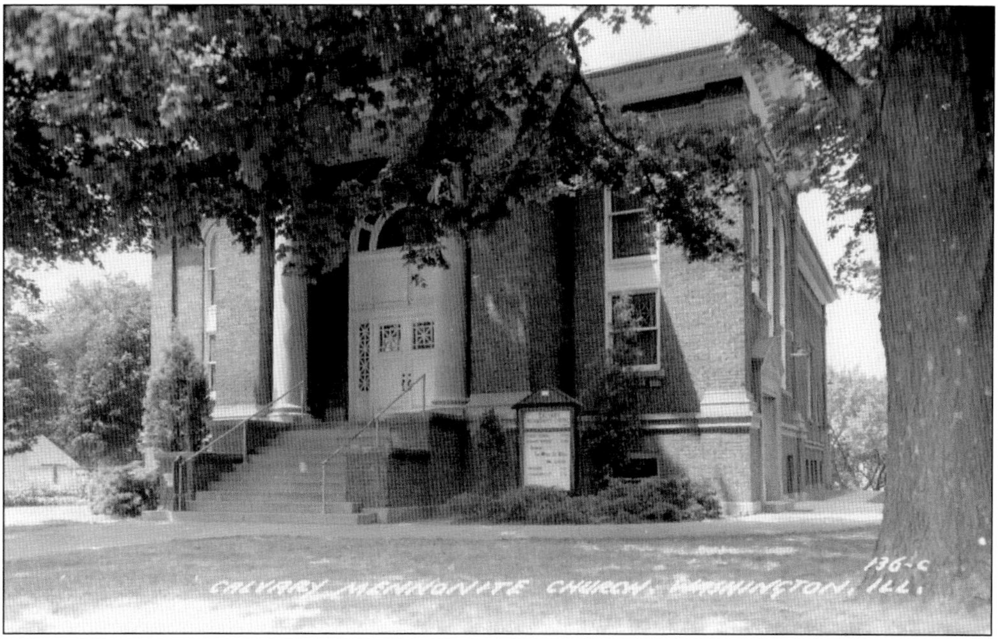

Classical Revival Plan. Pilasters on each of the corners on either side of the building frame what would be the transept portion of a church with a cruciform footprint. Classical treatments and details also exist at the side entry. A significant stone band wraps the building at the first-level floor line.

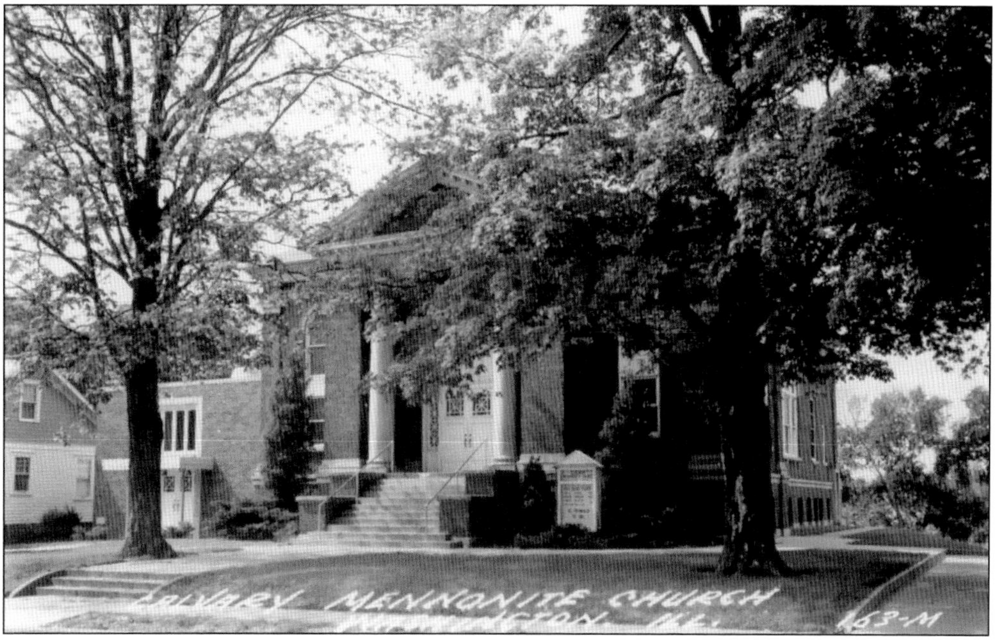

The Church and Context. The Calvary Mennonite Church is set back at a comparable distance to that of the surrounding residential context. A large walk leads from the front entry down to the sidewalk and out to the street. A drive to the side allows vehicular traffic, parking, and deliveries to head to the back of the building where such operations can be concealed from the street.

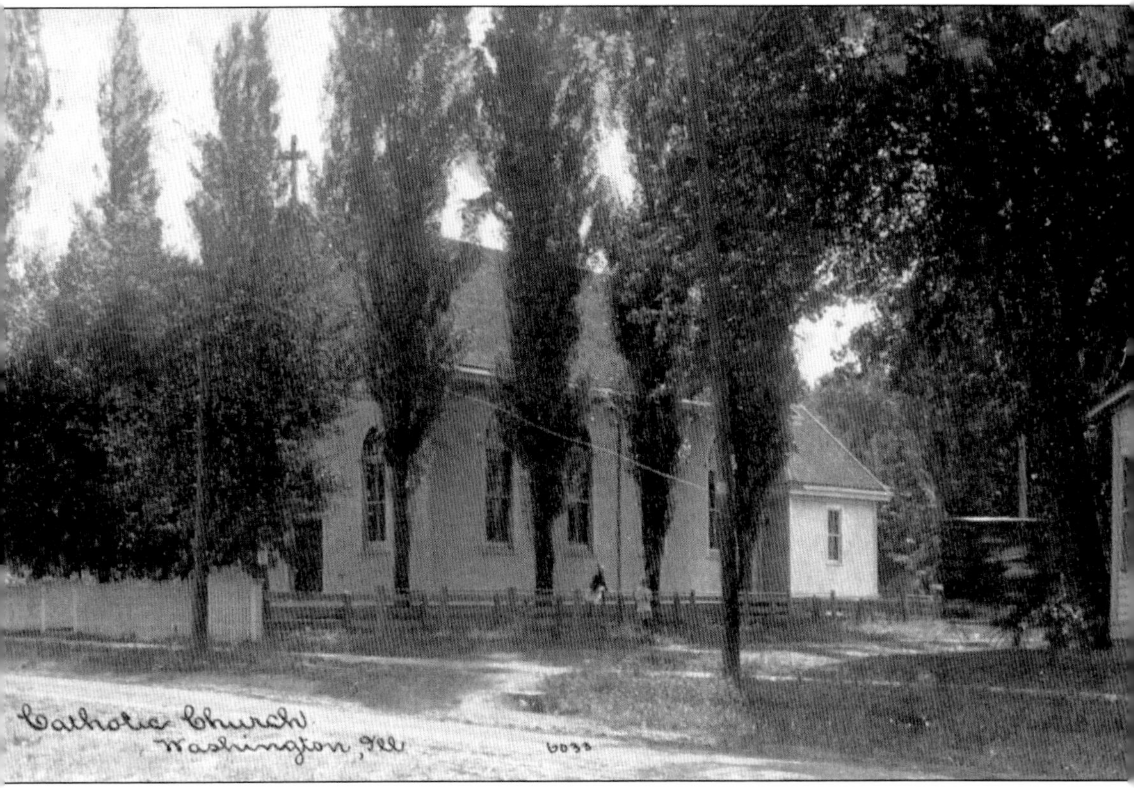

CATHOLIC CHURCH. Although there had been another Catholic church built along Jefferson Street on land donated by A. H. Danforth and Company, this building would be the home of St. Patrick's Church before the current building was constructed in 1966. This particular church building was of simple construction with a large pitched roof that would increase the height of the interior space. A cross adorns the top of the roof, and large windows look out onto the street and neighboring residents.

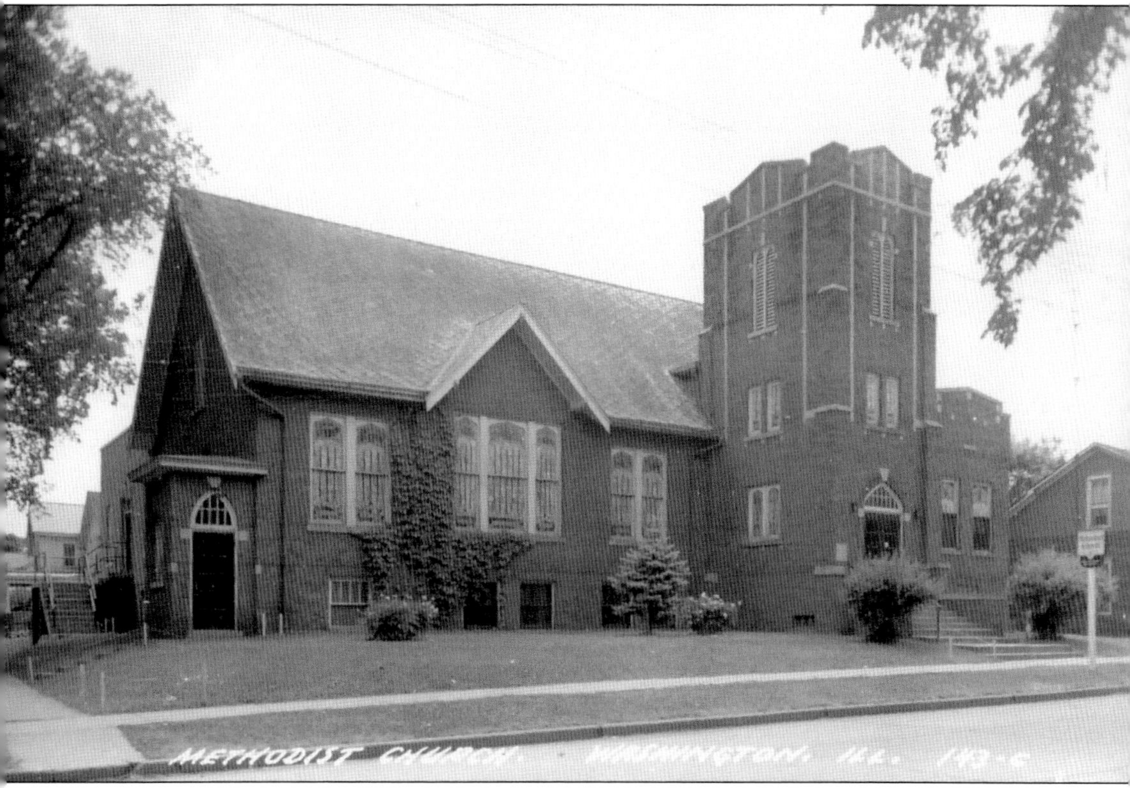

METHODIST CHURCH. This building was completed in 1925, and much like the Evangelical church found across the street, it was designed in the Gothic Revival style and was composed primarily of brick. The massing of each steeple and main worship space is similar, but the details are more simplified. The church entry found at the base of the steeple opens out on to Walnut Street, and a walk leads down to the sidewalk.

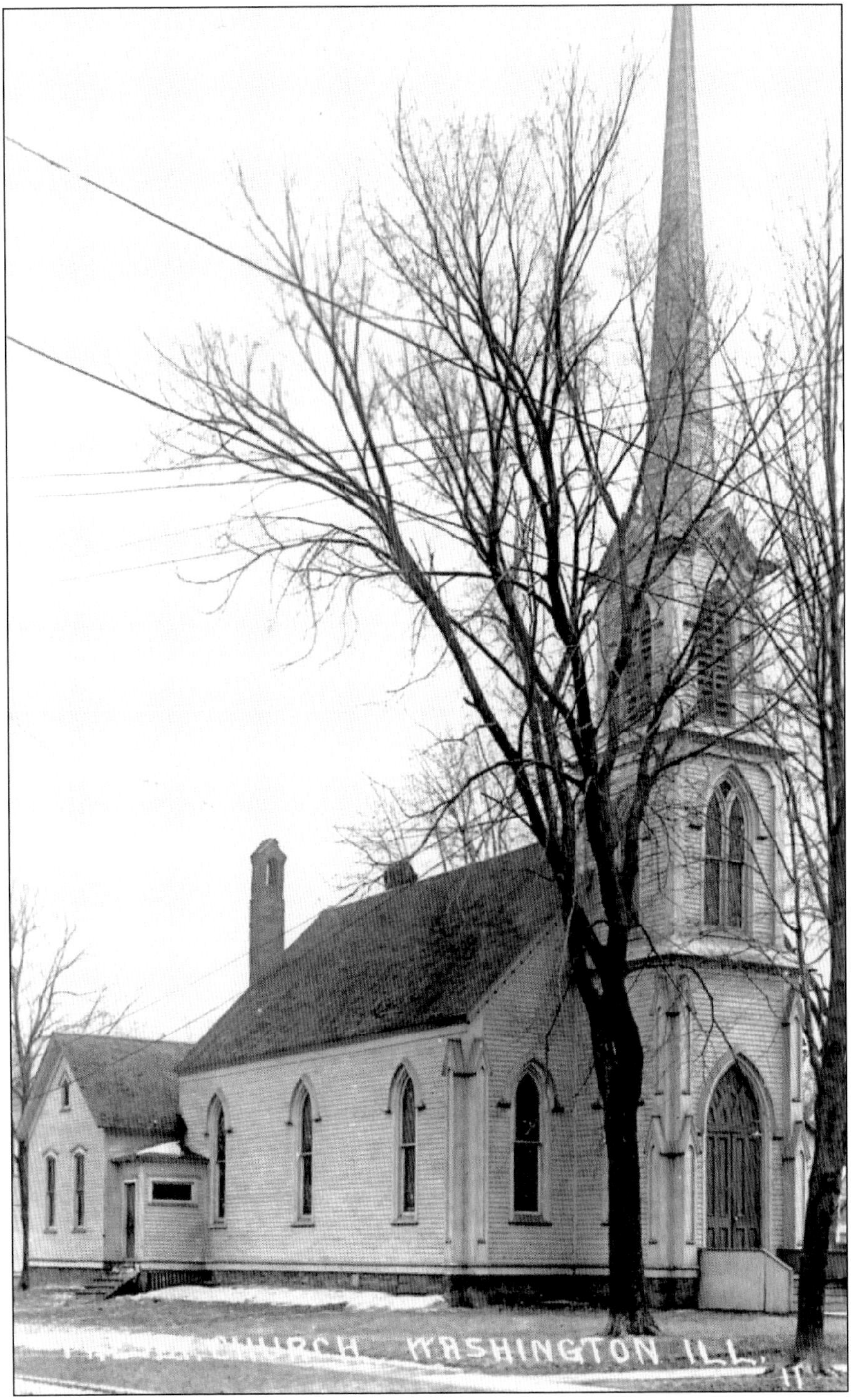

PRESBYTERIAN CHURCH. Two preceding churches built in 1837 and then in 1850 on the corner of Walnut and Elm Streets came before this building was constructed in 1871. The building is not large but the entry and steeple demand attention. The building was designed using the Gothic Revival style.

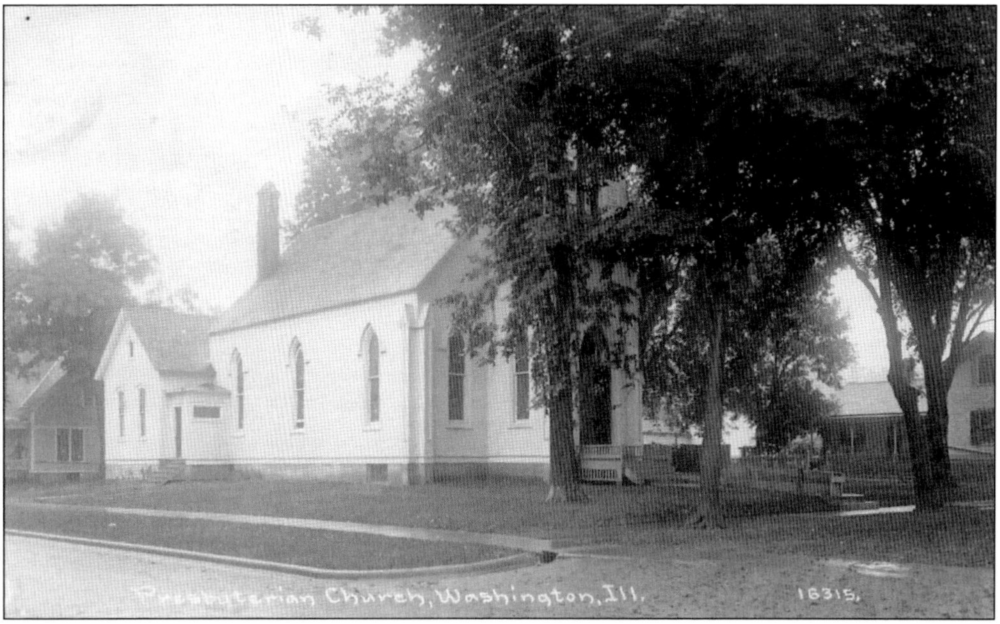

PRESBYTERIAN CHURCH, MASSING AND SITE. Tall windows for the primary worship space look out onto the street. The building is set back in a similar fashion to that of the surrounding residential context. A steeply pitched roof, common in many church designs, gives the interior space an added sense of height.

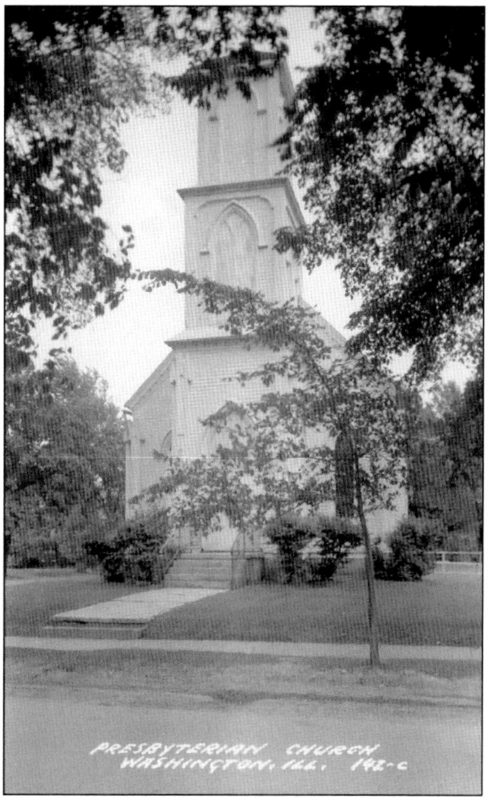

PRESBYTERIAN CHURCH ALTERATIONS. As the years went by, significant changes were made to the exterior of the church. The second-story windows on the steeple were removed along with the louvers above. The steeple was capped with a hipped roof without gabled dormers, and the spire was removed. This change was the most significant. As church steeples reach up into the sky they let others from outside the area know there is a community congregated below.

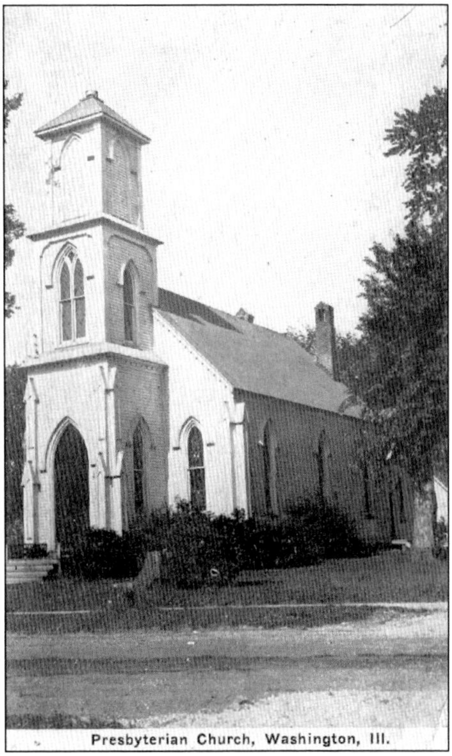

PRESBYTERIAN CHURCH, NEIGHBORS. Regardless of the changes made, the church building is still handsomely detailed and extremely well proportioned. Its smaller scale fits well within the surrounding context, and its presence along the street is strong. Its entry opens out to the sidewalk and invites all those living within the neighborhood to come inside.

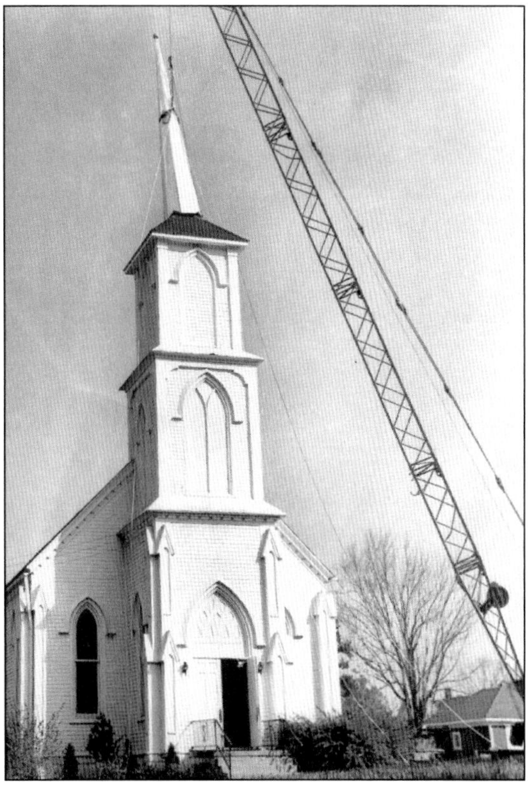

SPIRE REPLACED. Fortunately the spire was indeed replaced. As seen in the photograph, the crane is hoisting the new one into place on top of the church steeple. One can see an immediate difference in how it positively affects the entire composition of the church's exterior elevation as it had originally been intended. (Courtesy of the Washington Historical Society.)

CHRISTIAN CHURCH. One of the oldest congregations in the community built this church on the burned rubble of its predecessor during the 1870s. The church is located on North High Street, a block away from the square. Constructed primarily of wood, the church was built in the Gothic Revival style and closely resembles the appearance of the Presbyterian church on the corner of Walnut and Elm Streets. A significant entry stands at the base of the church steeple and opens into the main worship space.

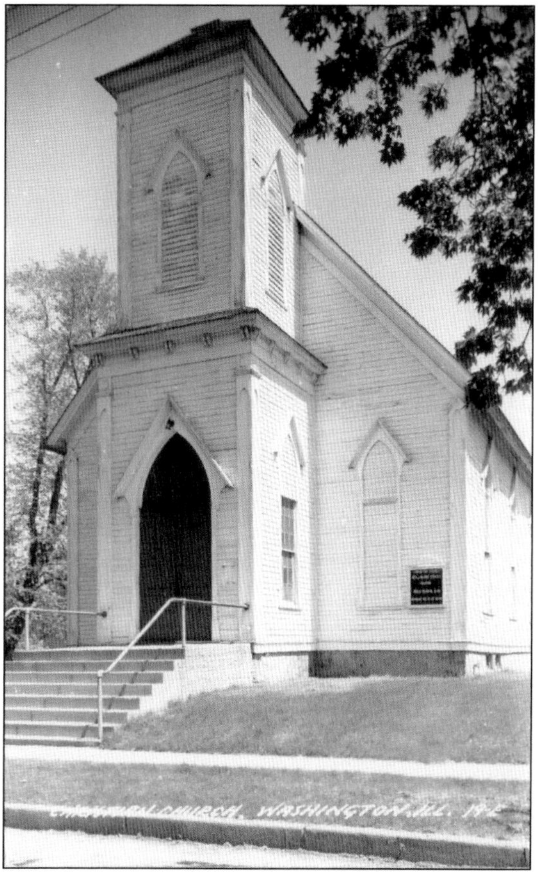

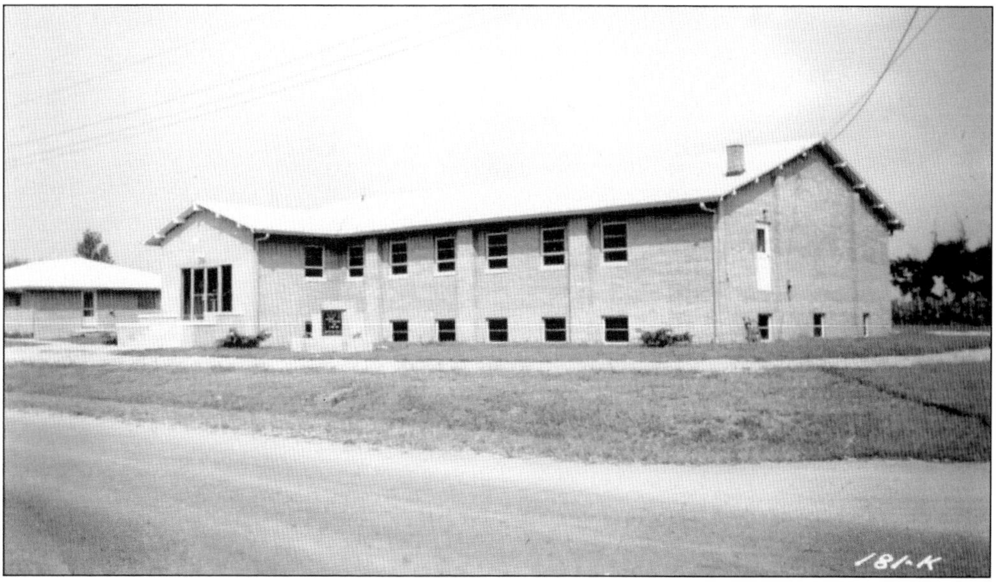

GRACE BIBLE CHURCH. This church building is primarily constructed of brick and was completed in the late 1950s. Purlins protrude out and add an interesting design element to the exterior. A large entry opens out onto the street and sidewalk.

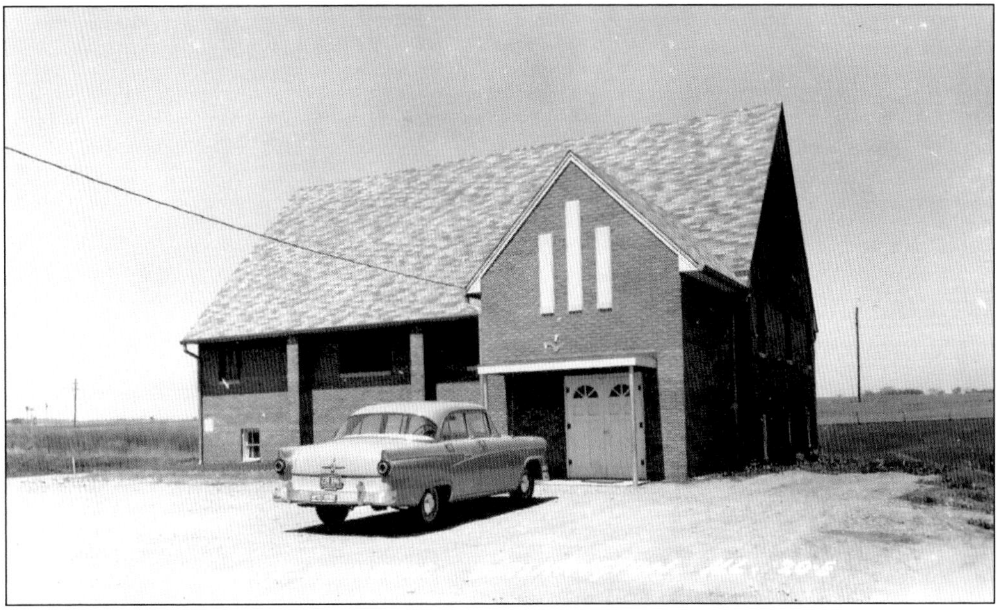

THE FIRST BAPTIST CHURCH. Originally known as the Washington Missionary Baptist Church, construction of this brick building occurred throughout the 1950s. The building shows hints of references to the Gothic style with structural columns protruding out like buttresses. The church is located along a stretch of Peoria Street where the emphasis is placed more on vehicular traffic rather than neighborhood-oriented pedestrian travel.

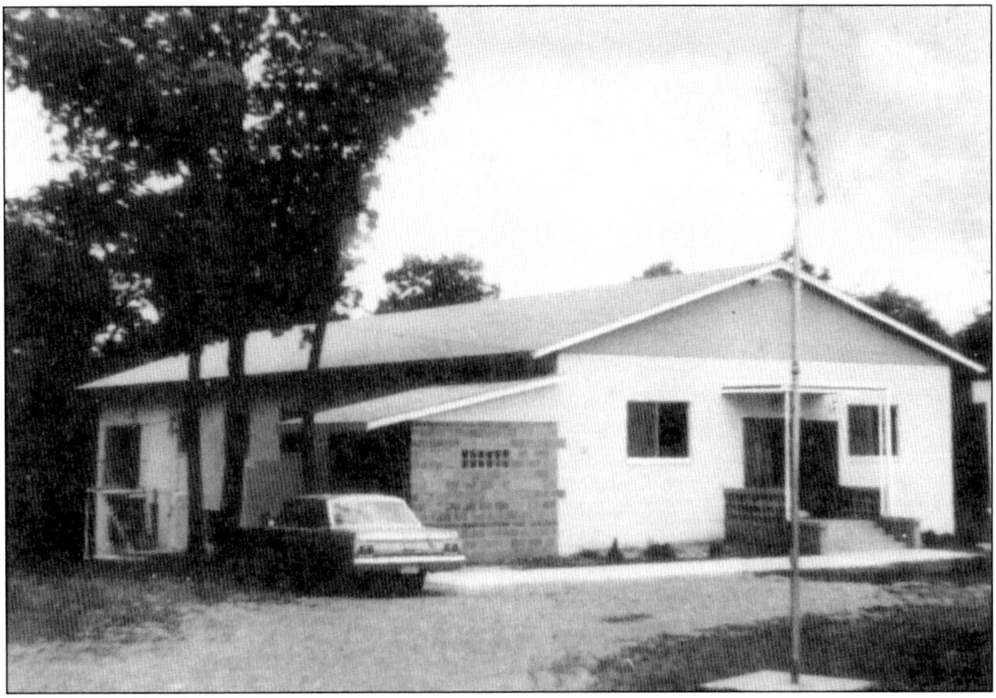

CAMP GOOD NEWS. Located in the northern portion of the community, Camp Good News has played host to generations of local young people who escape to the rural religious retreats each summer. Campers participate in a number of different recreational and worship activities.

Nine

The Schools

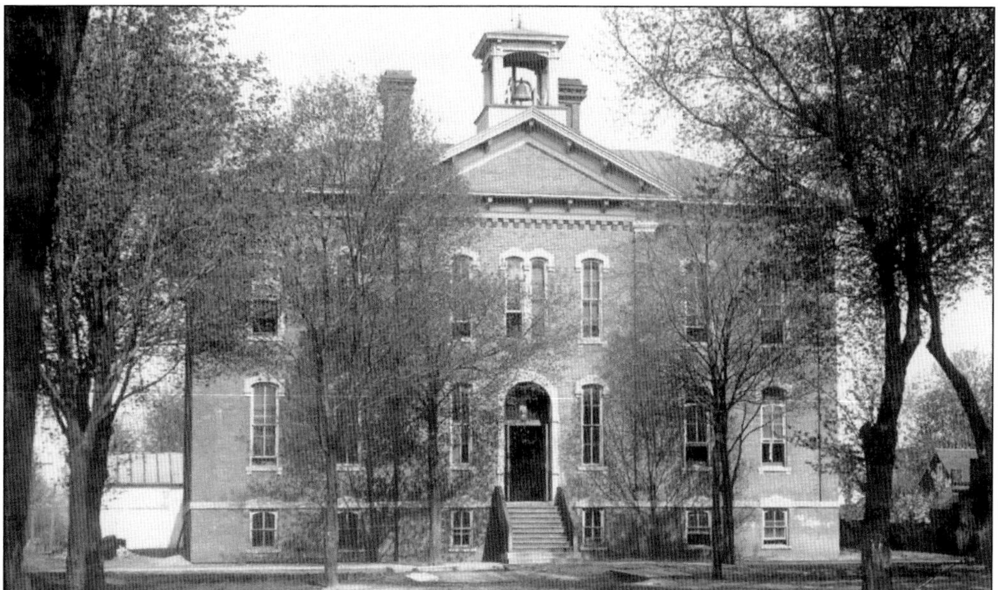

Washington Public School. In 1876, a new two-story building was constructed and would house both the grammar and high schools. Students from around the area would attend school in this eight-classroom building located on a five-acre site donated by the town founder, William Holland.

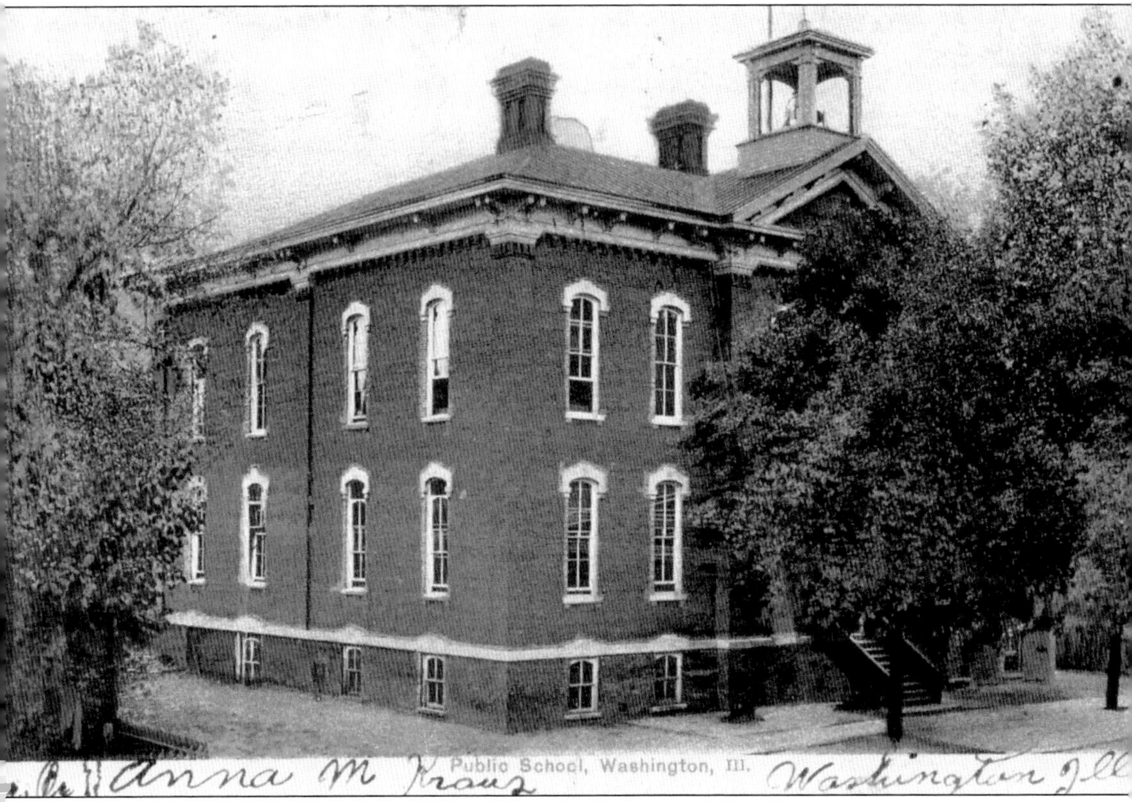

THE SCHOOL BUILDING. This primarily brick building was composed of simple massing yet on a grandiose scale. Pilasters rose up at the corners of the building and again toward the middle of the facade where they visually supported the pediment. A bell tower was placed atop the pediment and provided a signal for students, teachers, and the surrounding neighborhood.

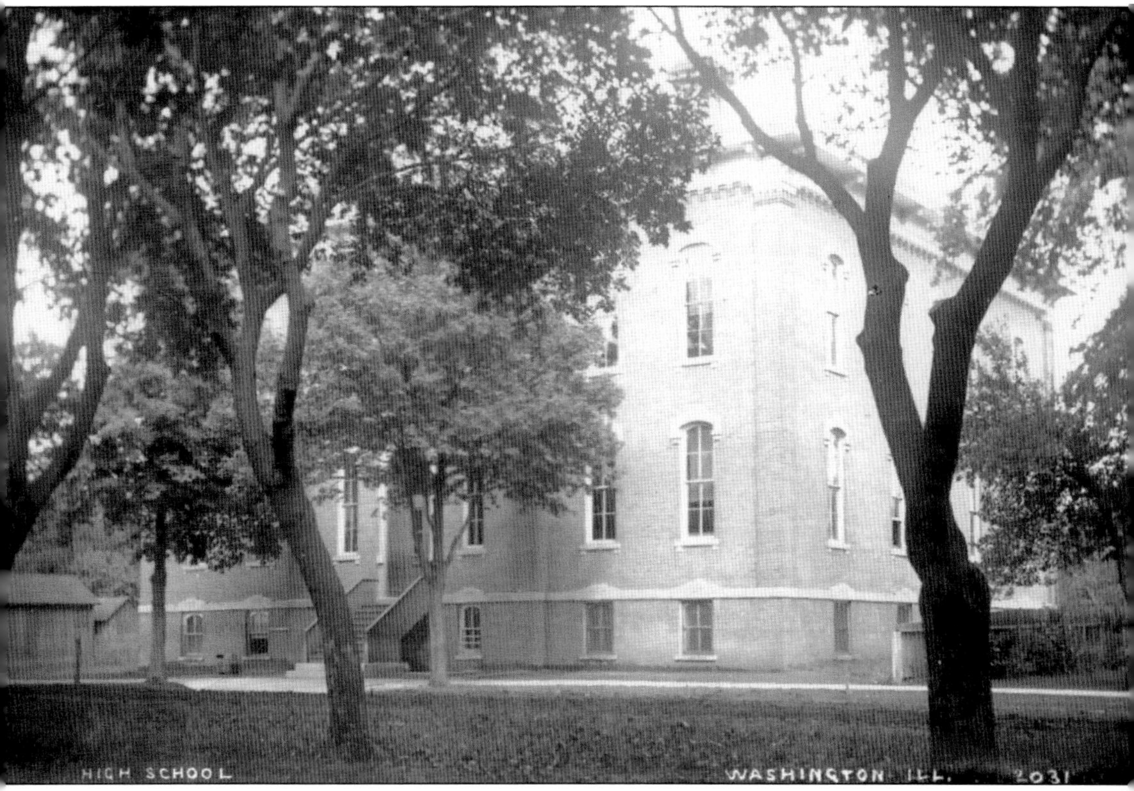

THE CAMPUS. The school building was situated on a site that was amid a residential neighborhood where the community could look after the educational progress and growth of the community's young people. Children had the option of walking with ease to and from school. The school doors opened out onto a dedicated park space that both the neighborhood and the school enjoyed. From its early days the community understood the importance of a good education for their young people and the beautiful, well-designed schools were constructed in a way in which that could be facilitated.

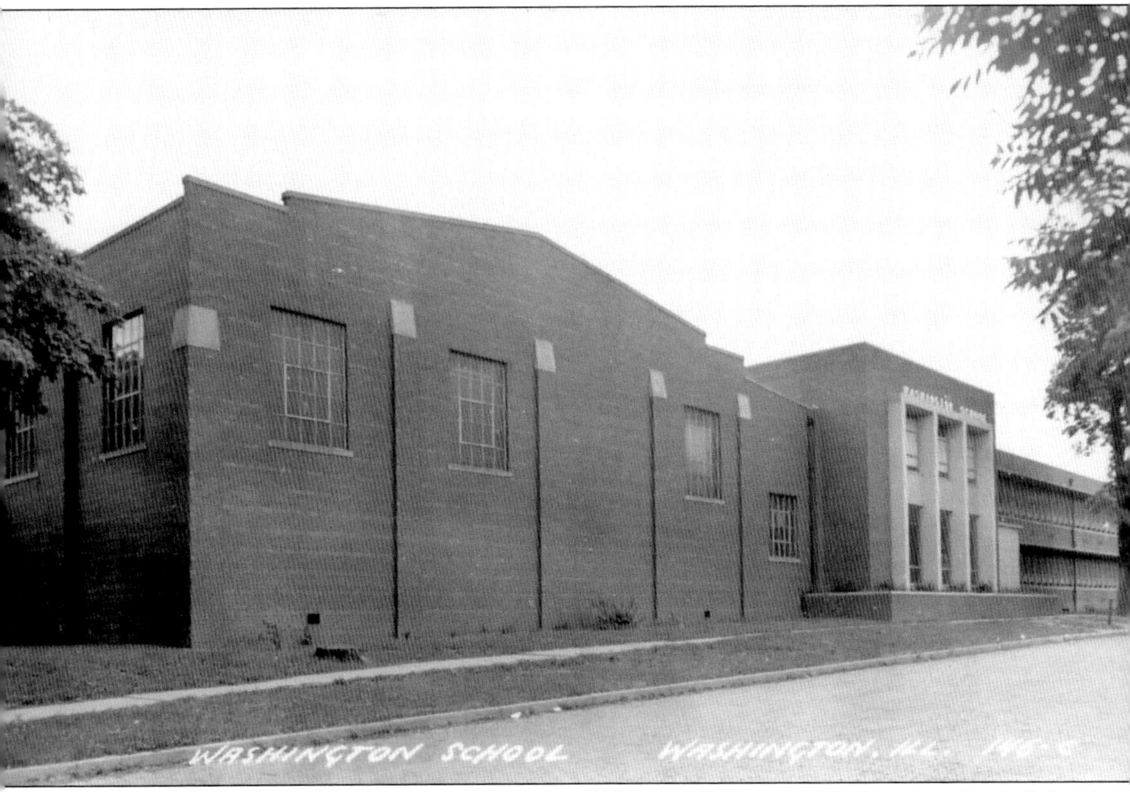

THE NEW WASHINGTON GRADE SCHOOL, 1953. In 1953, a new Washington Grade School was constructed on the site of the 1876 high school. Not unlike the new high school and grade schools that had been constructed before it, Washington Grade School took design cues from the popular modern movement of the time, utilizing elements of the international style. Large and numerous windows line the western face of the building. Concrete sunshades sit atop these windows and protect the interior spaces from direct sunlight. The gymnasium, seen in the foreground, had been built many years before in 1934.

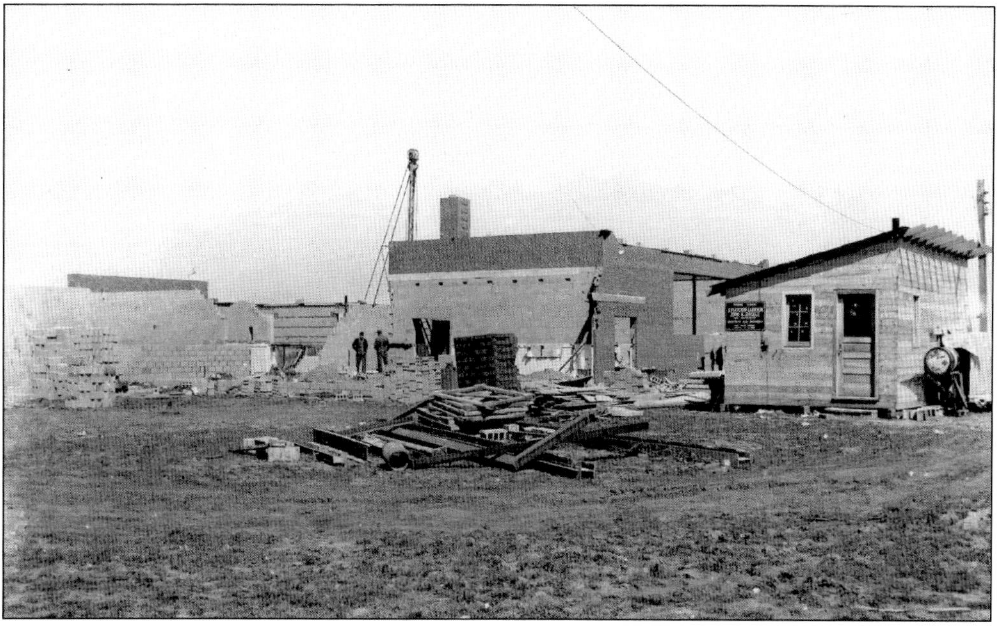

Pleasant View Construction. In 1948, Pleasant View District 622 was formed via the combination of several rural Washington Township school districts. In 1949, the school building itself was constructed on a four-acre site at the intersection of Guth and Pleasant View Roads. An addition to the building would be made in 1962. The image shows the walls of the eastern portion of the building being constructed. This space would eventually become the gymnasium. (Courtesy of the Washington Historical Society, photograph by Leo Clark.)

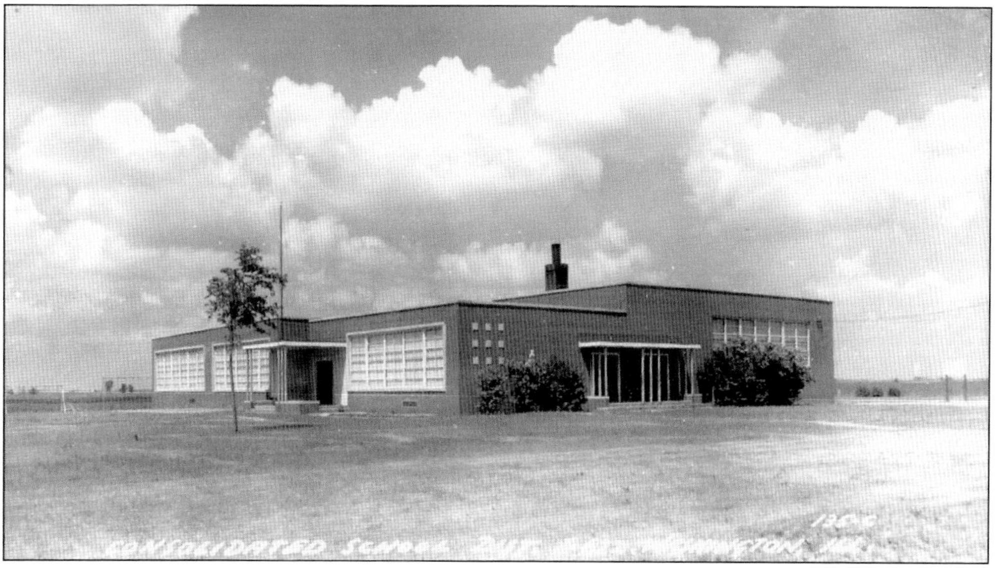

Pleasant View Modern Style. The building, much like the new high school, was designed in the modern, international style. A very rectilinear massing accentuated the functionality of the building. Each entry includes a simple planar canopy form supported by a series of steel tube columns. Numerous large windows allowed generous amounts of sunlight into interior spaces while providing for increased natural ventilation. As opposed to school buildings from an earlier time, there was no decorative ornamentation to be found.

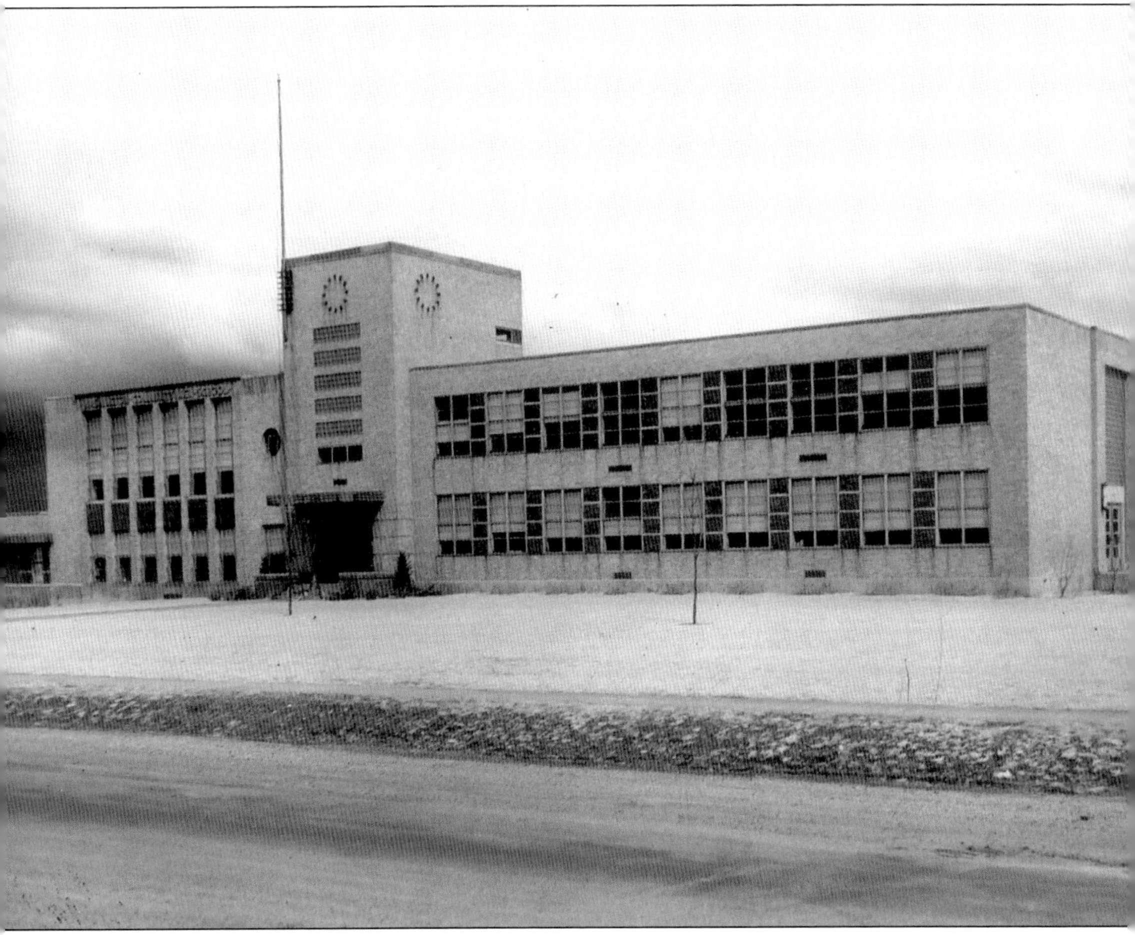

The New High School, 1942. With the population of the community rapidly growing, it was decided that a new high school would be needed. In 1942, a new high school building to accommodate 400 students was constructed on Bondurant Street. The new building was designed in the modern international style, which was characterized by a radically simplified form, an increased use of glass, a rejection of ornament, and reflected an increased emphasis on mechanization as the automobile and its production gained a romantic status amid the American public. (Courtesy of the Washington Historical Society, photograph by Leo Clark.)

Ten

The People

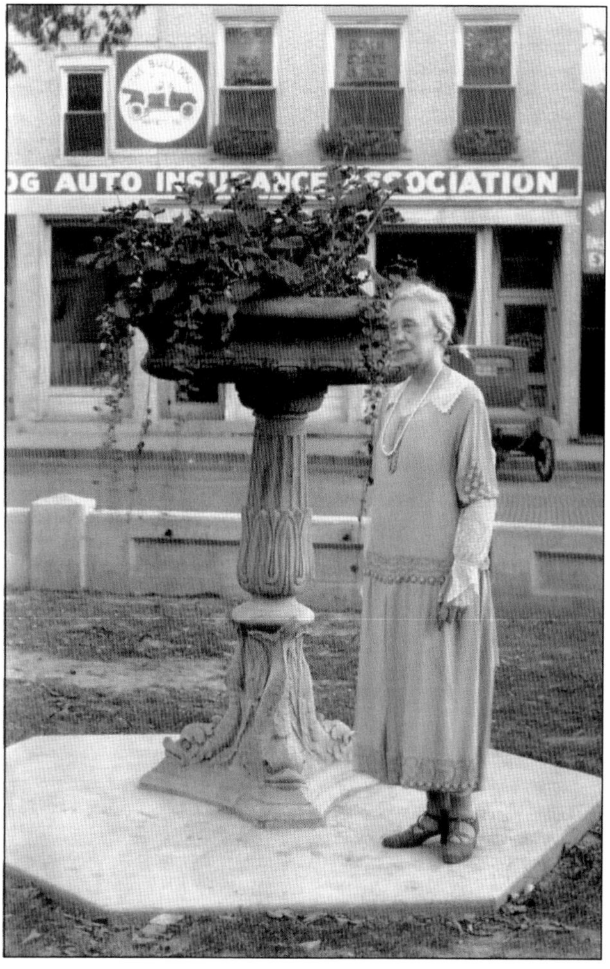

Miss Mary. There were very few early citizens of Washington that had as profound an affect on the growing community as Mary Italin, or "Miss Mary" to many throughout the community. Of the four graduates from the school built in 1876 on land donated by William Holland himself, Italin was one. After graduation she was given a teaching job at the school, and she would be employed at the school for the next 60 years. She is seen here in front of an urn placed within the square park space in her honor. (Courtesy of the Washington Historical Society.)

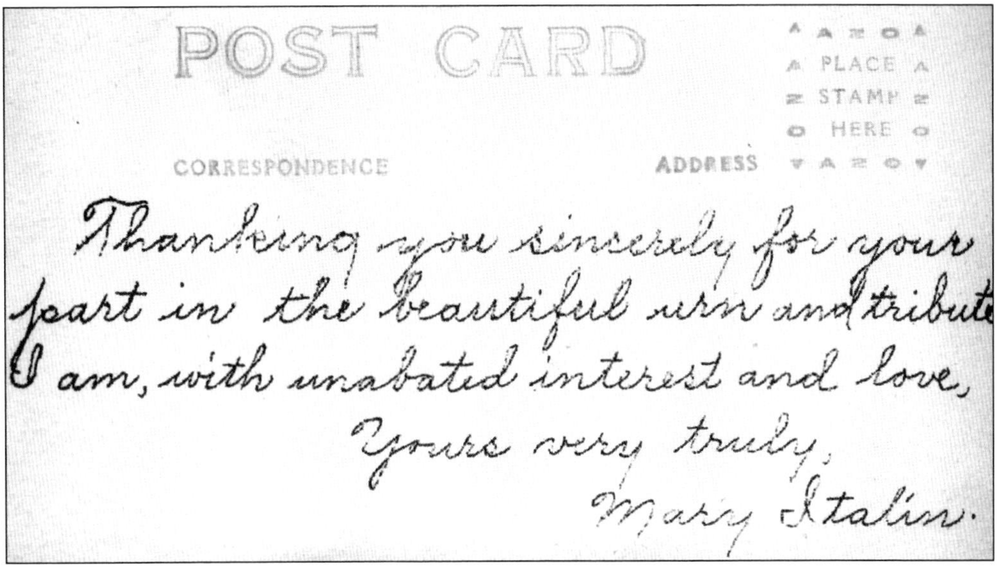

POST CARD

PLACE STAMP HERE

CORRESPONDENCE ADDRESS

Thanking you sincerely for your part in the beautiful urn and tribute I am, with unabated interest and love,

Yours very truly,

Mary Italin.

Yours Very Truly. On the back of the postcard, Mary "Miss Mary" Italin writes a sincere thank-you to all that paid her tribute. On August 11, 1925, the citizens of Washington recognized her amazing service to the community. The number of young minds that she helped shape was immense, and through her teachings she made a profound effect on the future that those young minds went about creating in Washington for many years. (Courtesy of the Washington Historical Society.)

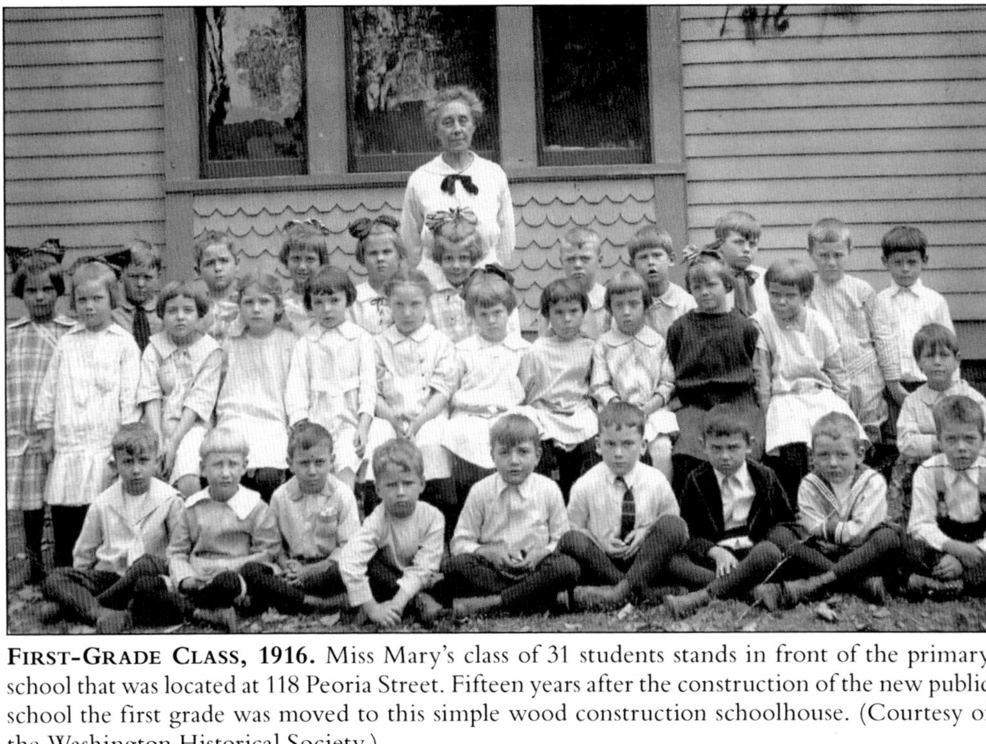

First-Grade Class, 1916. Miss Mary's class of 31 students stands in front of the primary school that was located at 118 Peoria Street. Fifteen years after the construction of the new public school the first grade was moved to this simple wood construction schoolhouse. (Courtesy of the Washington Historical Society.)

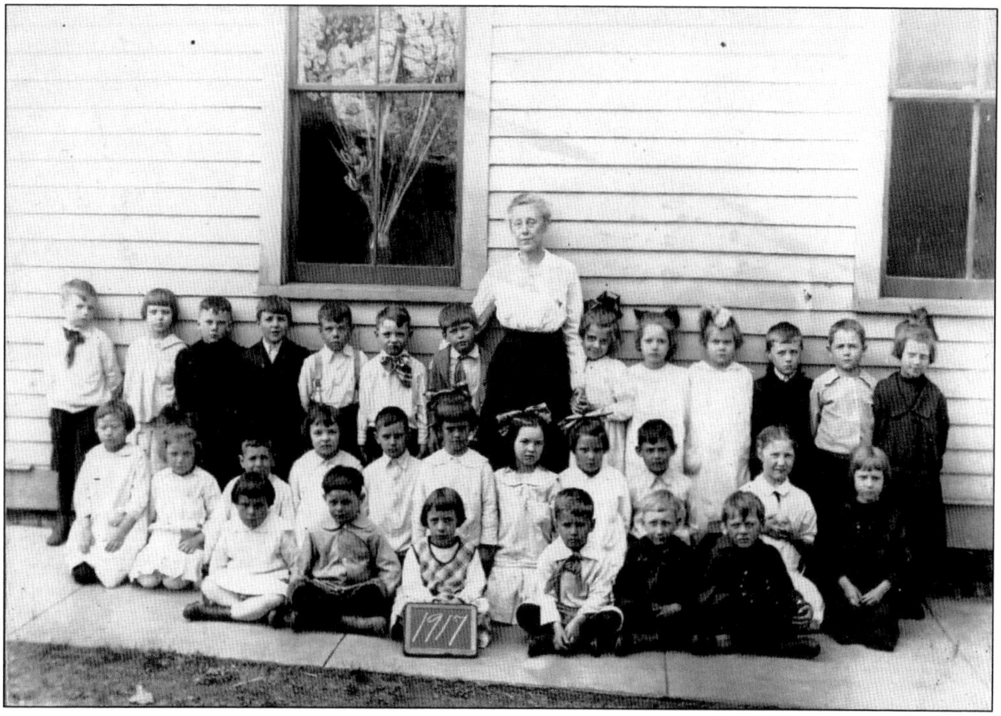

FIRST-GRADE CLASS, 1917. A 1917 class photograph shows Miss Mary's class of 30 students lined up outside on the sidewalk in front of the primary school located on Peoria Street. (Courtesy of the Washington Historical Society.)

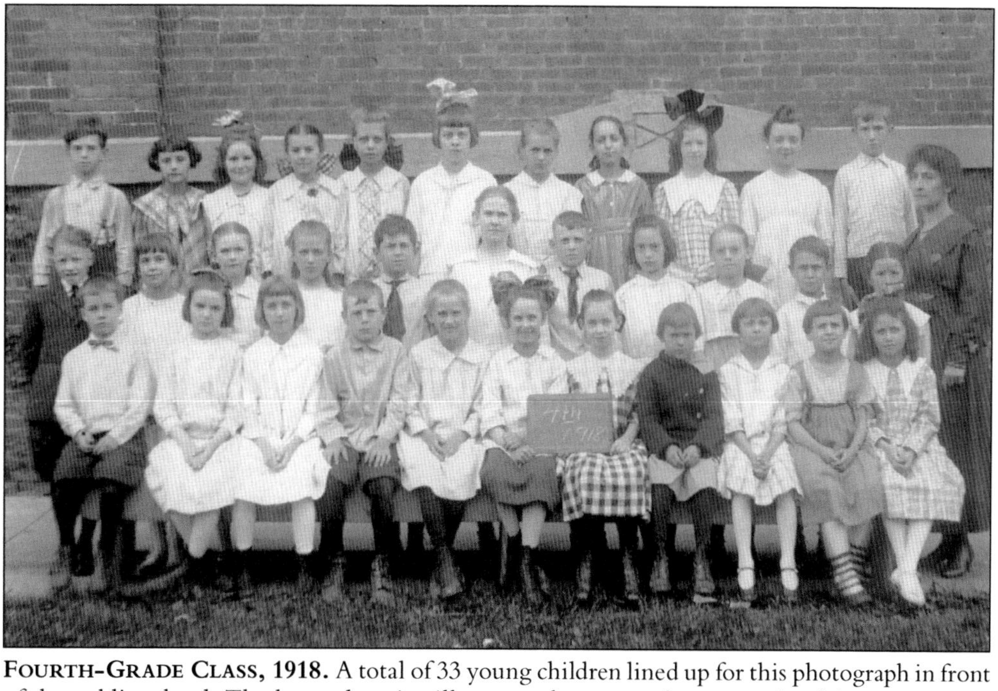

FOURTH-GRADE CLASS, 1918. A total of 33 young children lined up for this photograph in front of the public school. The large class size illustrates the tremendous growth of the community during the early portion of the century. (Courtesy of the Washington Historical Society.)

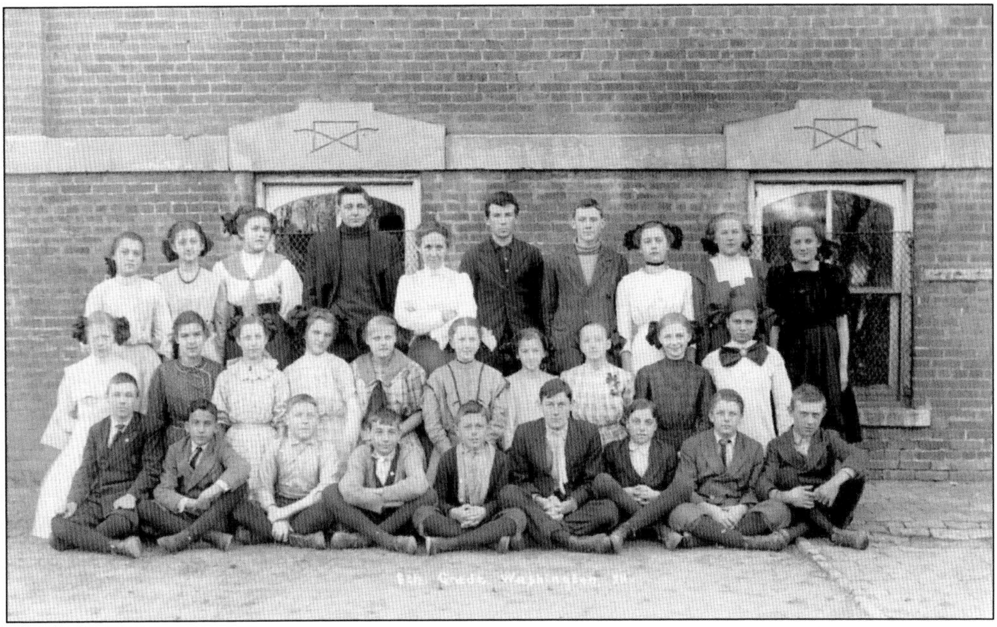

EIGHTH-GRADE CLASS. These 28 students were in their last year of grade school before some of them made the move into high school. At this time the high school was also held within the same building as the District 52 grade school. An addition was made to the building in 1912, and some of the space was rented by what would become the high school, formally known as Washington Community High School District 308 by 1920. (Courtesy of the Washington Historical Society.)

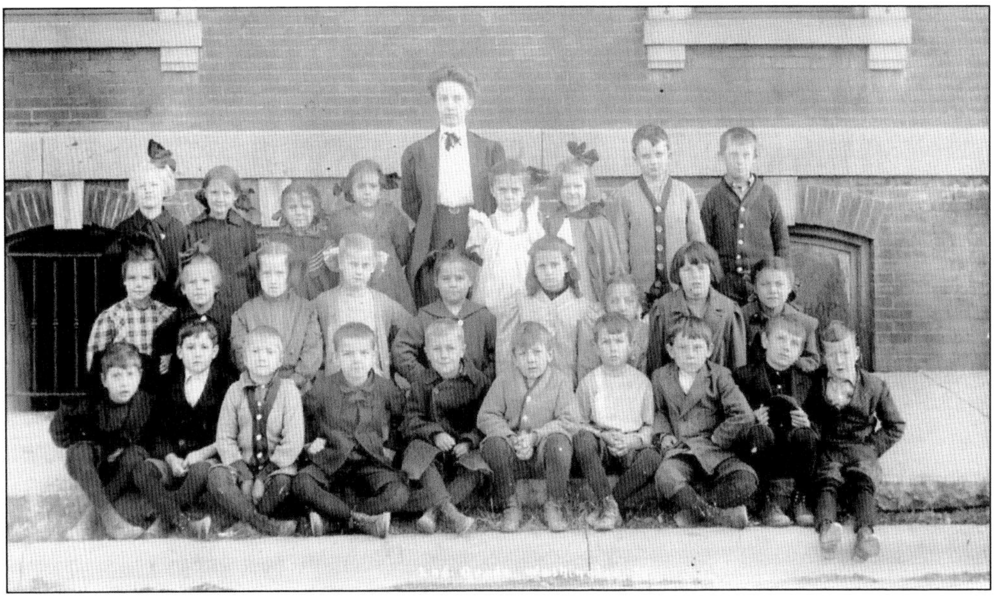

SECOND-GRADE CLASS, 1920S. This photograph shows a second-grade class of 27 with their teacher. What is interesting about the photograph is the location where it was shot. The students and teacher are not in front of the school on Spruce Street nor are they in front of the primary school on Peoria Street. The group is posed in front of the west facing side of the Denhart Bank building on North Main Street. (Courtesy of the Washington Historical Society.)

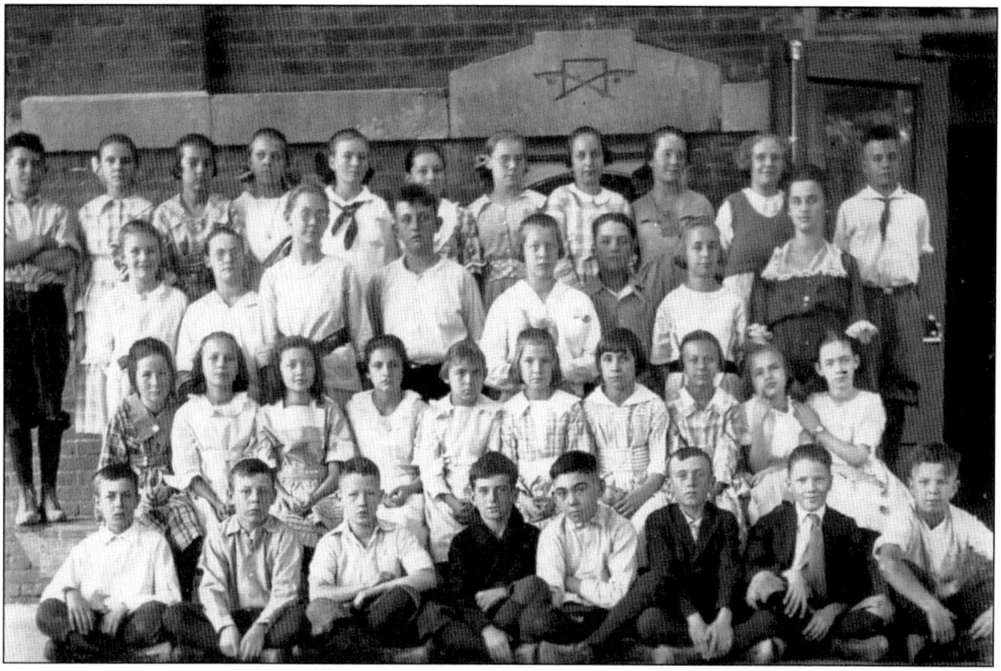

SEVENTH-GRADE CLASS, 1920. This seventh-grade class stands outside of the school on Spruce Street. The class size, like many of the others, was large at 36. The number of girls in the class far outnumber the boys. (Courtesy of the Washington Historical Society.)

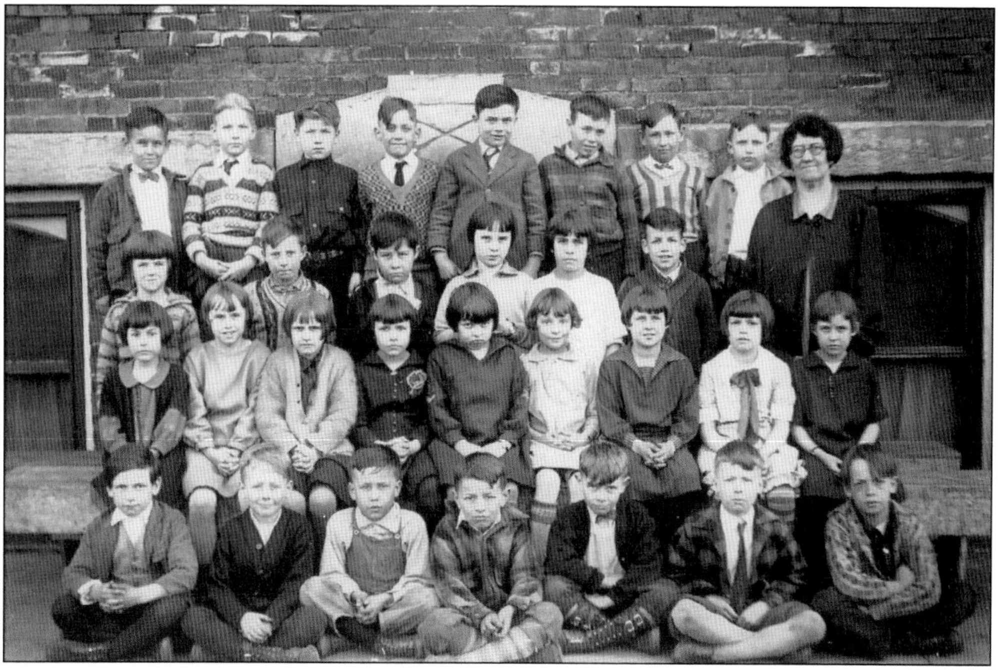

UNHAPPY GRADE SCHOOL CLASS. A class photograph in front of the grade school on Spruce Street shows a group of happy and not-so-happy young minds. Over their shoulders, wear on the building is evident as the masonry shows signs of needing tuck pointing and the bricks themselves are efflorescing. (Courtesy of the Washington Historical Society.)

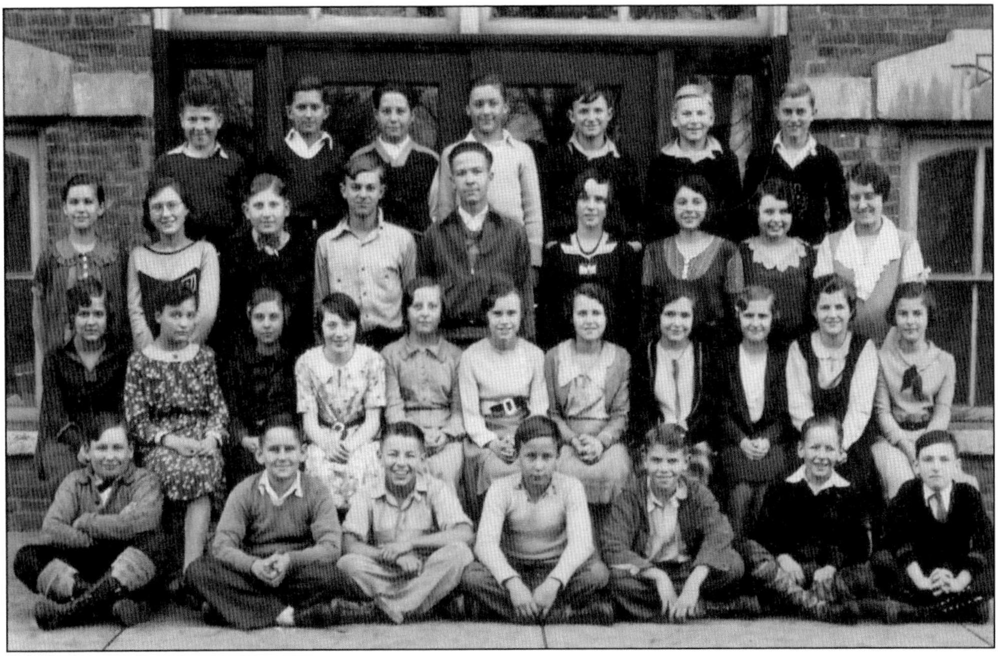

HAPPIER GRADE SCHOOL CLASS. The same teacher yet a different class pose for this photograph, and all 33 students appear much happier than the last group. Over the class's shoulders stands one of the entries into the grade school. (Courtesy of the Washington Historical Society.)

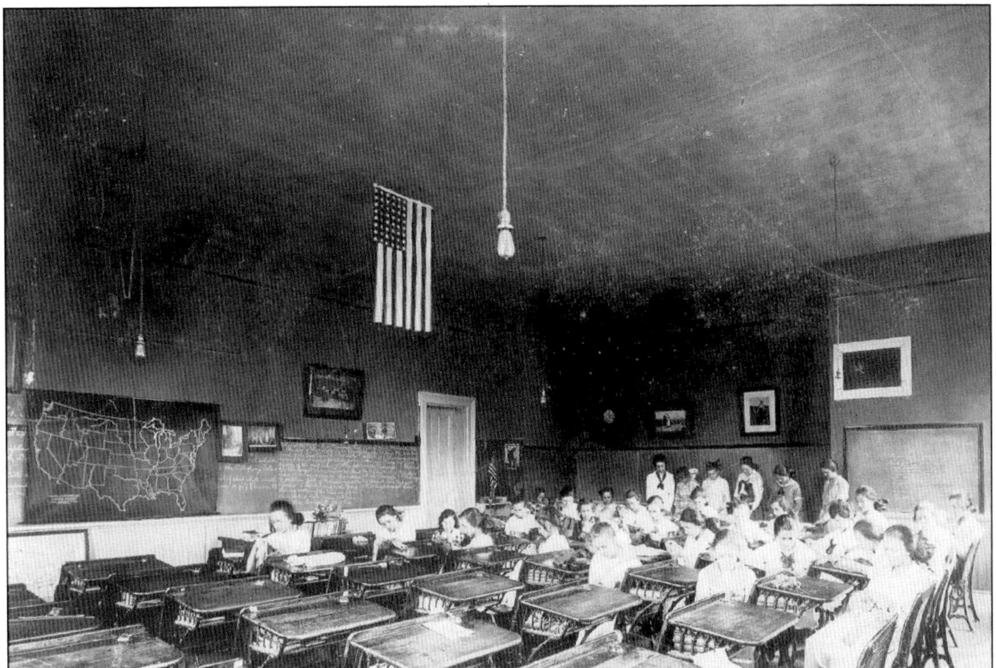

THE CLASSROOM. This classroom shows students and teacher at a moment of prayer. Carbon filament light bulbs hang from the ceiling along with a 48-star American flag. As seen from the exterior, the scale of the building is very generous and that comes through into the interior where classroom ceilings are extremely tall. (Courtesy of the Washington Historical Society.)

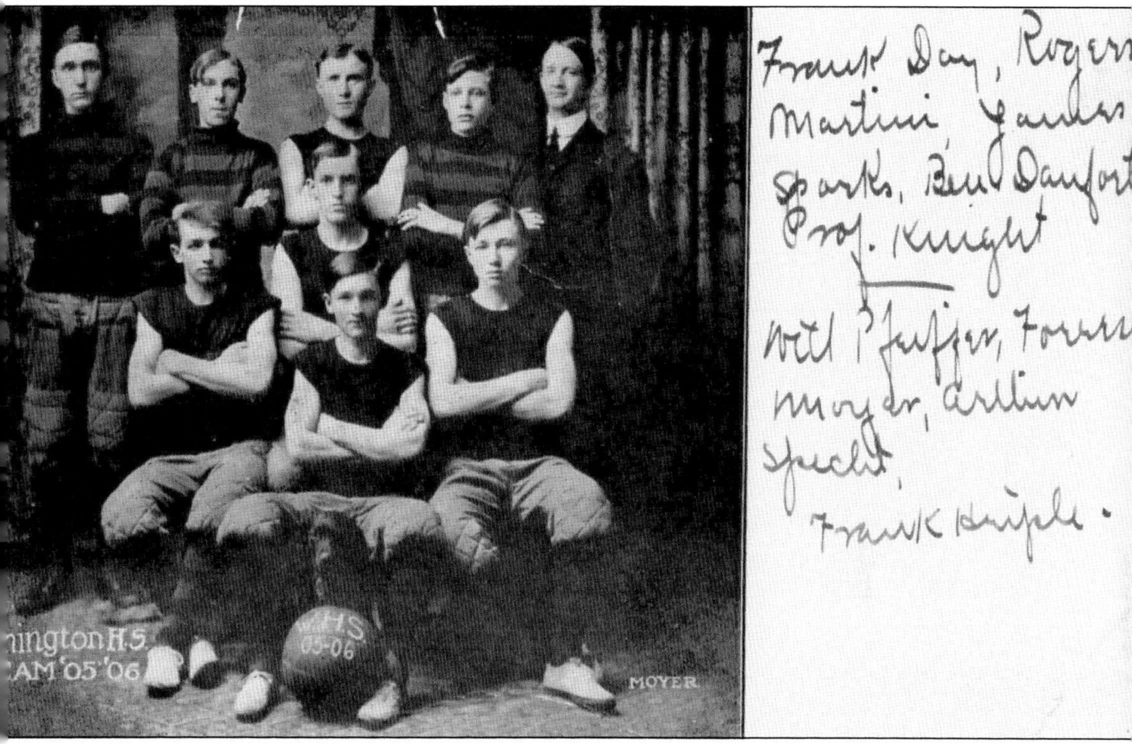

Birth of Washington High School Basketball. The arrival of a new science teacher brought about the birth of basketball in Washington. Prof. Lee I. Knight would coach the first high school basketball games in 1903, and in 1906, he would bring about the construction of the community's first gymnasium that sat 300 spectators. His 1905–1906 team won 30 straight games and went on to defeat what was known as Bradley College 26-24. Knight can be seen standing in the second row to the right.

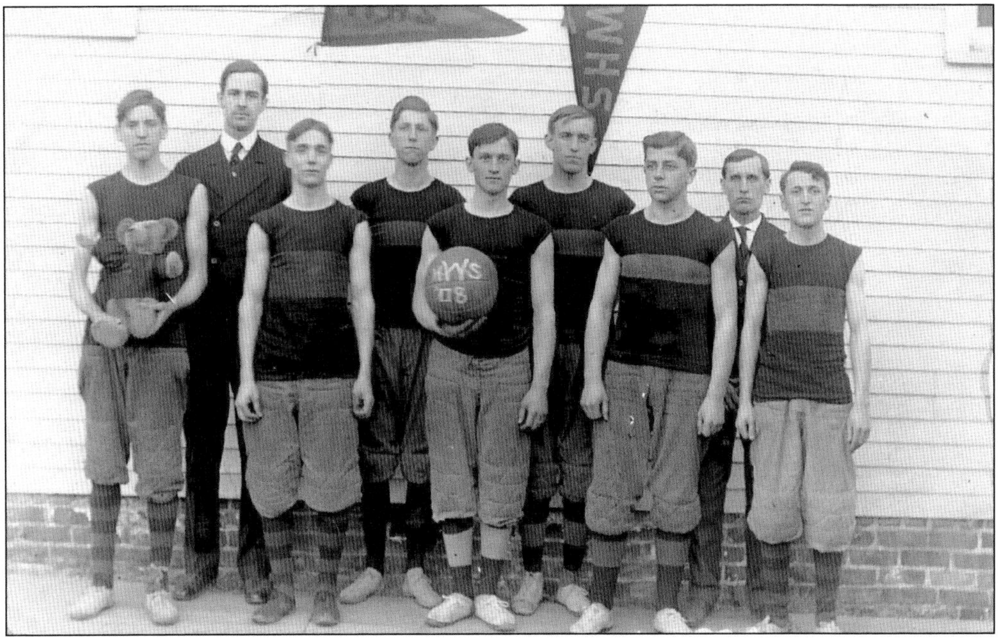

WASHINGTON HIGH SCHOOL BASKETBALL, 1908. In this season an extraordinary thing happened during a game against Brimfield. The basketball team reached the 100-point milestone while limiting the opposition to two points.

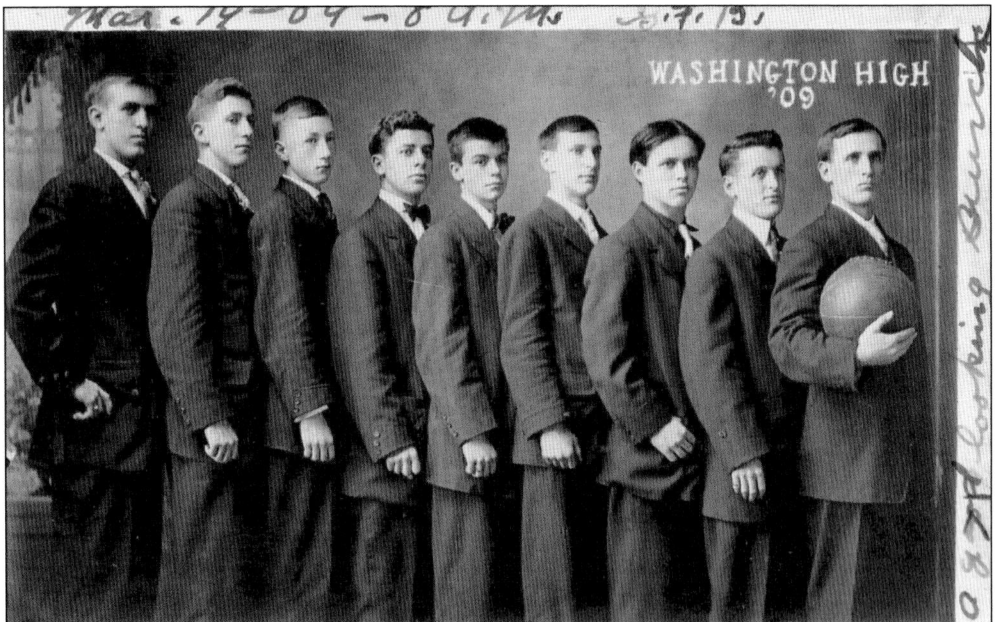

WASHINGTON HIGH SCHOOL BASKETBALL, 1909. During this season the Illinois High School Athletic Association established a tournament setting for its postseason championships. After defeating Decatur at home the team went on to the state championships in Bloomington where they lost to Hinsdale by five points.

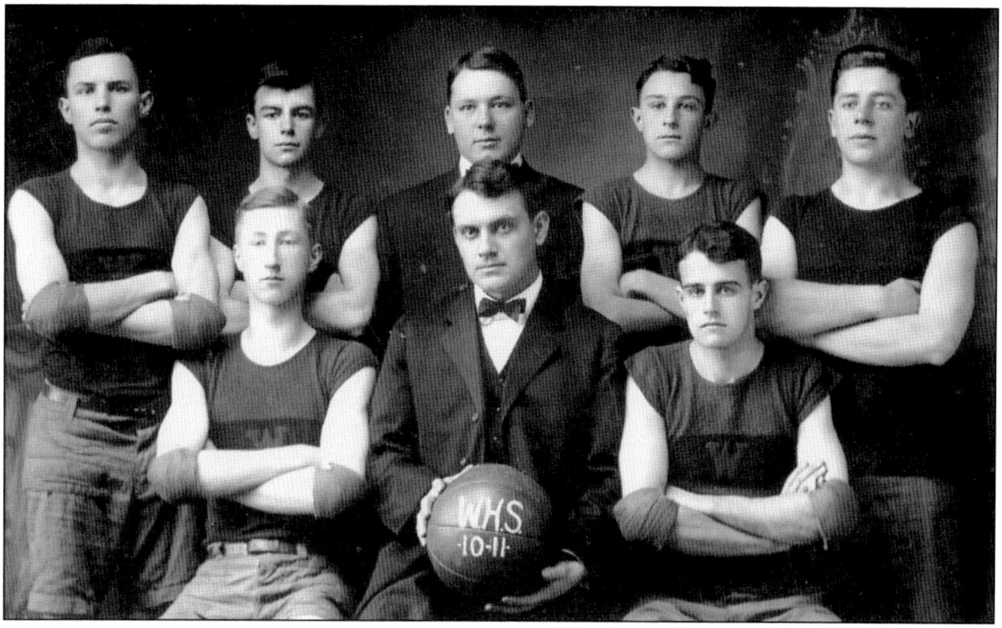

WASHINGTON HIGH SCHOOL BASKETBALL, 1910–1911. This team of six was to be one of the best in the school's early history. However, after beating Streator 41-29 to win the Central Illinois Championship the team, weakened by falling ill with the mumps, fell to defeat against Paris.

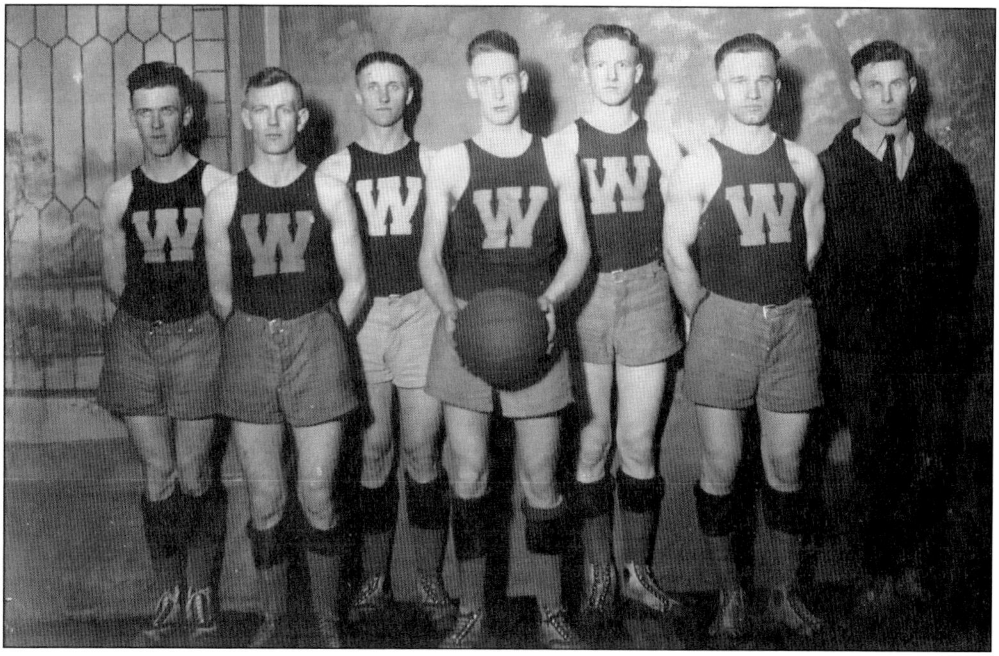

WASHINGTON HIGH SCHOOL BASKETBALL. A number of different coaches and a number of different home courts were a part of the early history of the Washington basketball program. By 1929, the team's original home was condemned, which forced them to play their games entirely on the road. In 1931, what was the Danforth Hotel and City Building was converted into a gymnasium. The team called this place home until 1934, when they moved into a new gymnasium adjacent to the grade school. (Courtesy of the Washington Historical Society.)

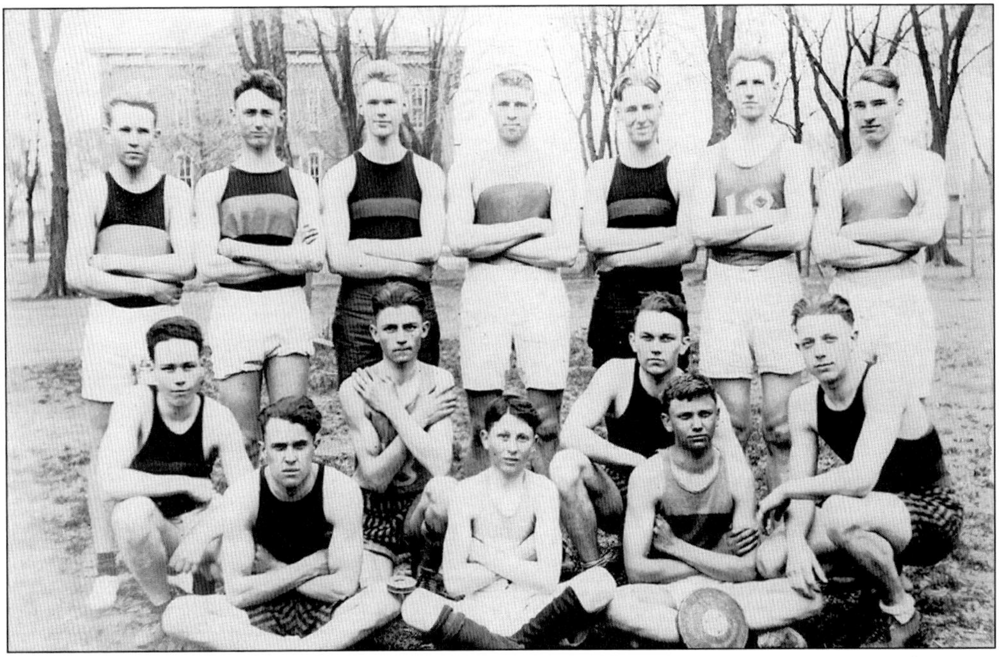

TRACK AND FIELD TEAM. Track competition came to the high school in 1903 via the same individual that had brought basketball, Prof. Lee I. Knight. By 1912, Washington was participating in the Tazewell County Meet, which at the time was attended by nearly 2,000 people. A track was placed in the grade school playground before the 1920s. In the photograph one can see the grade school building looming over the team's shoulders. (Courtesy of the Washington Historical Society.)

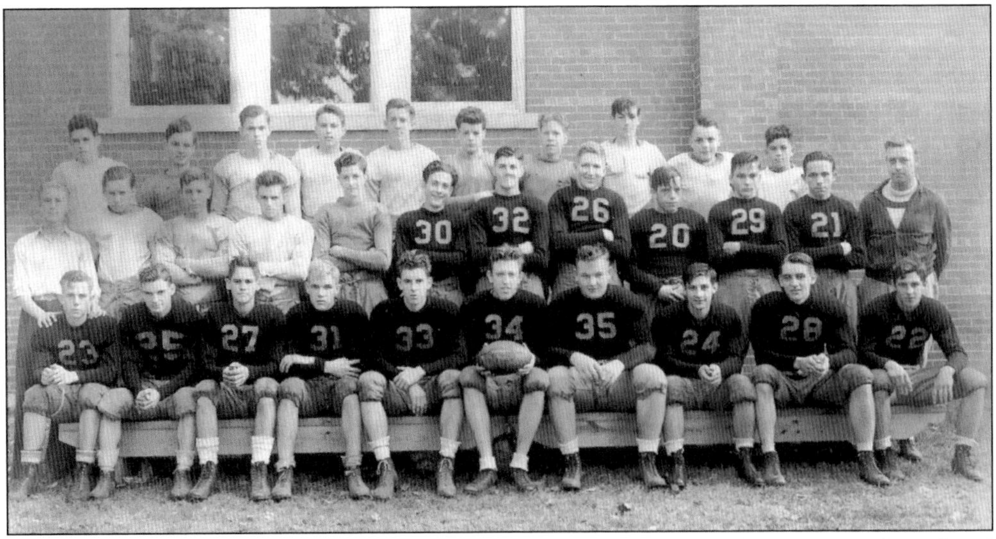

WASHINGTON HIGH SCHOOL FOOTBALL. Although football in Washington was first played at the school in 1902, an injury to a player postponed any further football activity until 1923. In 1938, Golden Babcook took over the coaching duties and held the position until 1953. The team seen in this photograph, taken on October 5, 1938, was his first and had a winning record. In 1962, the high school would develop a field at its Bondurant location and it would be named after Golden Babcook. (Courtesy of the Washington Historical Society.)

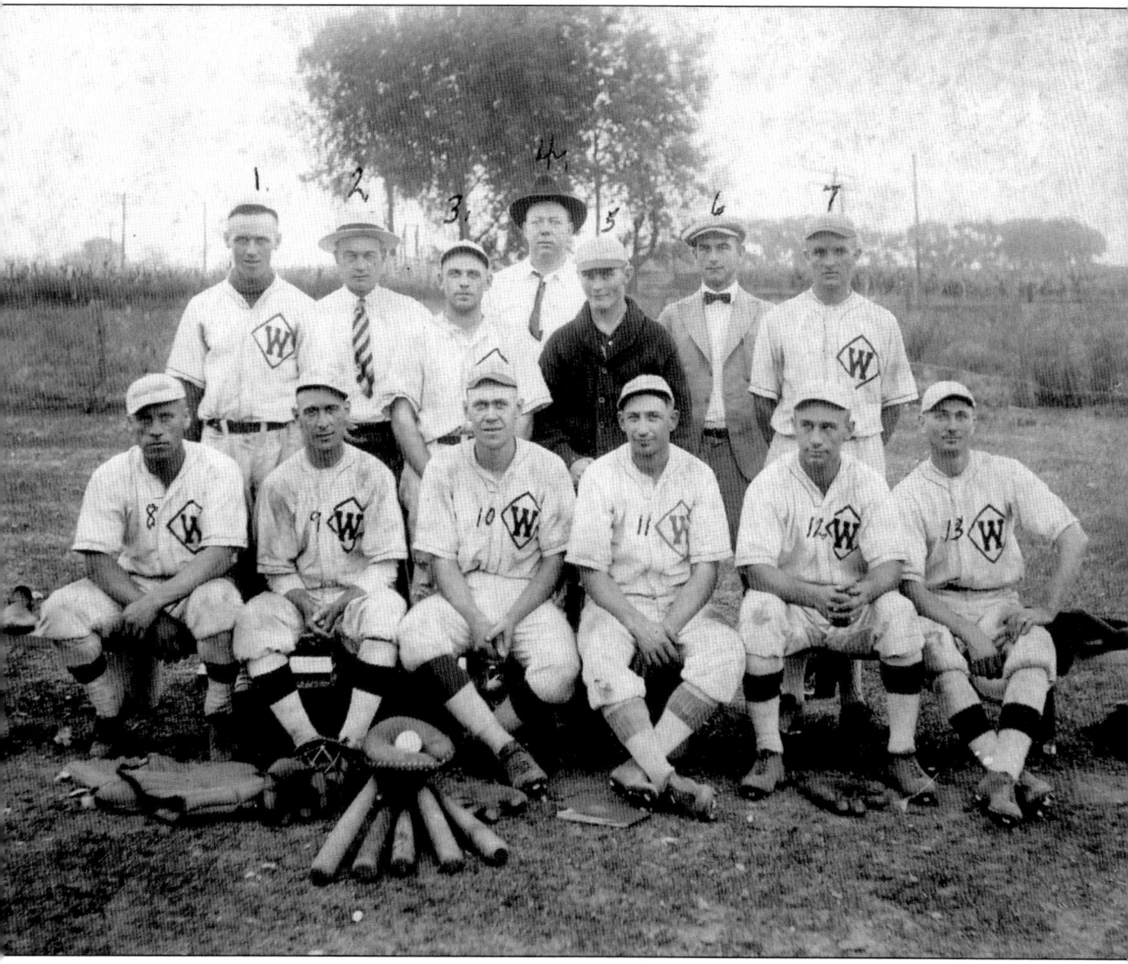

BASEBALL IN WASHINGTON. Organized baseball in Washington began at the beginning of the 20th century with the play of the Clippers at Highland Park Field. Legend has it that the independent Clippers were to play a big game against a team from El Paso and retained the services of an excellent pitcher out of Roanoke. After some alleged betting on the game before a loss by Washington, the pitcher was accused of throwing the game. After that the Clippers were not supported in Washington. Such an incident brings forth memories of the 1919 World Series and the Chicago White Sox. After the demise of the Clippers, along came the Washington Bulldogs, as shown in the photograph above. Sponsored by the Bulldog Insurance Company, the Bulldogs were widely considered one of the toughest teams in Central Illinois to beat during the 1920s and drew large crowds to each of their games played at Sullivan Field, located on Walnut Street. (Courtesy of the Washington Historical Society.)

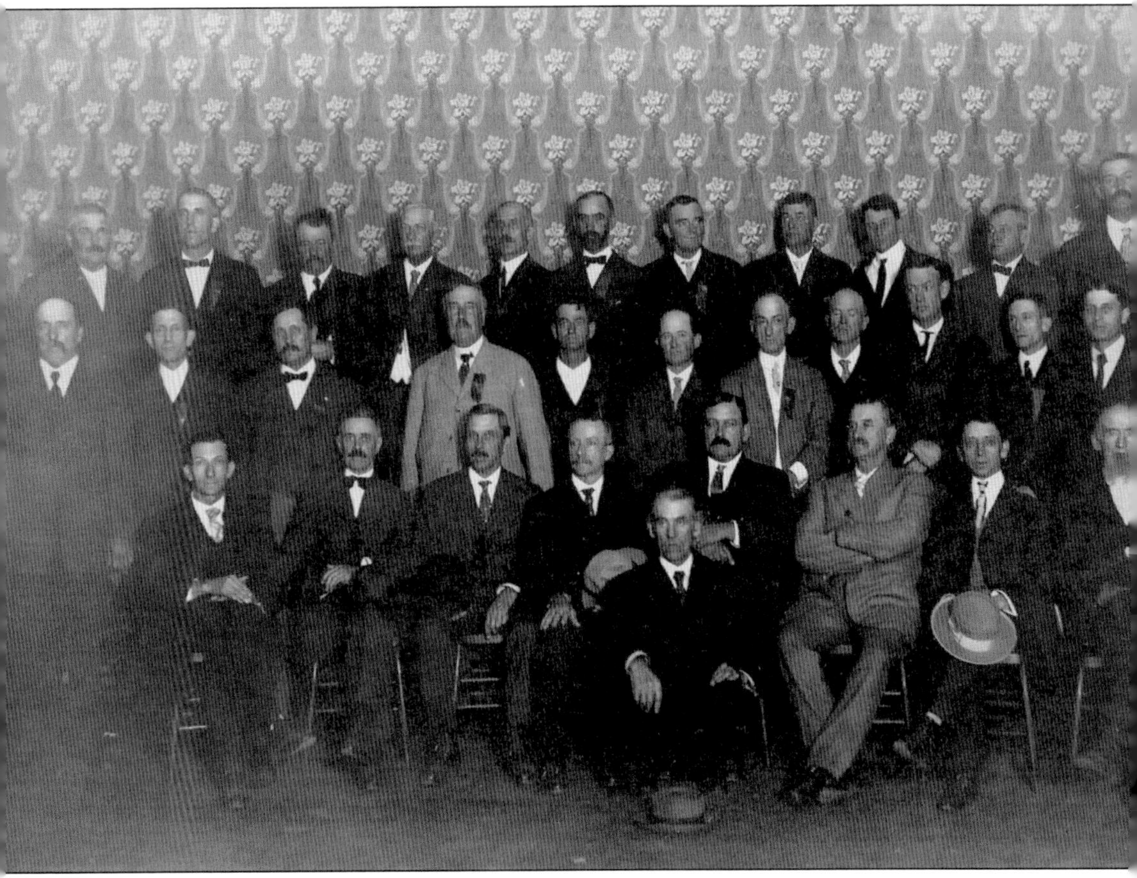

WASHINGTON BUSINESS ELITE. This is a rare sitting for a photograph of some of Washington's most prominent businessmen, many of whom played large roles in the formation and growth of the community from its very beginning. Names such as Tobias, Holland, Anthony, Roehm, Rapp, and Heiple fill out the roster. (Courtesy of the Washington Historical Society.)

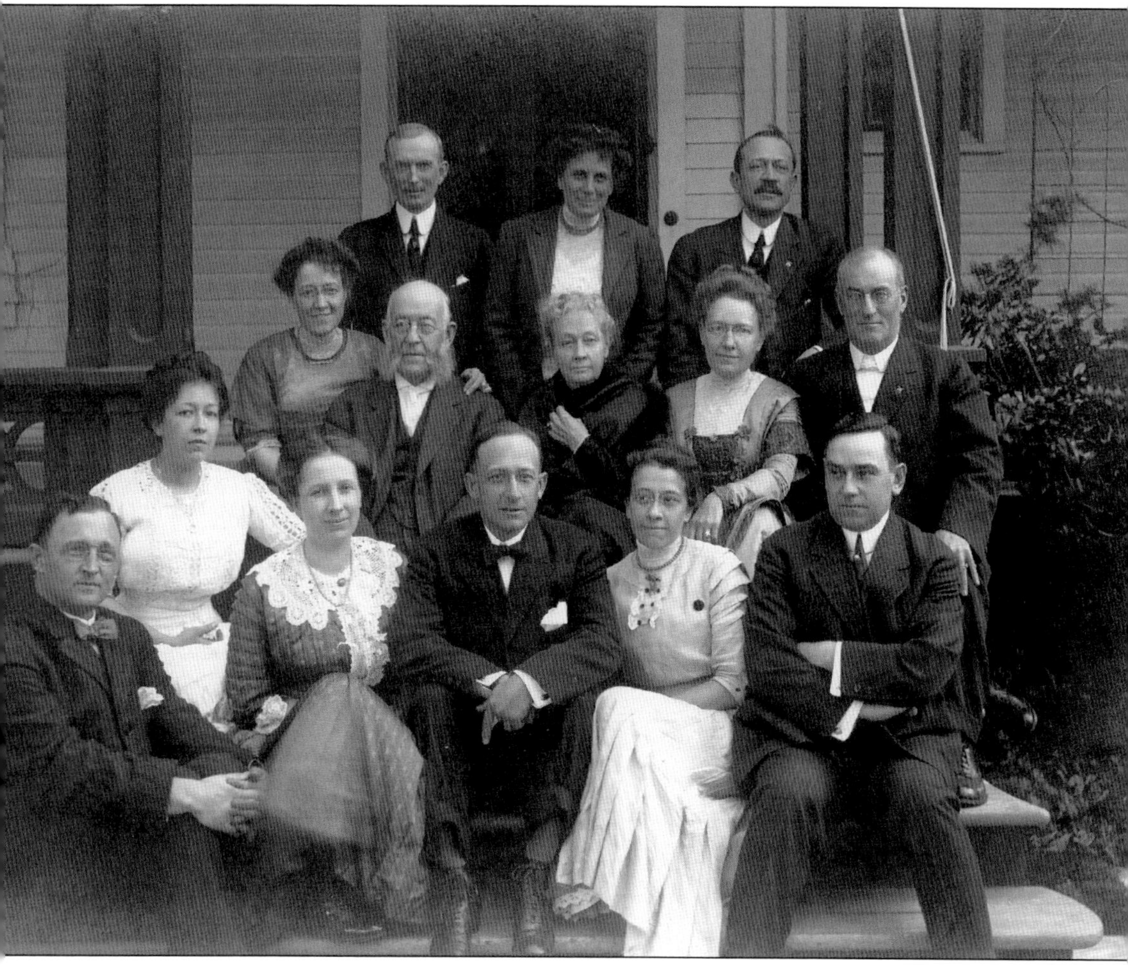

THE ALMON GEORGE DANFORTH FAMILY. One of the most prominent families to reside in Washington sat down on the front steps of their home for this photograph. In the back row, Asa Hamilton Danforth sits next to his wife, Mabel, and George Chester Danforth. The second row includes Almon George Danforth, and the front row includes George Stimson and his wife, Mary Telva Danforth Stimson. (Courtesy of the Washington Historical Society.)

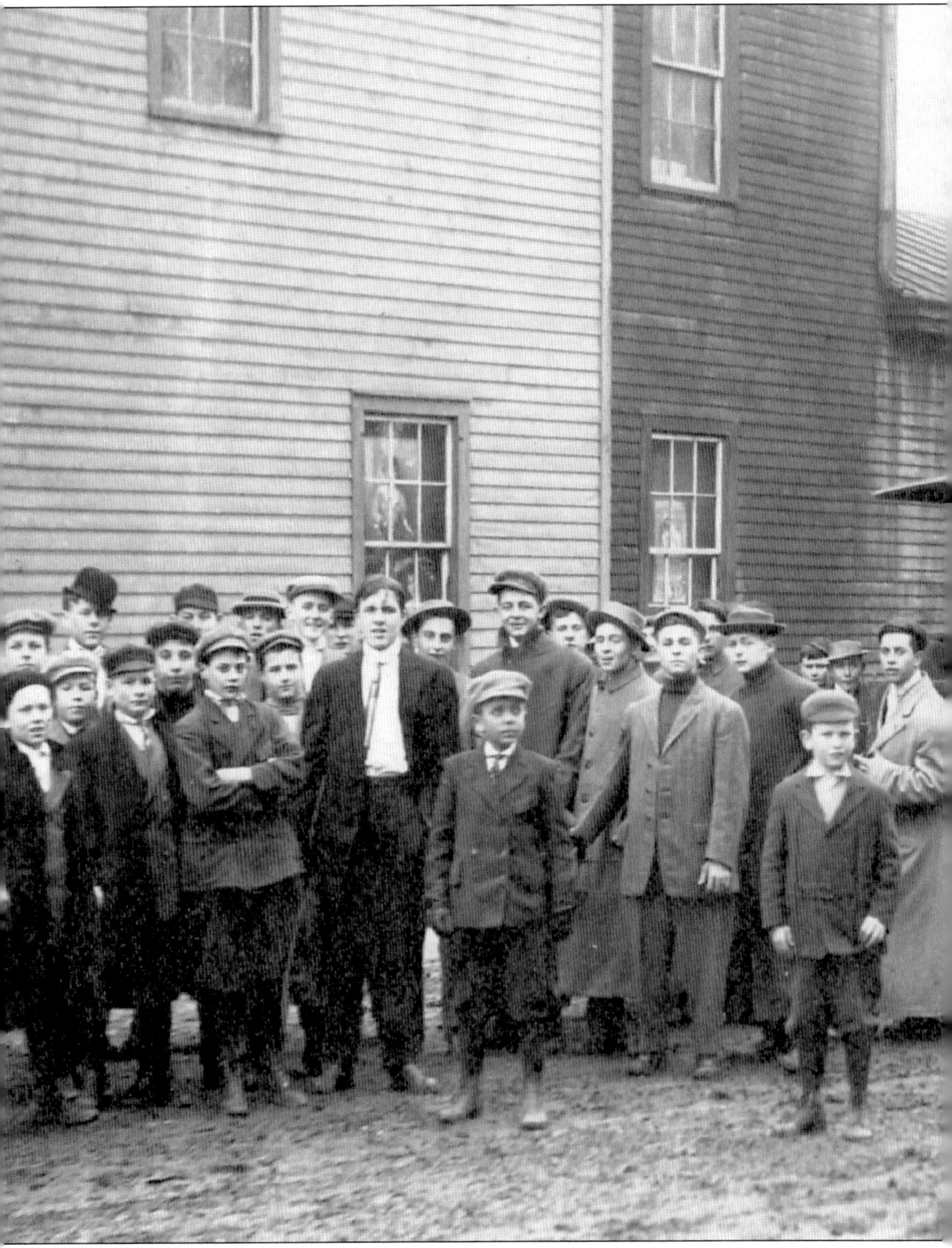

PEORIA STREET SCENE. An early-1900s image shows a group of young men and boys crowding proudly around in order to fit into the photographer's shot. The view looking southwest shows

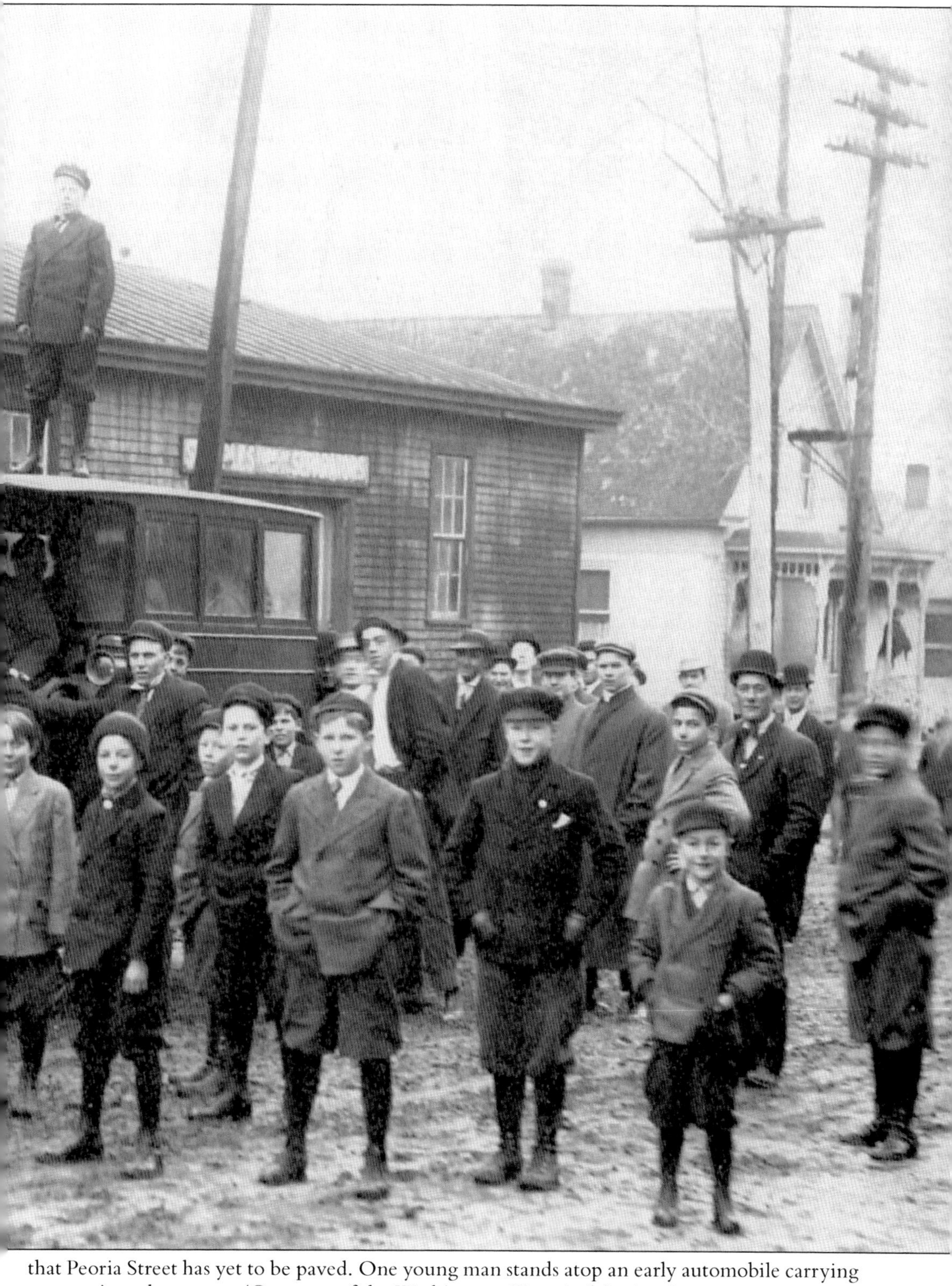

that Peoria Street has yet to be paved. One young man stands atop an early automobile carrying a group into the square. (Courtesy of the Washington Historical Society.)

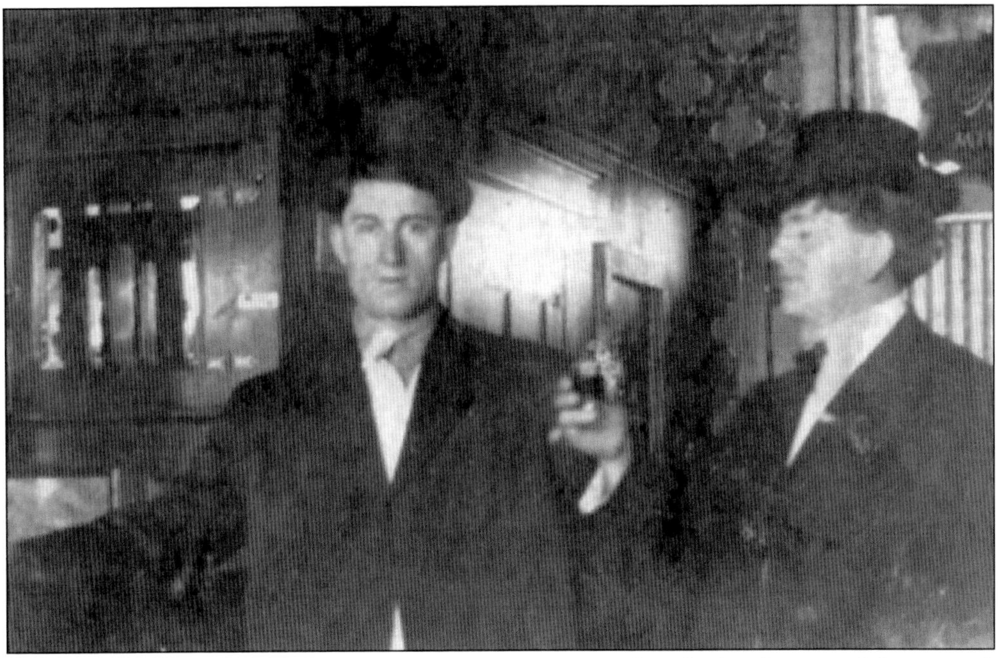

WASHINGTON SALOON PATRONS. Two young men stand at the bar in one of the square's handful of saloons posing in such a way that beckons the beginning of the *Cheers* television show sound track. Both wearing stylish attire from the time, one of the gentlemen seems to be raising a toast. Over their shoulders a Blatz Beer Company of Milwaukee advertisement hangs on the wall. (Courtesy of the Washington Historical Society.)

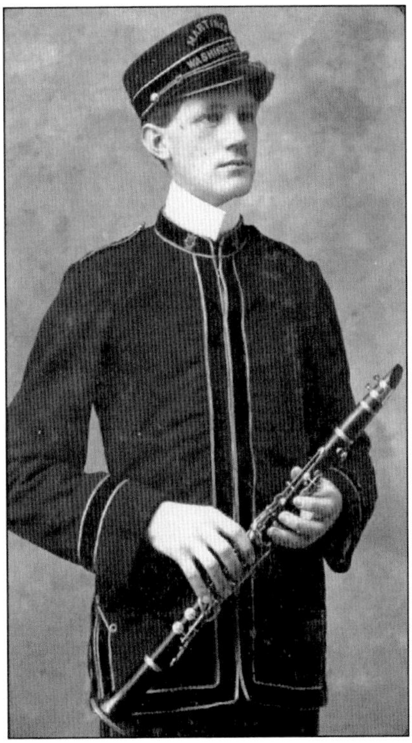

THE MARTINI BAND. German-born Meinhardt Martini, who originally settled in Deer Creek, came to Washington and worked his way into the grocery and shoe business on the square. Having great musical talent, especially amid the brass section, Martini went about starting a band. Martini bought the instruments and taught the lessons, and with this, Washington had its own formal musical entertainment. Undoubtedly the band at some point entertained a crowd atop the bandstand in the park on the square. This photograph portrays one of the band's clarinet players. (Courtesy of the Washington Historical Society.)

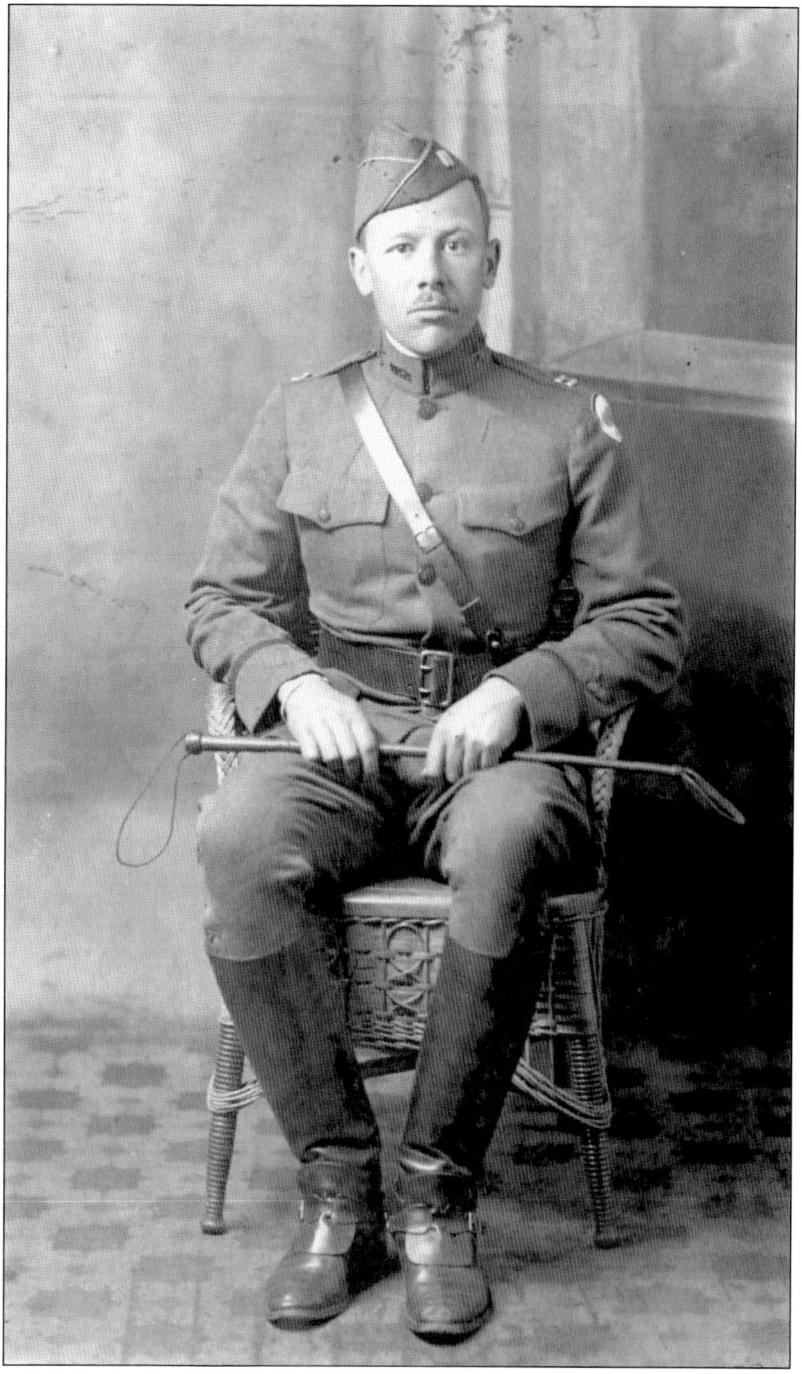

FRED SWEITZER. The son of Peter and Rachel Sweitzer was a member of the 92nd Division at Camp Grant. Fred Sweitzer served as regimental adjutant, 365th Infantry through World War I, and spent three months on the front line. After the war, he helped organize and became elected commander of Washington Post No. 100 in 1919. Sweitzer also served as the justice of the peace for the community for 24 years from 1924 to 1948. (Courtesy of the Washington Historical Society.)

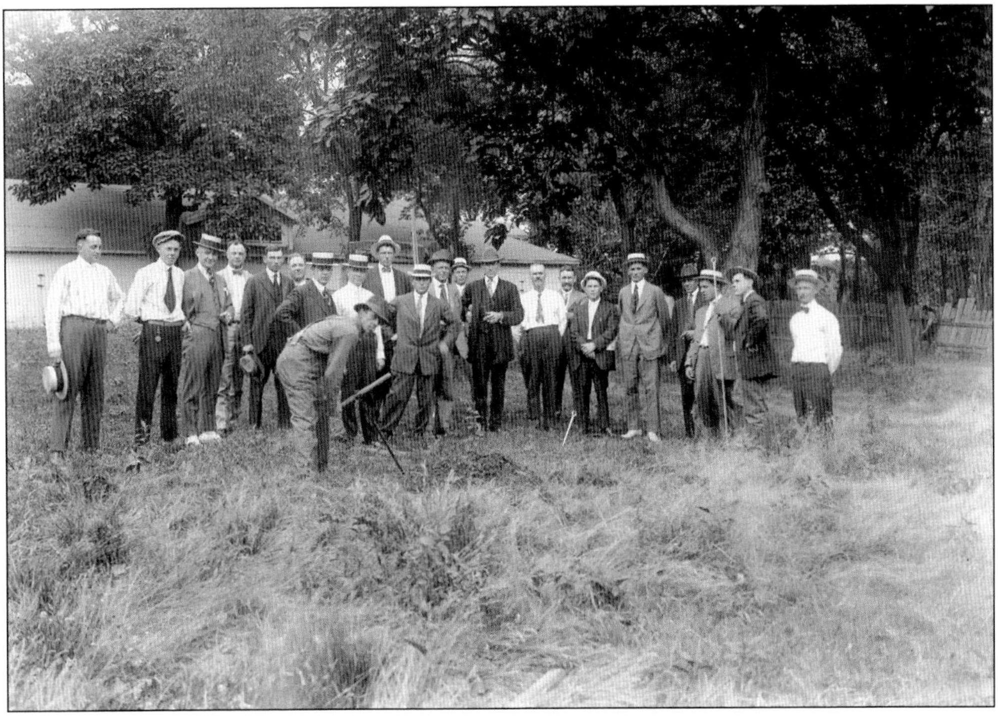

Gathering for a Task. This group of men in the 1920s, many sporting the popular boater hats of the times, is gathered together to take on a task that the man bent over in the foreground is preparing. That task, as seen in the second photograph is uprooting a tree. Much like a ceremonial groundbreaking, the men may be clearing the way for new construction. (Courtesy of the Washington Historical Society.)

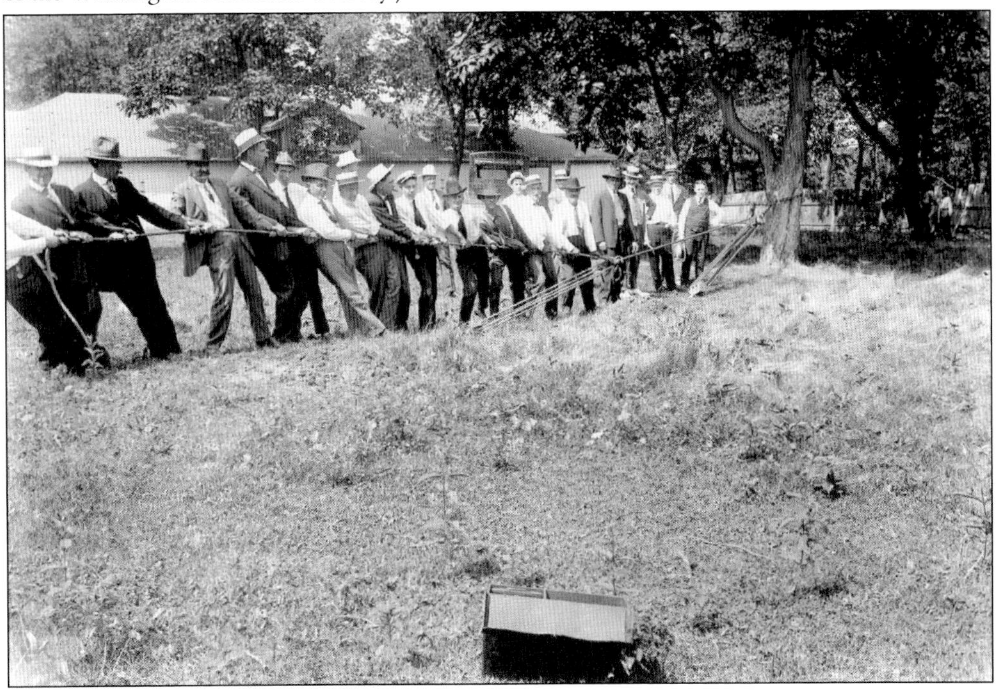

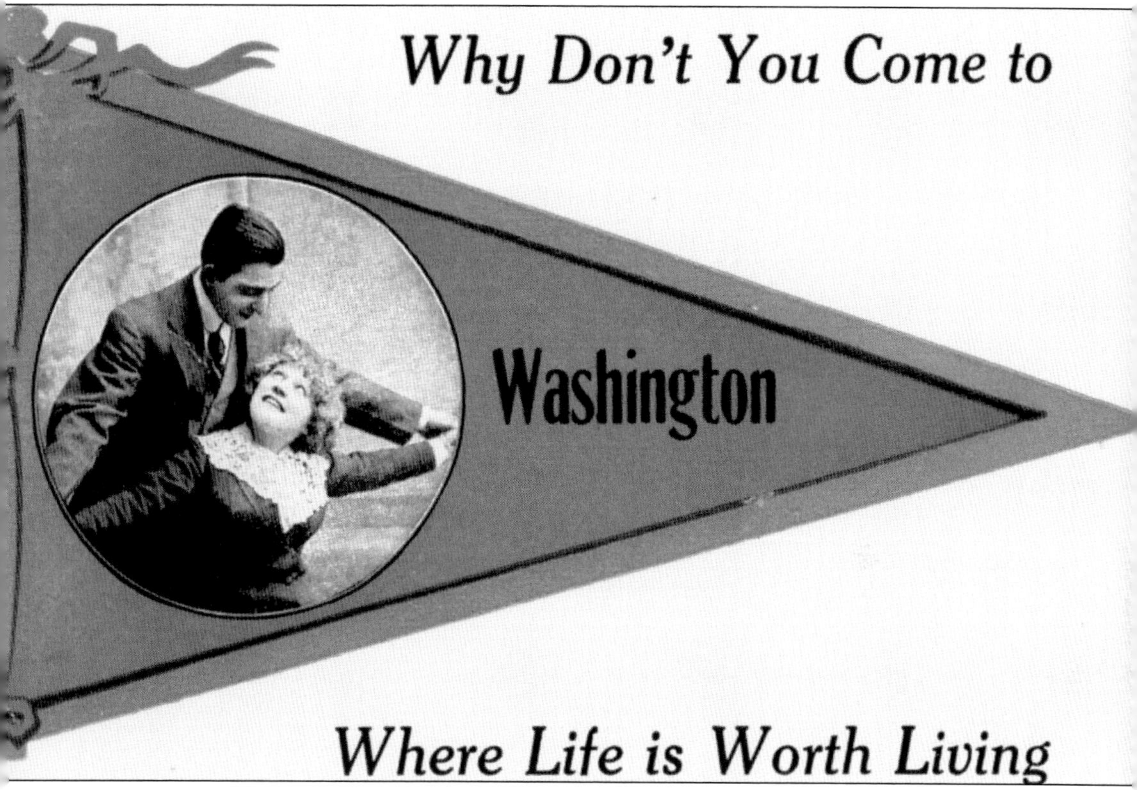

THE GOOD LIFE. A postcard probably used for hundreds of different communities of all scales with just a change of name on the pennant expresses and advertises the quality of life in Washington. In Washington, the community lived up to the advertisement. Three major rails and a beautiful and very wonderful public square surrounded by a strong network of streets lined by beautiful houses has made Washington a place where life is indeed worth living. The question for the future will be: can future generations create such wonderful development like what made Washington so special and worth caring for all of these years?